ULTIMATE
ANNUALS

ULTIMATE
ANNUALS

ULTIMATE FANTASTIC FOUR
Writer: **Mike Carey**
Pencils: **Stuart Immonen**
Inks: **Wade VonGrawbadger**
Colors: **Paul Mounts**
Art & Colors, Moleman Sequences: **Frazer Irving**
Letters: **Virtual Calligraphy's Randy Gentile**
Cover: **Stuart Immonen & Richard Isanove**

ULTIMATE X-MEN
Writer: **Robert Kirkman**
Art: **Salvador Larroca**
Art, Bonus Feature: **Leinil Francis Yu**
Colors: **Jason Keith**
Colors, Bonus Feature: **Dean White**
Letters: **Virtual Calligraphy's Joe Caramagna**
Cover: **Salvador Larroca & Richard Isanove**

THE ULTIMATES
Writer: **Charlie Huston**
Pencils, Present Day: **Mike Deodato Jr.**
Pencils, Flashbacks: **Ryan Sook**
Inks, Present Day: **Joe Pimentel**
Inks, Flashbacks: **Wade VonGrawbadger with Scott Koblish**
Colors, Present Day: **Rain Beredo**
Colors, Flashbacks: **June Chung**
Letters: **Virtual Calligraphy's Joe Caramagna**
Cover: **Mike Deodato Jr. & Richard Isanove**

ULTIMATE SPIDER-MAN
Writer: **Brian Michael Bendis**
Penciler: **Mark Brooks**
Inker: **Jaime Mendoza with Mark Morales**
Victor Olazaba & Mark Brooks
Colors: **Laura Martin with Larry Molinar**
Letters: **Virtual Calligraphy's Cory Petit**
Cover: **Mark Brooks & Richard Isanove**

Associate Editor: **John Barber**
Editor: **Ralph Macchio**

Collection Editor: **Jennifer Grünwald**
Assistant Editor: **Michael Short**
Associate Editor: **Mark D. Beazley**
Senior Editor, Special Projects: **Jeff Youngquist**
Vice President of Sales: **David Gabriel**
Production: **Jerron Quality Color**
Vice President of Creative: **Tom Marvelli**

Editor in Chief: **Joe Quesada**
Publisher: **Dan Buckley**

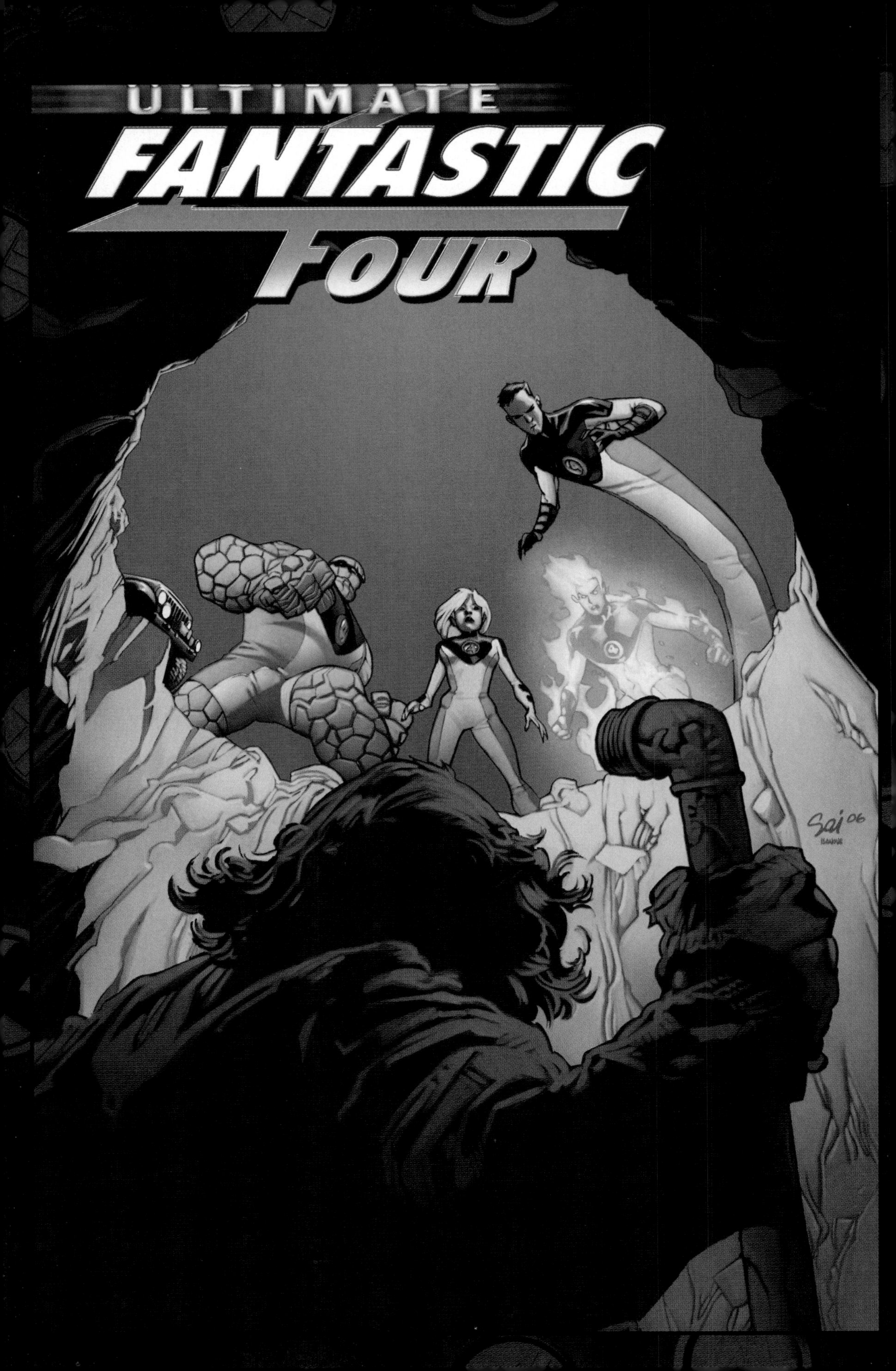
ULTIMATE
FANTASTIC
FOUR

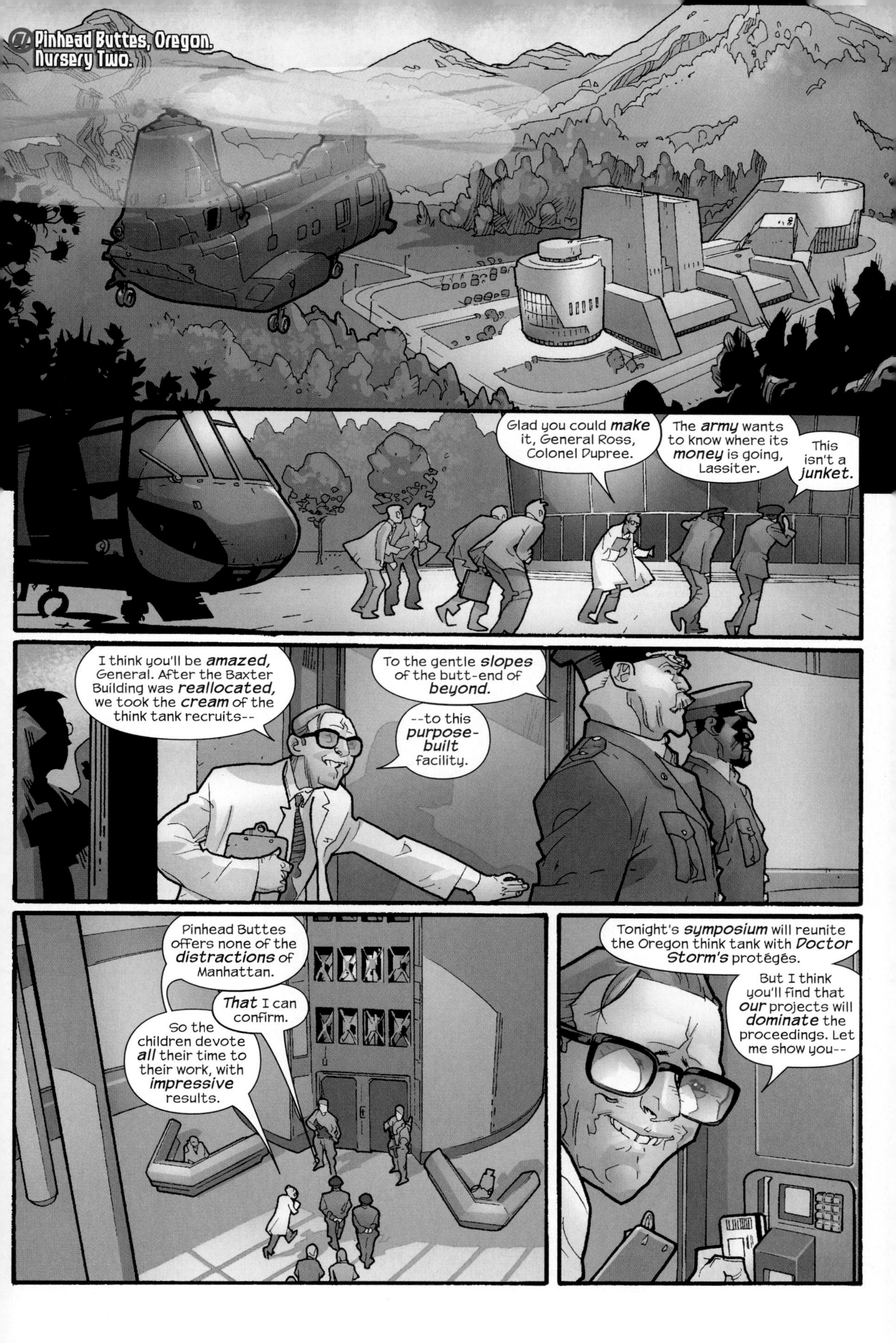

Pinhead Buttes, Oregon. Nursery Two.
Glad you could make it, General Ross, Colonel Dupree.
The army wants to know where its money is going, Lassiter.
This isn't a junket.
I think you'll be amazed, General. After the Baxter Building was reallocated, we took the cream of the think tank recruits--
To the gentle slopes of the butt-end of beyond.
--to this purpose-built facility.
Pinhead Buttes offers none of the distractions of Manhattan.
That I can confirm.
So the children devote all their time to their work, with impressive results.
Tonight's symposium will reunite the Oregon think tank with Doctor Storm's protégés.
But I think you'll find that our projects will dominate the proceedings. Let me show you--

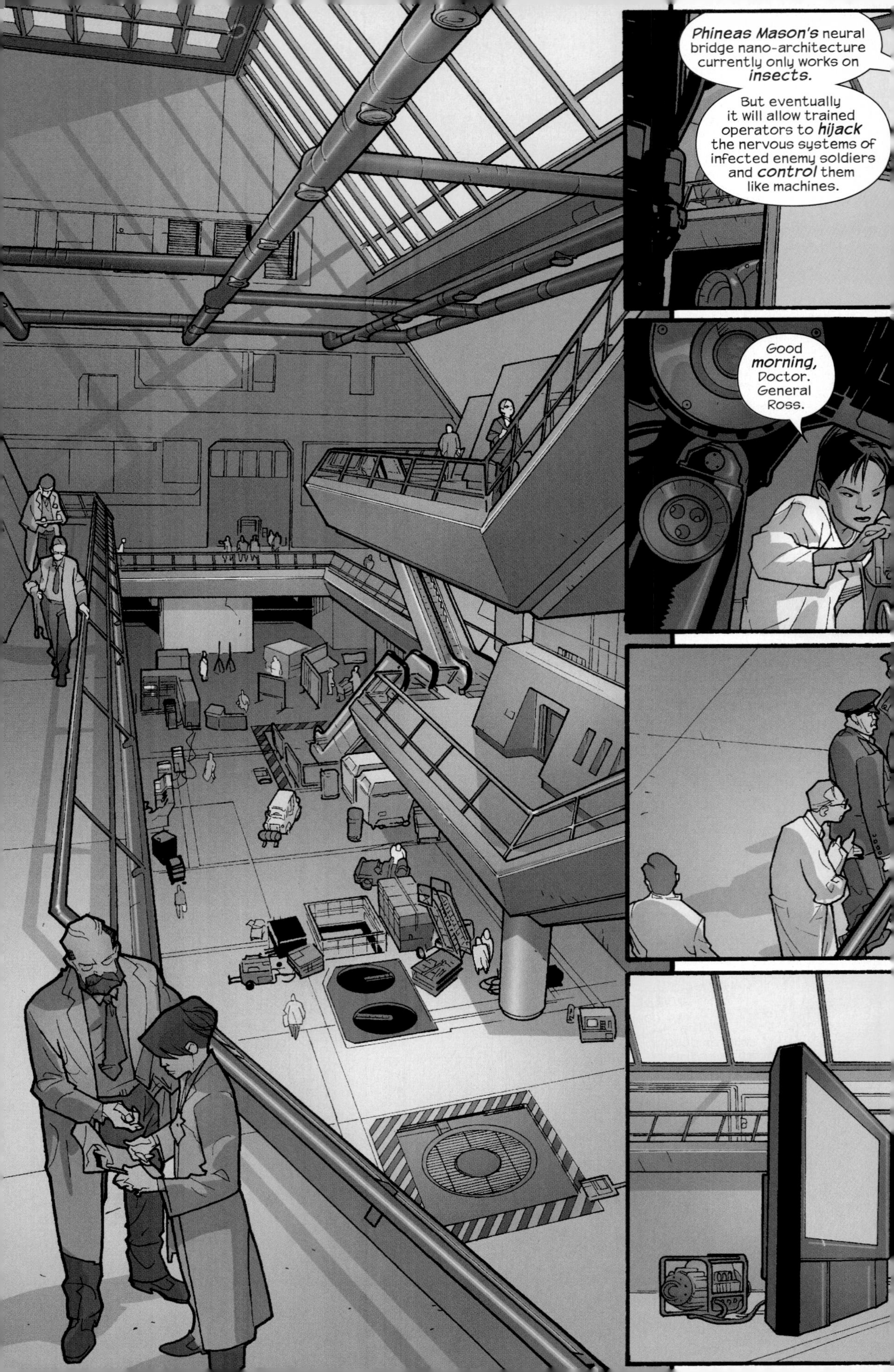

Phineas Mason's neural bridge nano-architecture currently only works on insects.
But eventually it will allow trained operators to hijack the nervous systems of infected enemy soldiers and control them like machines.
Good morning, Doctor. General Ross.

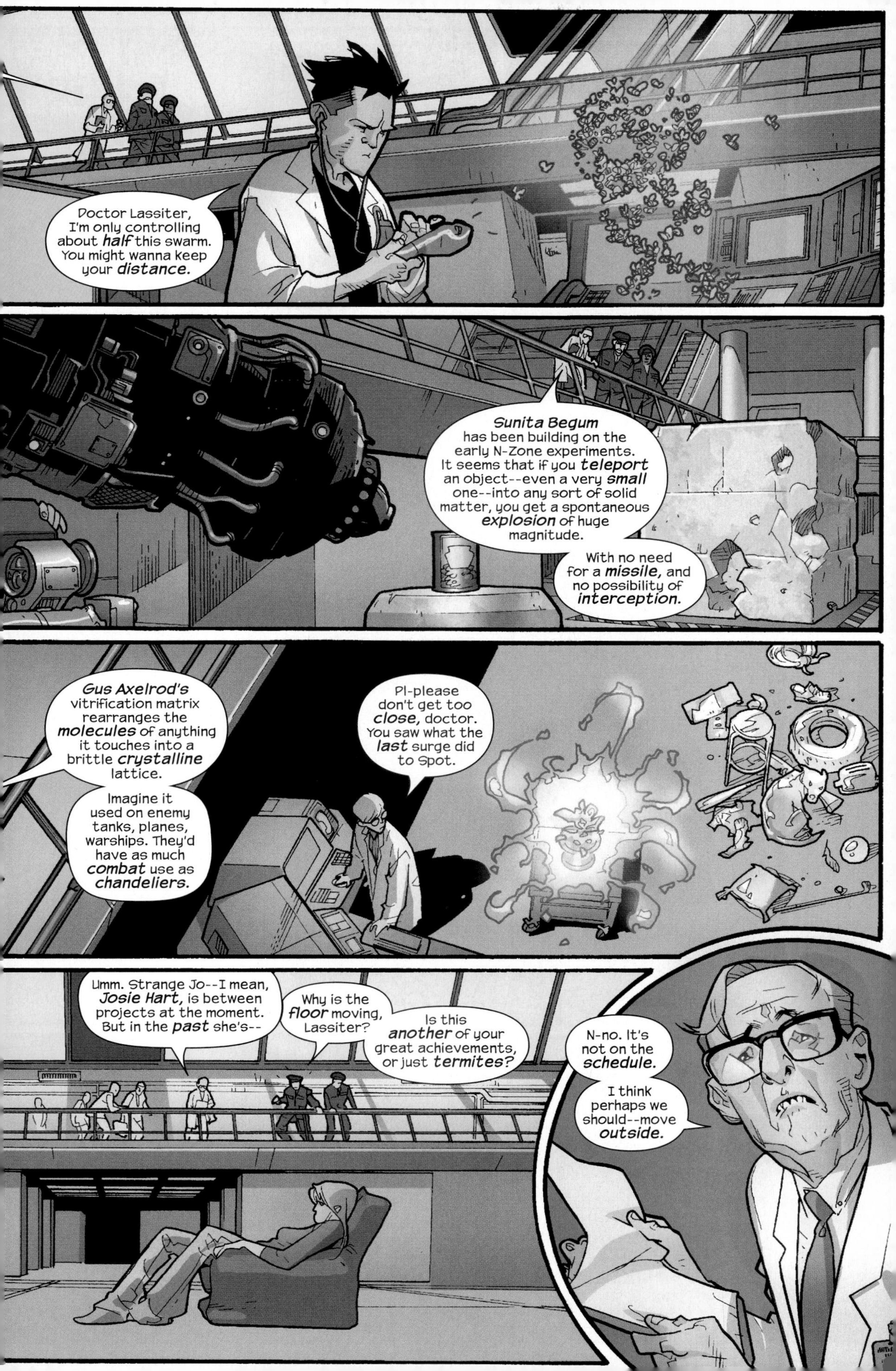

Doctor Lassiter, I'm only controlling about half this swarm. You might wanna keep your distance.
Sunita Begum has been building on the early N-Zone experiments. It seems that if you teleport an object--even a very small one--into any sort of solid matter, you get a spontaneous explosion of huge magnitude.
With no need for a missile, and no possibility of interception.
Gus Axelrod's vitrification matrix rearranges the molecules of anything it touches into a brittle crystalline lattice.
Imagine it used on enemy tanks, planes, warships. They'd have as much combat use as chandeliers.
Pl-please don't get too close, doctor. You saw what the last surge did to Spot.
Umm. Strange Jo--I mean, Josie Hart, is between projects at the moment. But in the past she's--
Why is the floor moving, Lassiter?
Is this another of your great achievements, or just termites?
N-no. It's not on the schedule.
I think perhaps we should--move outside.

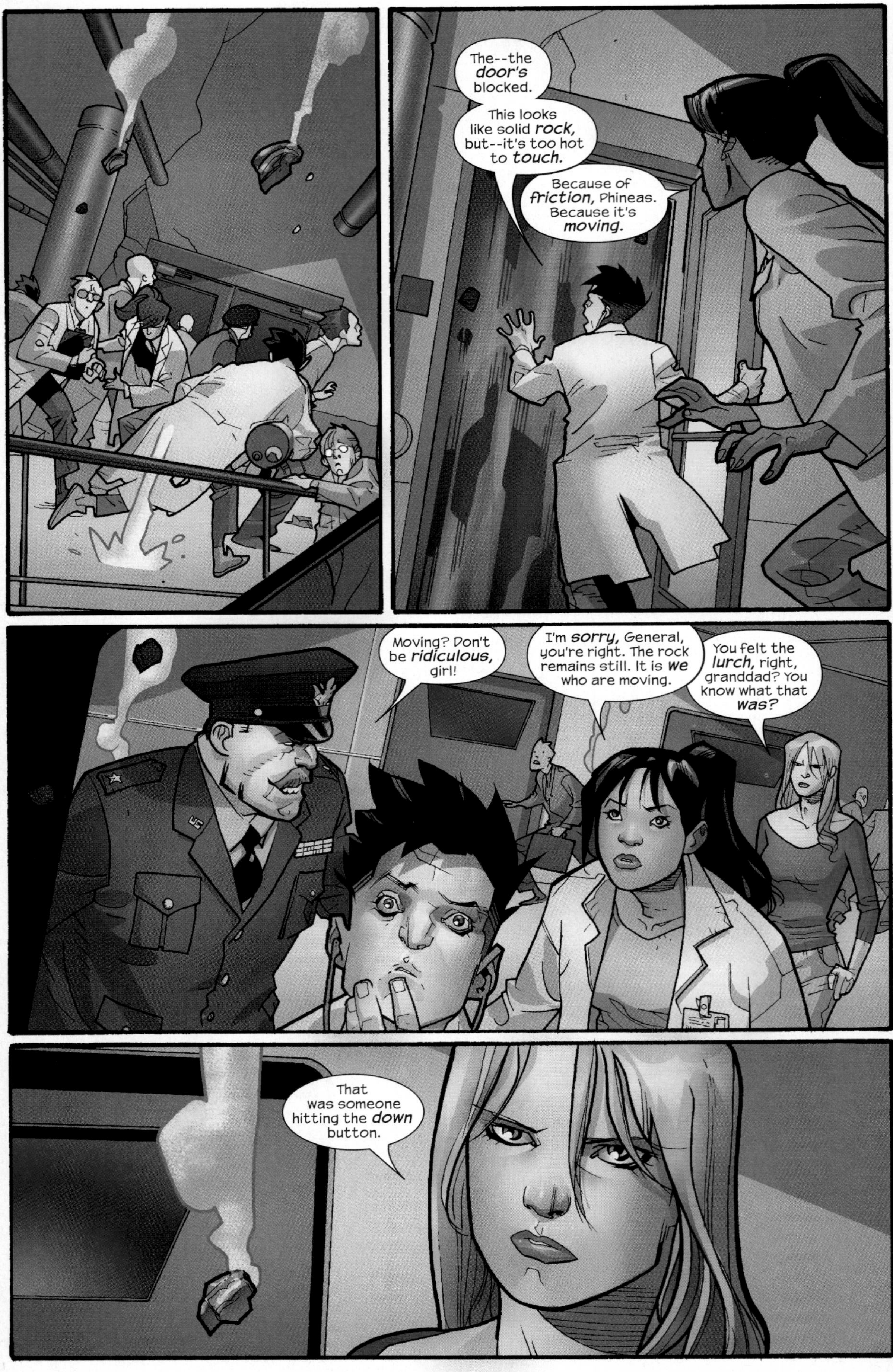
The--the door's blocked.
This looks like solid rock, but--it's too hot to touch.
Because of friction, Phineas. Because it's moving.
Moving? Don't be ridiculous, girl!
I'm sorry, General, you're right. The rock remains still. It is we who are moving.
You felt the lurch, right, granddad? You know what that was?
That was someone hitting the down button.

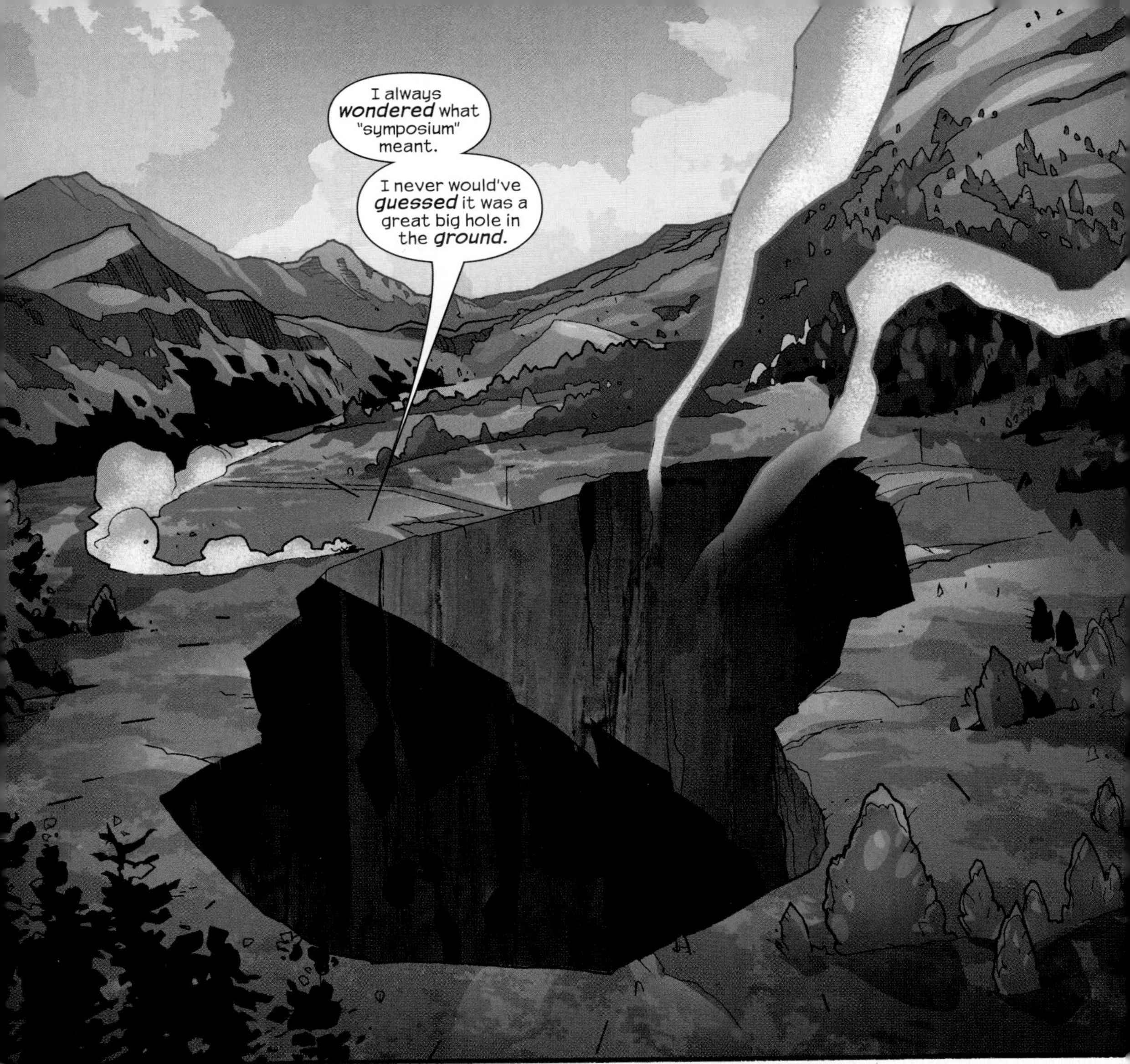
I always **wondered** what "symposium" meant.
I never would've **guessed** it was a great big hole in the **ground.**

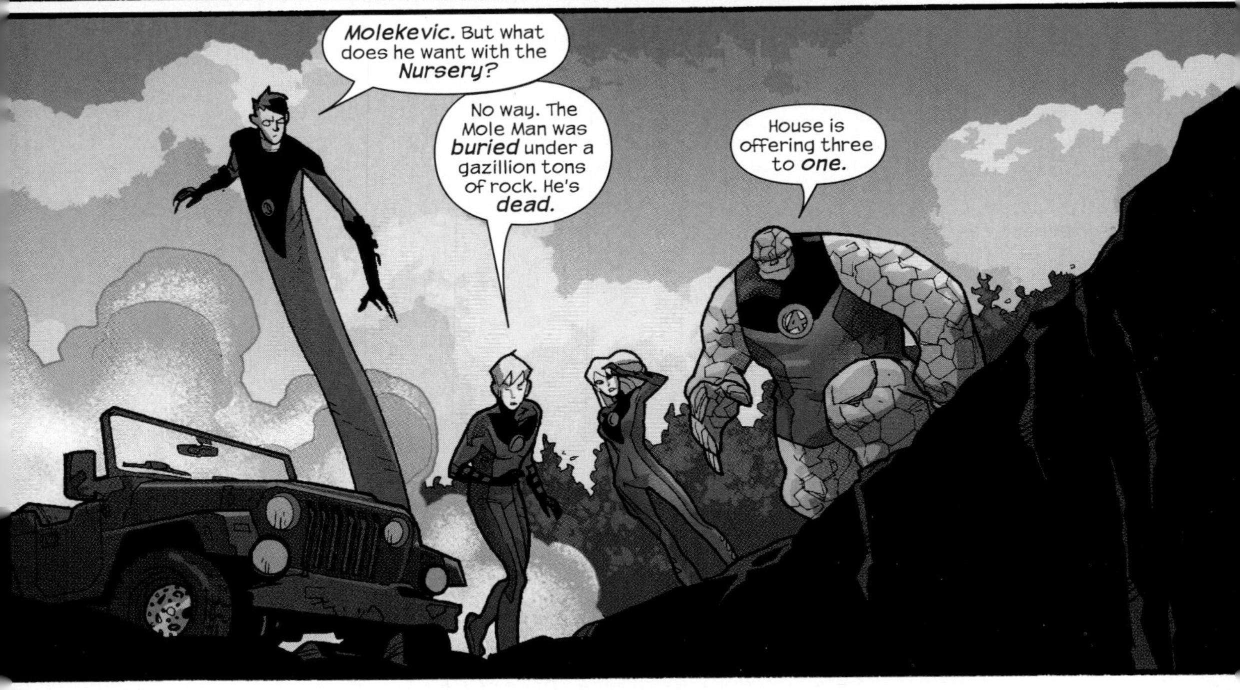
Molekevic. But what does he want with the **Nursery?**
No way. The Mole Man was **buried** under a gazillion tons of rock. He's **dead.**
House is offering three to **one.**

PREVIOUSLY IN ULTIMATE FANTASTIC FOUR:

Reed Richards, handpicked to join the Baxter Building think tank of young geniuses, spent his youth developing a teleport system that transported solid matter into a parallel universe. Its first full-scale test was witnessed by Reed, fellow think tank members Sue Storm and her brother Johnny, as well as Reed's childhood friend Ben Grimm.

There was an accident. The quartet's genetic structures were scrambled and recombined in a fantastically strange way. Reed's body stretches and flows like water. Ben looks like a thing carved from desert rock. Sue can become invisible. Johnny generates flame.

Dr. Arthur Molekevic was a teacher at the think tank. Called "Mole Man" by the students, he was fired five years before the Fantastic Four came into being. When the young heroes made their debut, they discovered Molekevic had created a monster army underground, and was lashing out against the surface world. The team stopped Mole Man, and believed he was crushed to death in a cave-in.

Months later, after the quartet went public and became celebrity super heroes, the rest of the think tank was moved out of the Baxter Building, for their own protection...a decision which has just proved ironic...

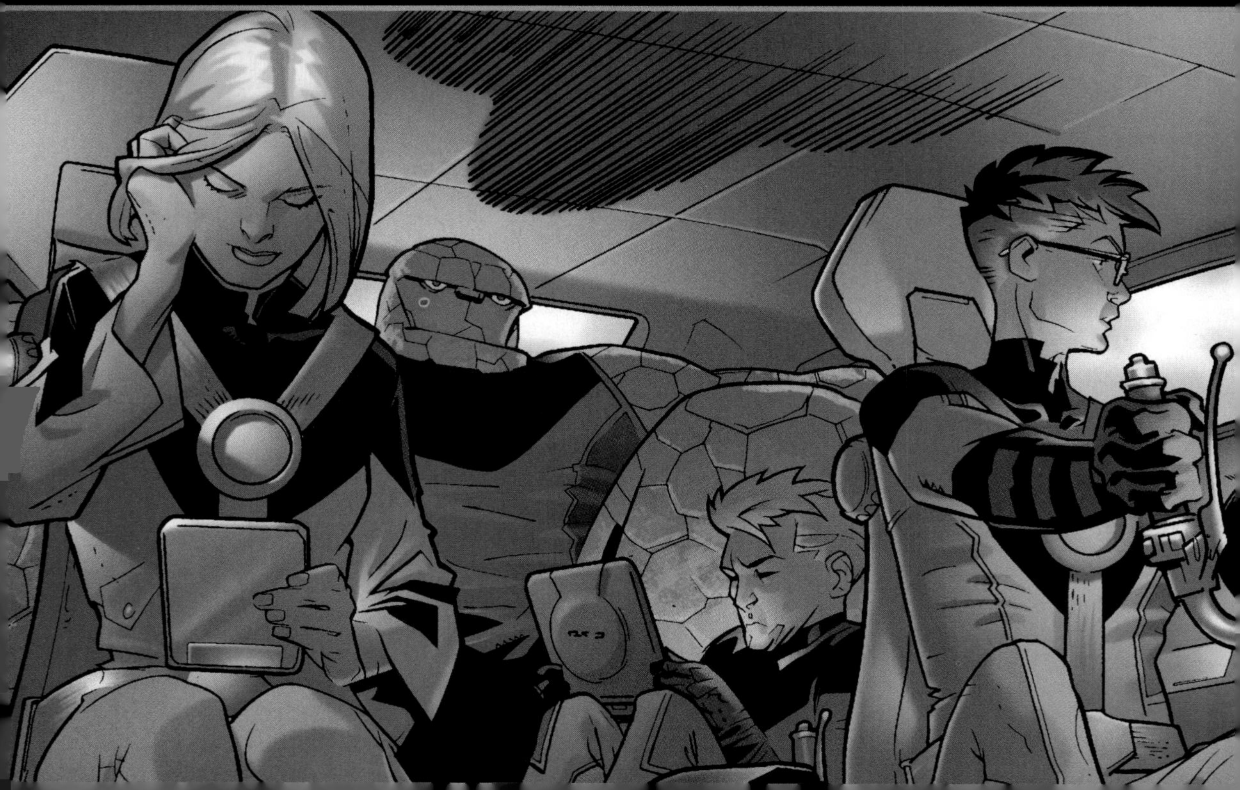

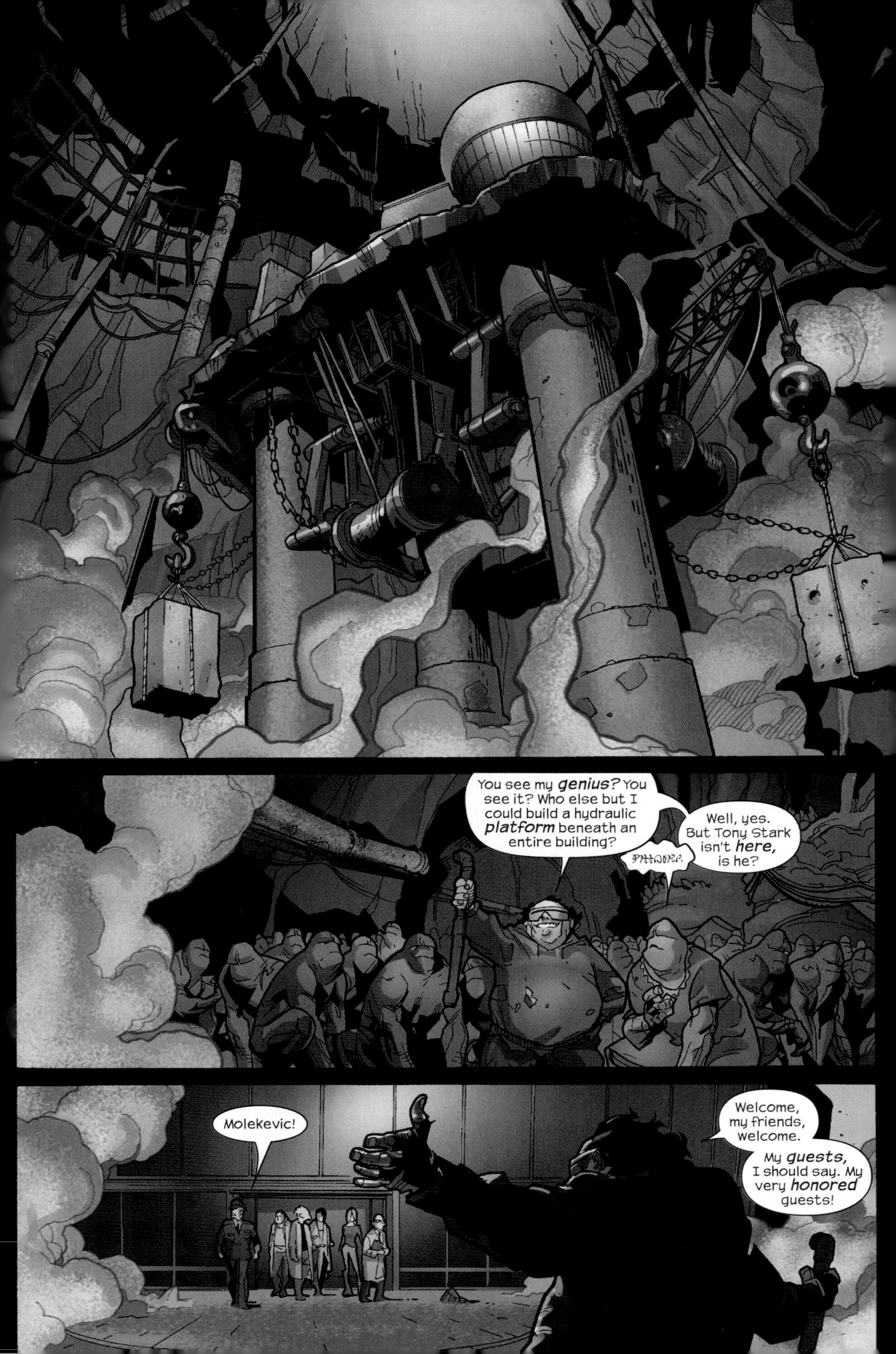
You see my genius? You see it? Who else but I could build a hydraulic platform beneath an entire building?
Well, yes. But Tony Stark isn't here, is he?
Molekevic!
Welcome, my friends, welcome.
My guests, I should say. My very honored guests!

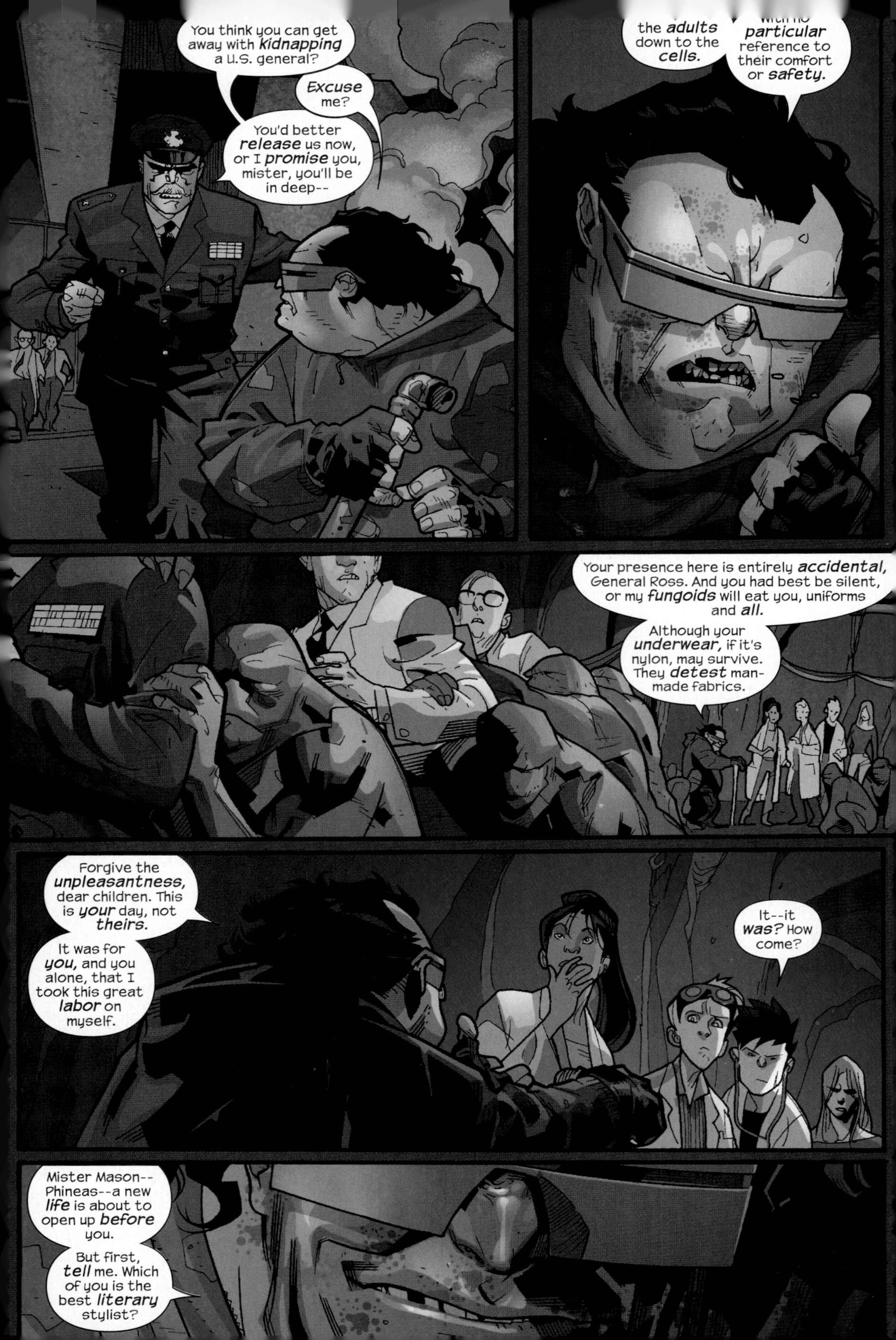

You think you can get away with kidnapping a U.S. general?
Excuse me?
You'd better release us now, or I promise you, mister, you'll be in deep--
the adults down to the cells.
particular reference to their comfort or safety.
Your presence here is entirely accidental, General Ross. And you had best be silent, or my fungoids will eat you, uniforms and all.
Although your underwear, if it's nylon, may survive. They detest man-made fabrics.
Forgive the unpleasantness, dear children. This is your day, not theirs.
It was for you, and you alone, that I took this great labor on myself.
It--it was? How come?
Mister Mason--Phineas--a new life is about to open up before you.
But first, tell me. Which of you is the best literary stylist?

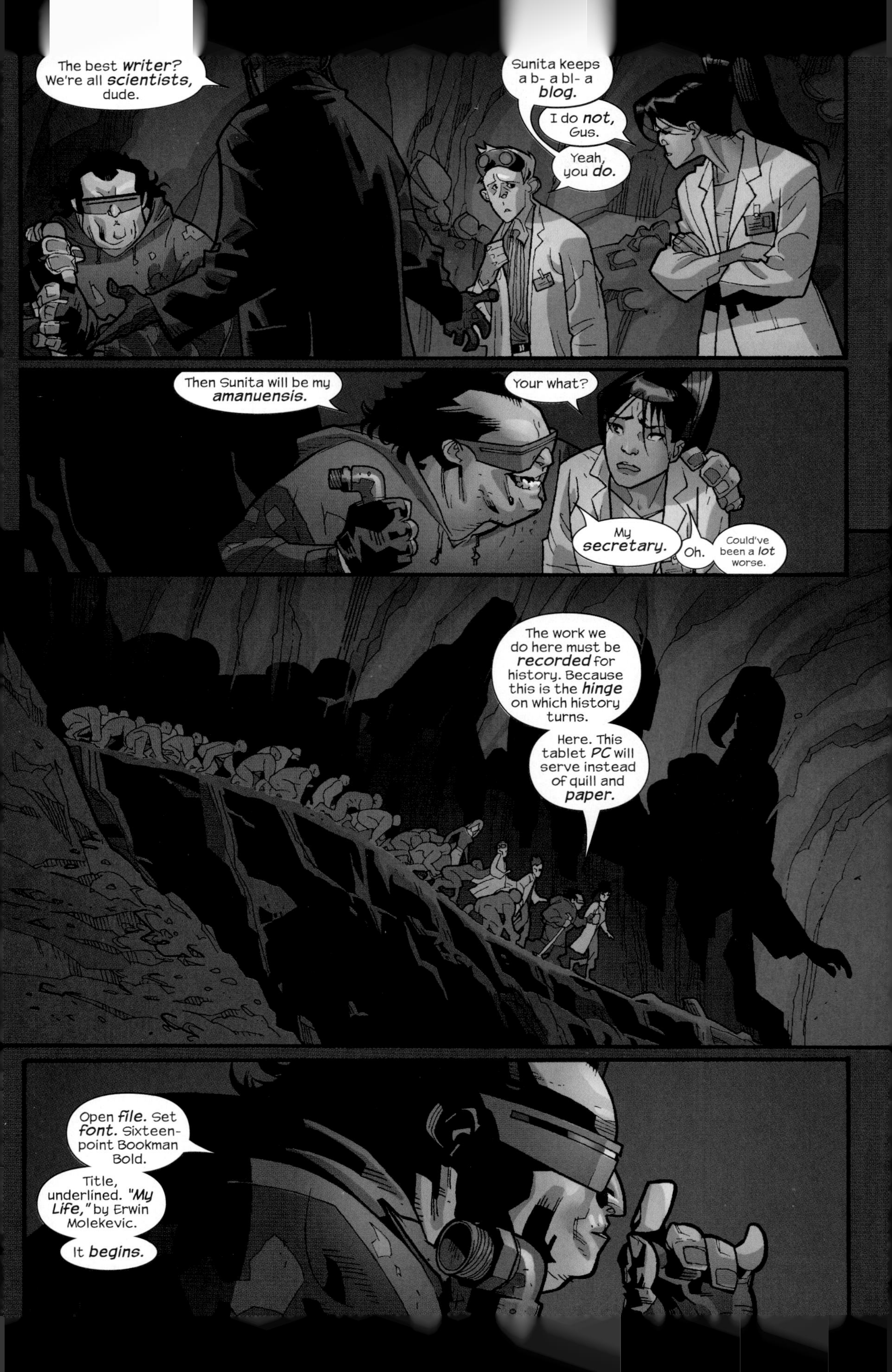

The best *writer*? We're all *scientists*, dude.
Sunita keeps a b- a bl- a *blog.*
I do *not,* Gus.
Yeah, you *do.*
Then Sunita will be my *amanuensis.*
Your what?
My *secretary.*
Oh.
Could've been a *lot* worse.
The work we do here must be *recorded* for history. Because this is the *hinge* on which history turns.
Here. This tablet *PC* will serve instead of quill and *paper.*
Open *file.* Set *font.* Sixteen-point Bookman Bold.
Title, underlined. *"My Life,"* by Erwin Molekevic.
It *begins.*

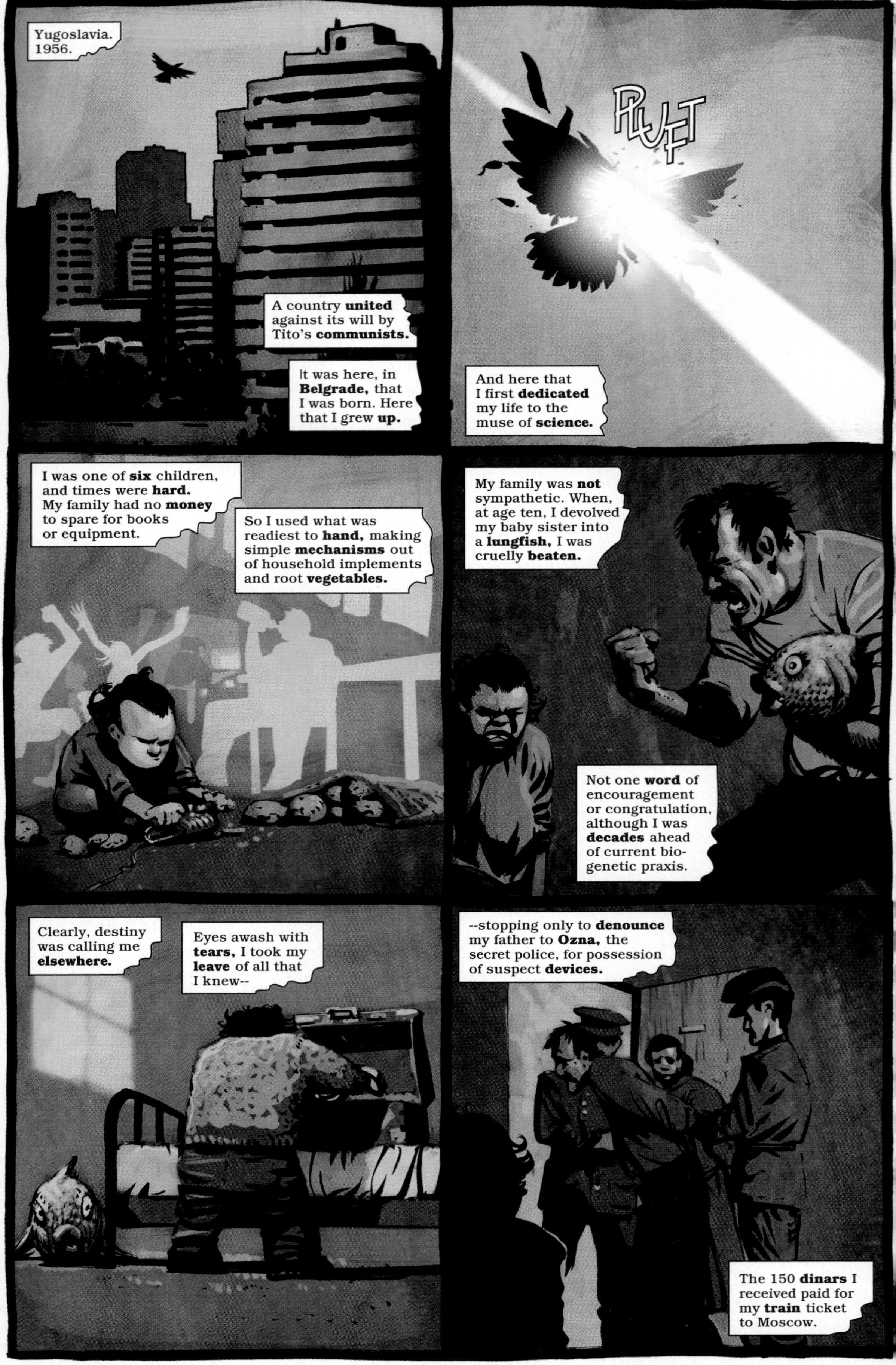

Yugoslavia. 1956.
A country united against its will by Tito's communists.
It was here, in Belgrade, that I was born. Here that I grew up.
PLUFT
And here that I first dedicated my life to the muse of science.
I was one of six children, and times were hard. My family had no money to spare for books or equipment.
So I used what was readiest to hand, making simple mechanisms out of household implements and root vegetables.
My family was not sympathetic. When, at age ten, I devolved my baby sister into a lungfish, I was cruelly beaten.
Not one word of encouragement or congratulation, although I was decades ahead of current bio-genetic praxis.
Clearly, destiny was calling me elsewhere.
Eyes awash with tears, I took my leave of all that I knew--
--stopping only to denounce my father to Ozna, the secret police, for possession of suspect devices.
The 150 dinars I received paid for my train ticket to Moscow.

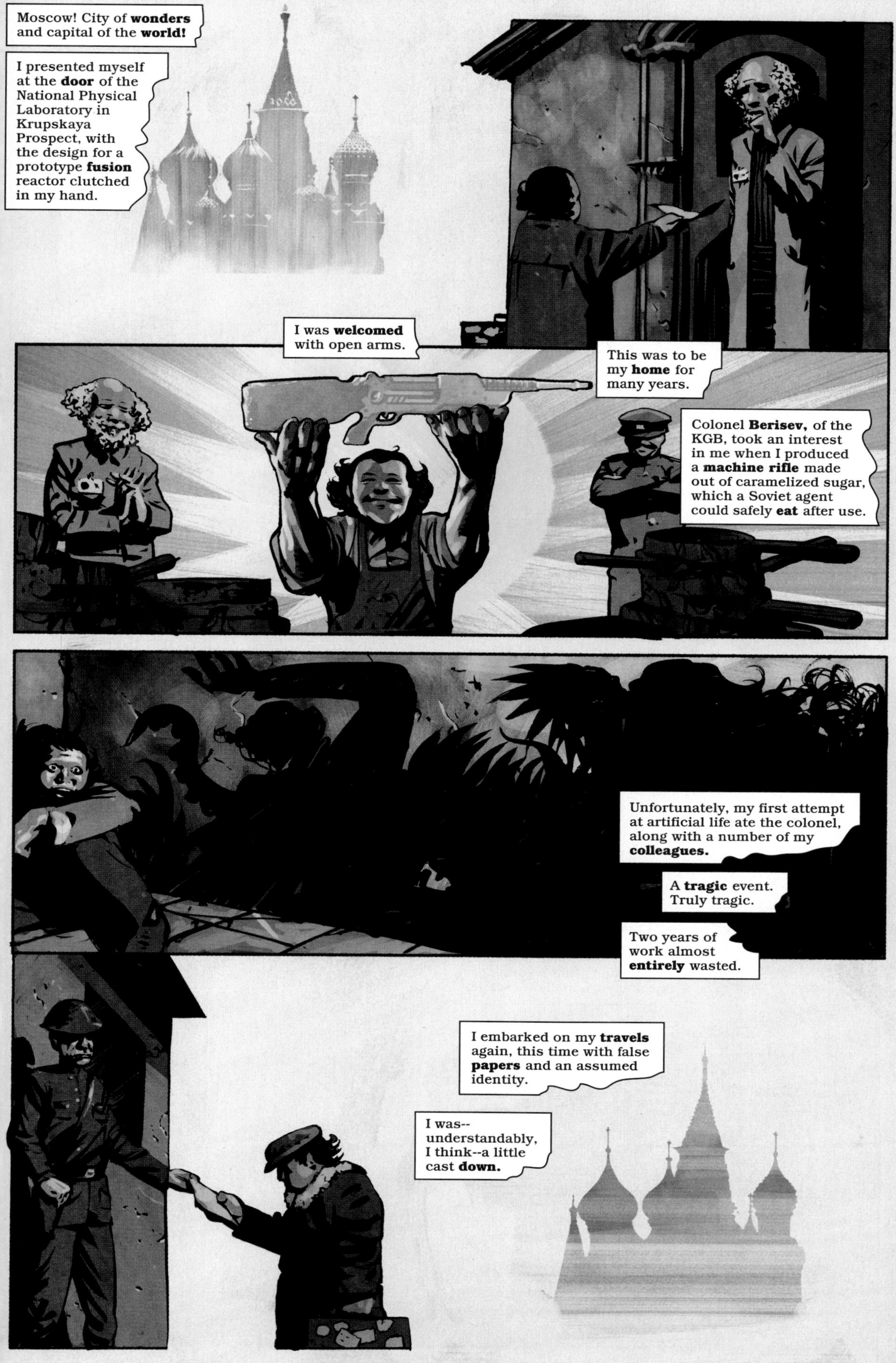

Moscow! City of wonders and capital of the world!
I presented myself at the door of the National Physical Laboratory in Krupskaya Prospect, with the design for a prototype fusion reactor clutched in my hand.
I was welcomed with open arms.
This was to be my home for many years.
Colonel Berisev, of the KGB, took an interest in me when I produced a machine rifle made out of caramelized sugar, which a Soviet agent could safely eat after use.
Unfortunately, my first attempt at artificial life ate the colonel, along with a number of my colleagues.
A tragic event. Truly tragic.
Two years of work almost entirely wasted.
I embarked on my travels again, this time with false papers and an assumed identity.
I was--understandably, I think--a little cast down.

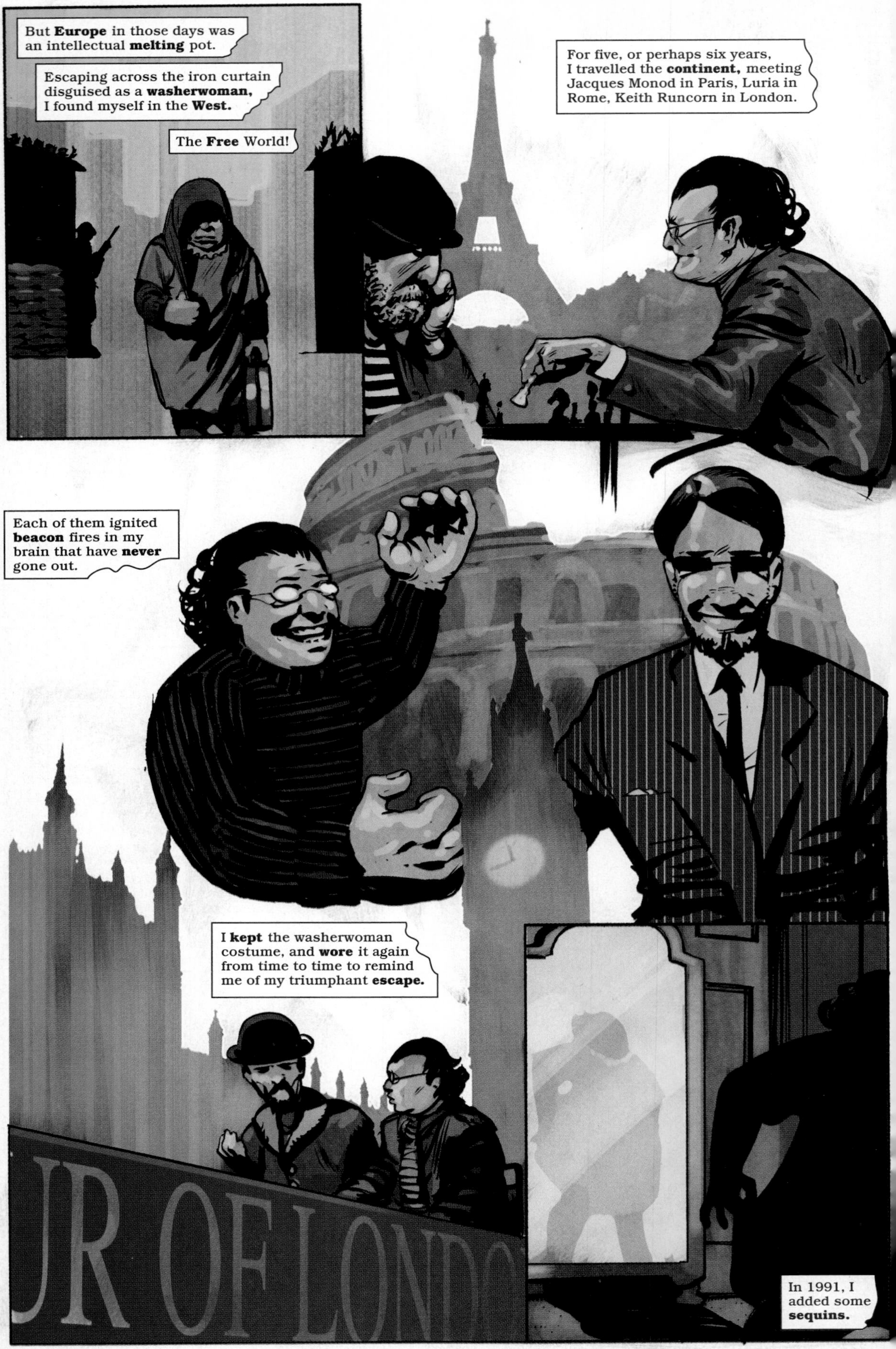
But Europe in those days was an intellectual melting pot.
Escaping across the iron curtain disguised as a washerwoman, I found myself in the West.
The Free World!
For five, or perhaps six years, I travelled the continent, meeting Jacques Monod in Paris, Luria in Rome, Keith Runcorn in London.
Each of them ignited beacon fires in my brain that have never gone out.
I kept the washerwoman costume, and wore it again from time to time to remind me of my triumphant escape.
JR OF LONDO
In 1991, I added some sequins.

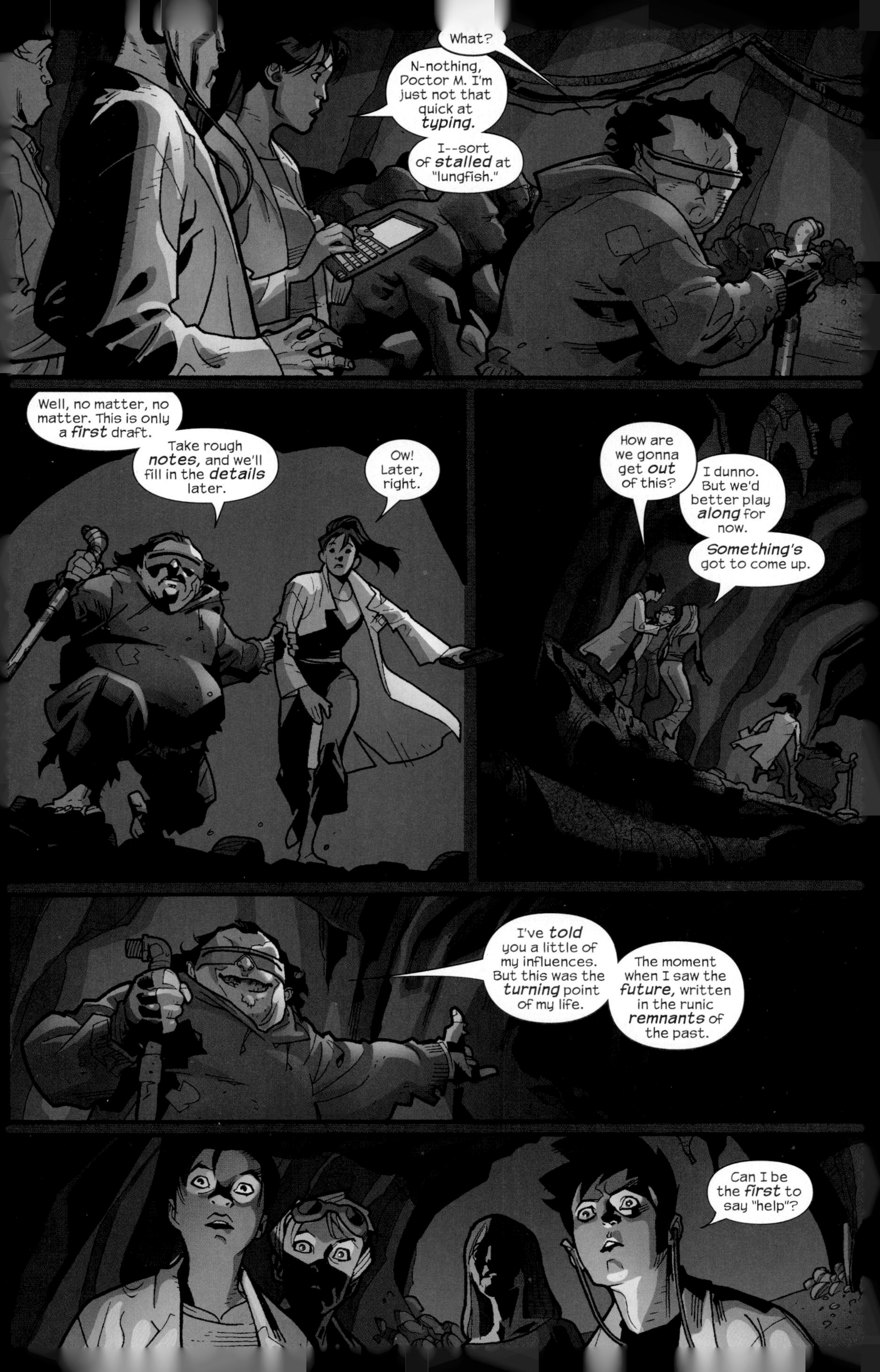
What?
N-nothing, Doctor M. I'm just not that quick at typing.
I--sort of stalled at "lungfish."
Well, no matter, no matter. This is only a first draft.
Take rough notes, and we'll fill in the details later.
Ow! Later, right.
How are we gonna get out of this?
I dunno. But we'd better play along for now.
Something's got to come up.
I've told you a little of my influences. But this was the turning point of my life.
The moment when I saw the future, written in the runic remnants of the past.
Can I be the first to say "help"?

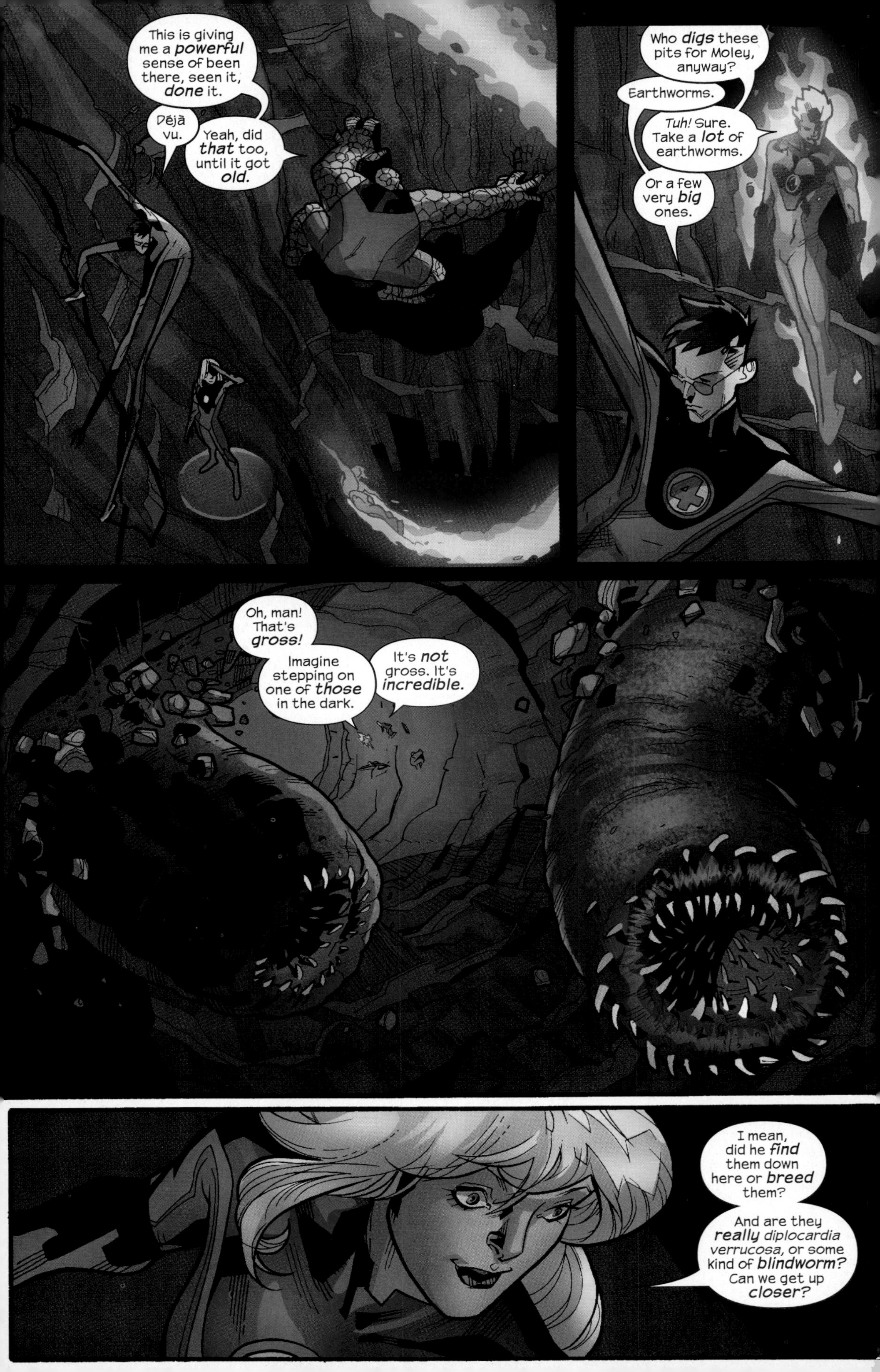
This is giving me a *powerful* sense of been there, seen it, *done* it.
Déjà vu.
Yeah, did *that* too, until it got *old.*
Who *digs* these pits for Moley, anyway?
Earthworms.
Tuh! Sure. Take a *lot* of earthworms.
Or a few very *big* ones.
Oh, man! That's *gross!*
Imagine stepping on one of *those* in the dark.
It's *not* gross. It's *incredible.*
I mean, did he *find* them down here or *breed* them?
And are they *really* *diplocardia verrucosa*, or some kind of *blindworm*? Can we get up *closer*?

Are you *sure* we're related?

What, you'd rather I *screamed* and made *barfing* noises?

Sure. Or *I* could make the barfing noises and you could *agree.* Then I'd say--

Oops. Not *good.*

Guys, I think I just *tripped* some kind of a--

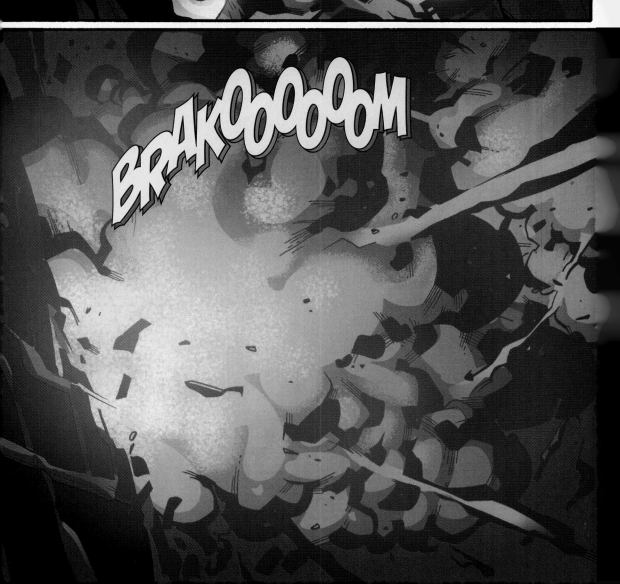

BRAKOOOOOOM

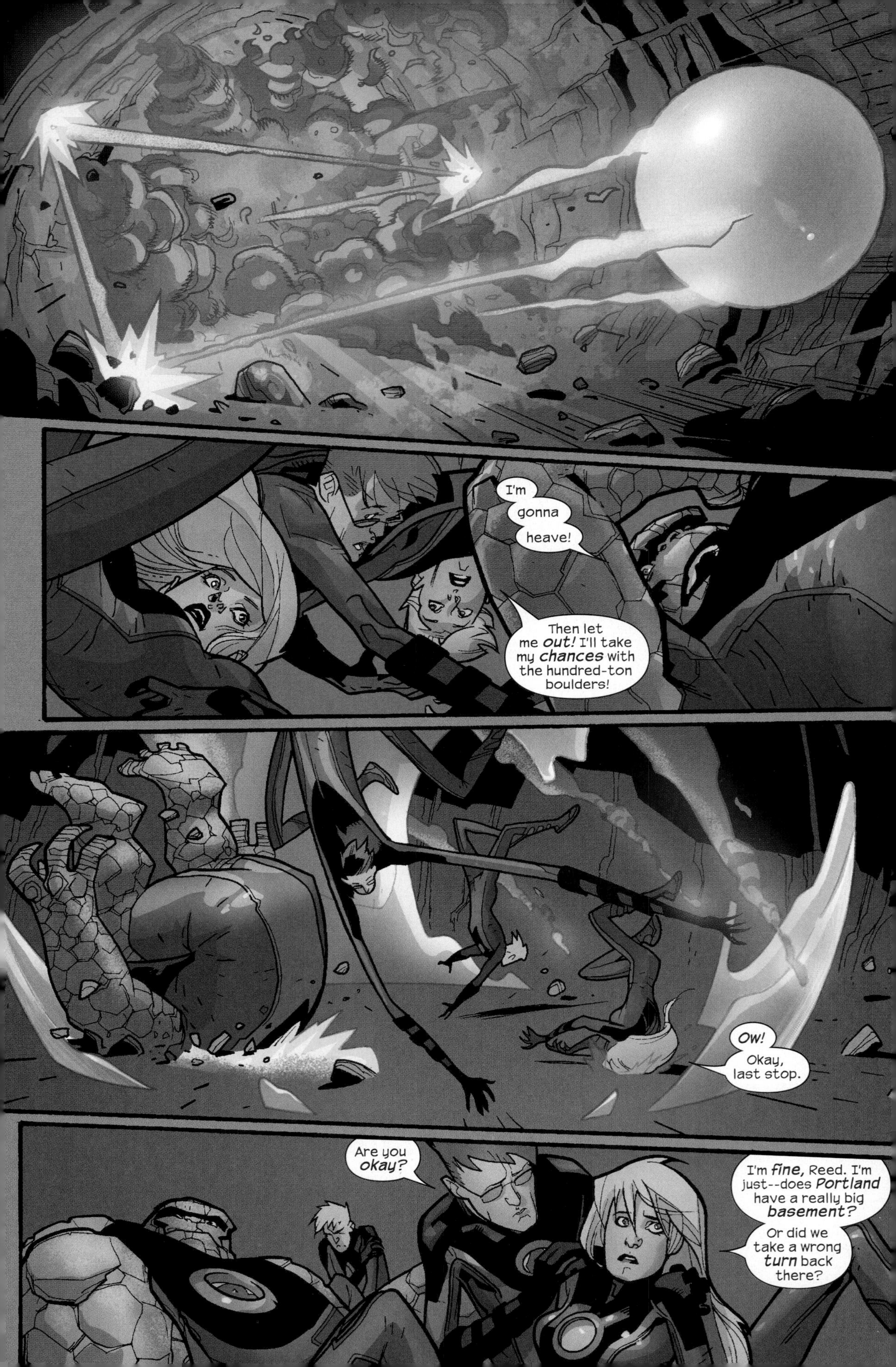
I'm
gonna
heave!
Then let me out! I'll take my chances with the hundred-ton boulders!
Ow!
Okay, last stop.
Are you okay?
I'm fine, Reed. I'm just--does Portland have a really big basement?
Or did we take a wrong turn back there?

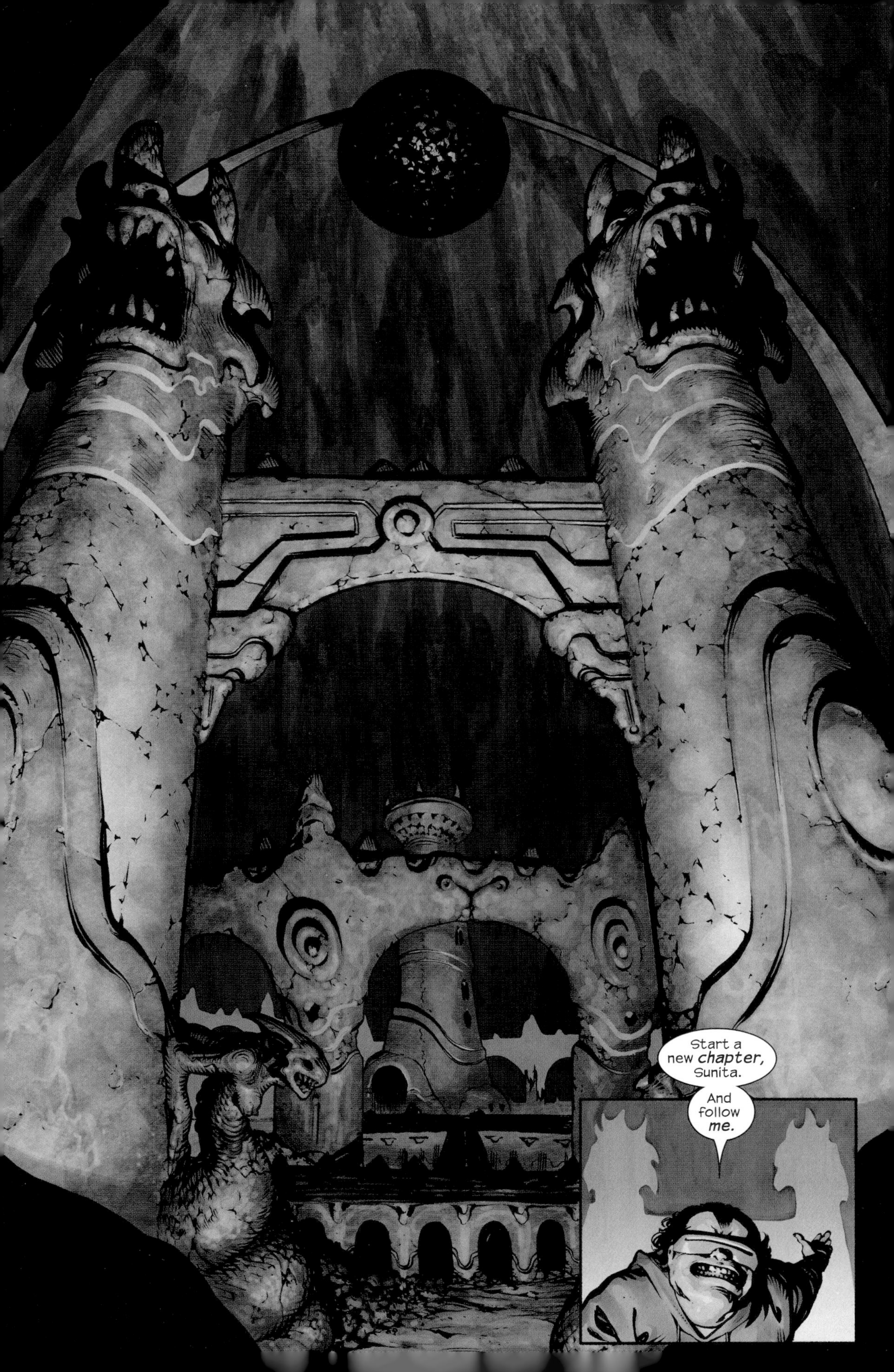

Start a new *chapter,* Sunita.
And follow *me.*

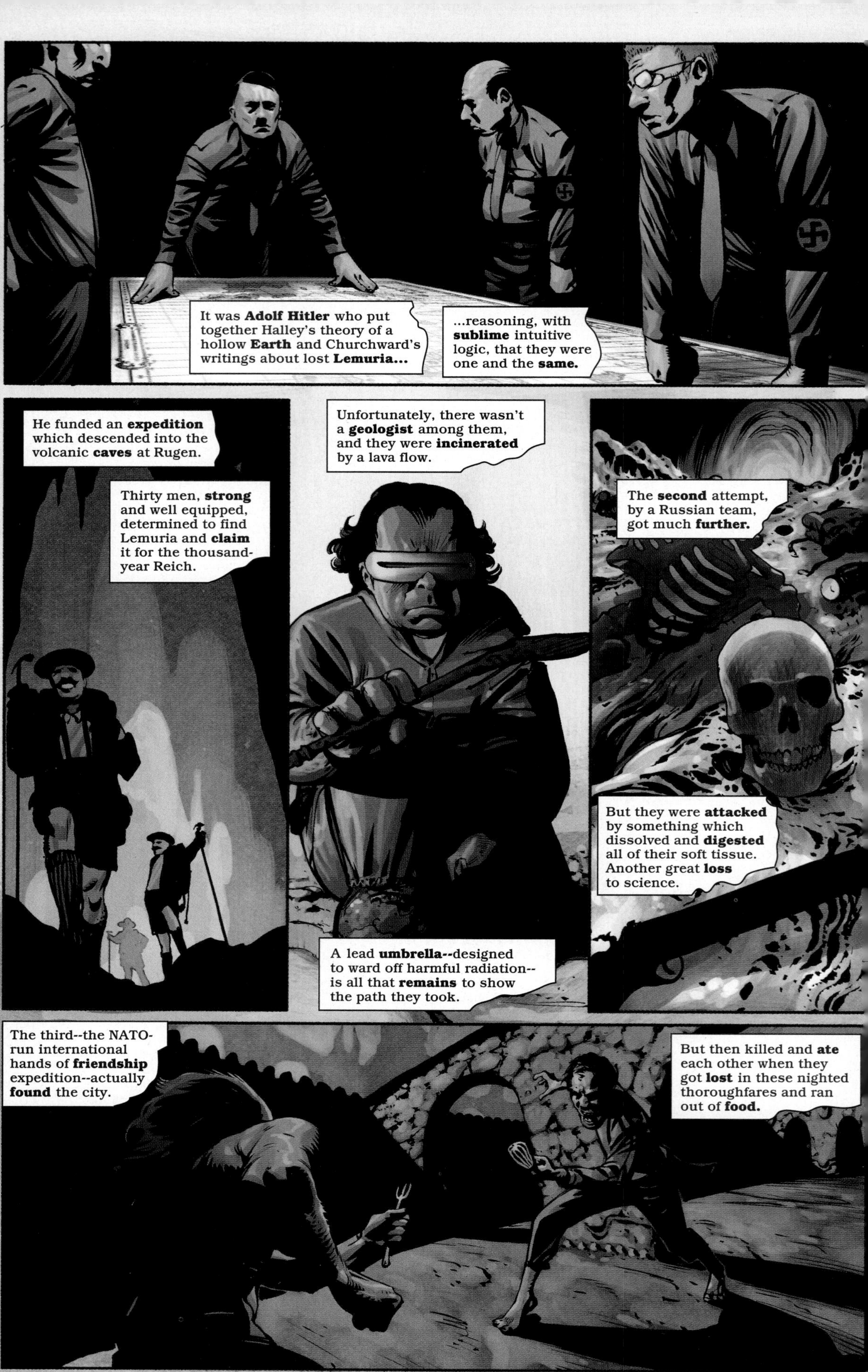
It was **Adolf Hitler** who put together Halley's theory of a hollow **Earth** and Churchward's writings about lost **Lemuria...**
...reasoning, with **sublime** intuitive logic, that they were one and the **same.**
He funded an **expedition** which descended into the volcanic **caves** at Rugen.
Thirty men, **strong** and well equipped, determined to find Lemuria and **claim** it for the thousand-year Reich.
Unfortunately, there wasn't a **geologist** among them, and they were **incinerated** by a lava flow.
A lead **umbrella--**designed to ward off harmful radiation--is all that **remains** to show the path they took.
The **second** attempt, by a Russian team, got much **further.**
But they were **attacked** by something which dissolved and **digested** all of their soft tissue. Another great **loss** to science.
The third--the NATO-run international hands of **friendship** expedition--actually **found** the city.
But then killed and **ate** each other when they got **lost** in these nighted thoroughfares and ran out of **food.**

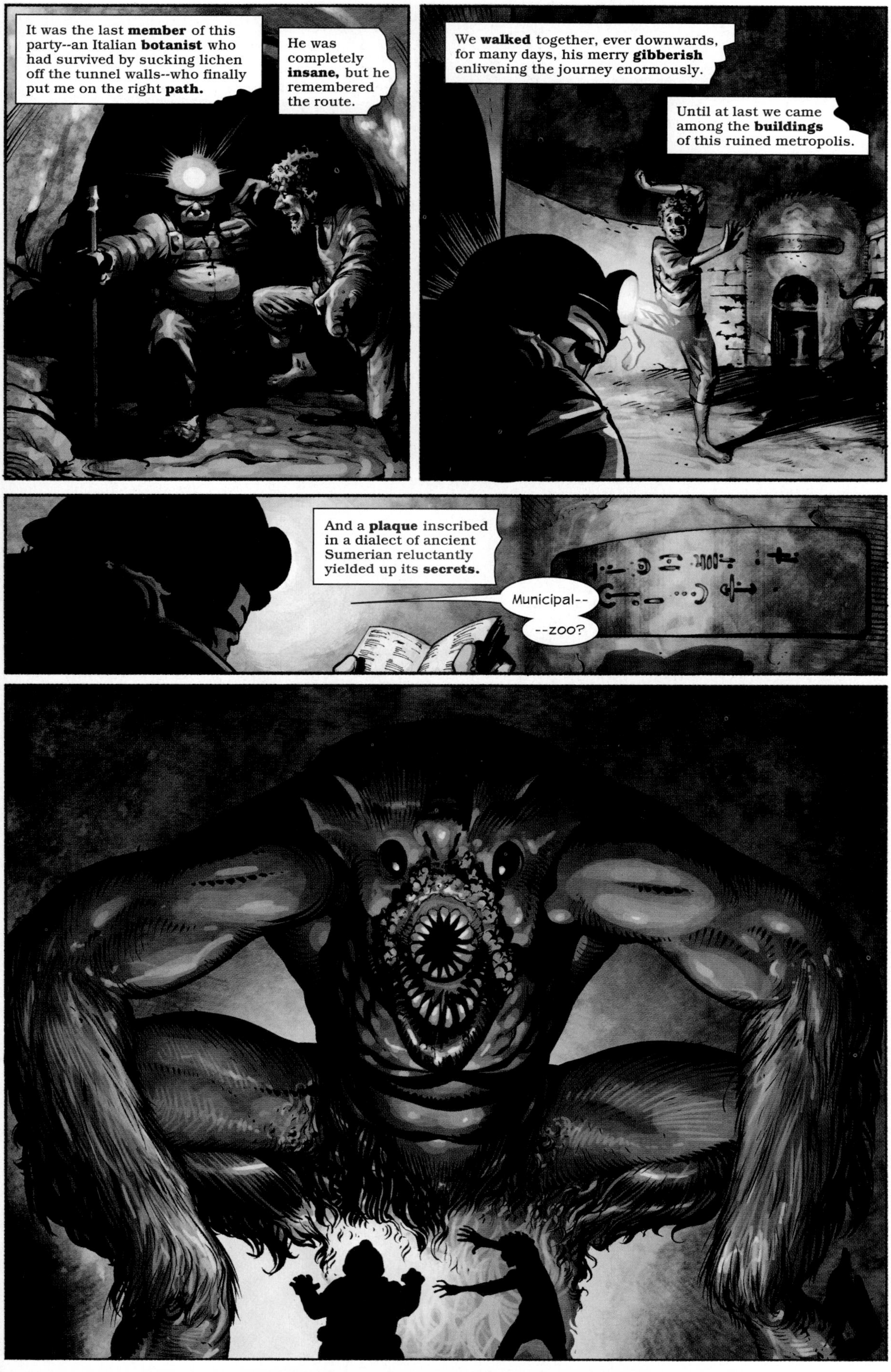
It was the last **member** of this party--an Italian **botanist** who had survived by sucking lichen off the tunnel walls--who finally put me on the right **path.**
He was completely **insane,** but he remembered the route.
We **walked** together, ever downwards, for many days, his merry **gibberish** enlivening the journey enormously.
Until at last we came among the **buildings** of this ruined metropolis.
And a **plaque** inscribed in a dialect of ancient Sumerian reluctantly yielded up its **secrets.**
Municipal--
--zoo?

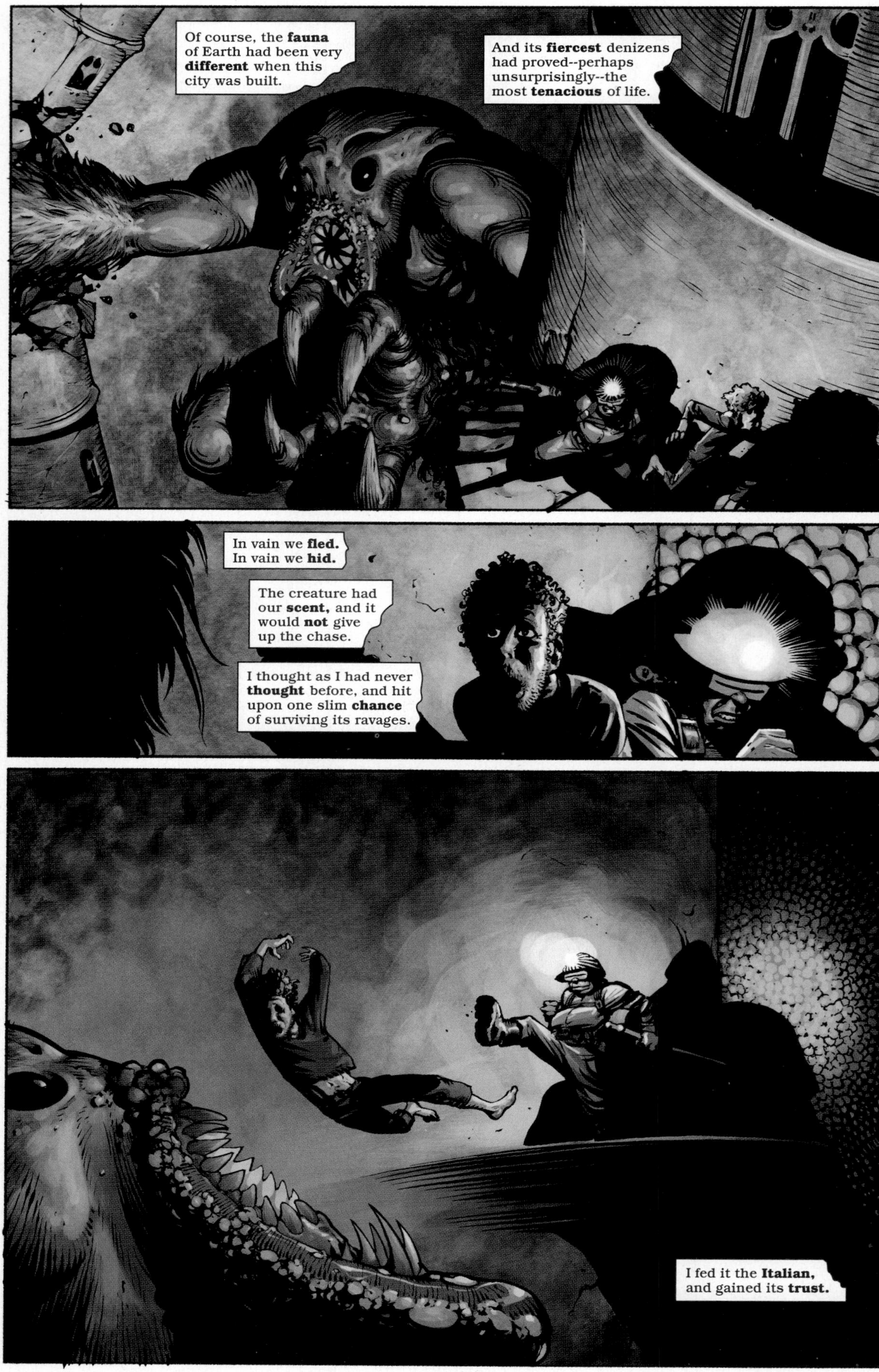
Of course, the **fauna** of Earth had been very **different** when this city was built.
And its **fiercest** denizens had proved--perhaps unsurprisingly--the most **tenacious** of life.
In vain we **fled.** In vain we **hid.**
The creature had our **scent,** and it would **not** give up the chase.
I thought as I had never **thought** before, and hit upon one slim **chance** of surviving its ravages.
I fed it the **Italian,** and gained its **trust.**

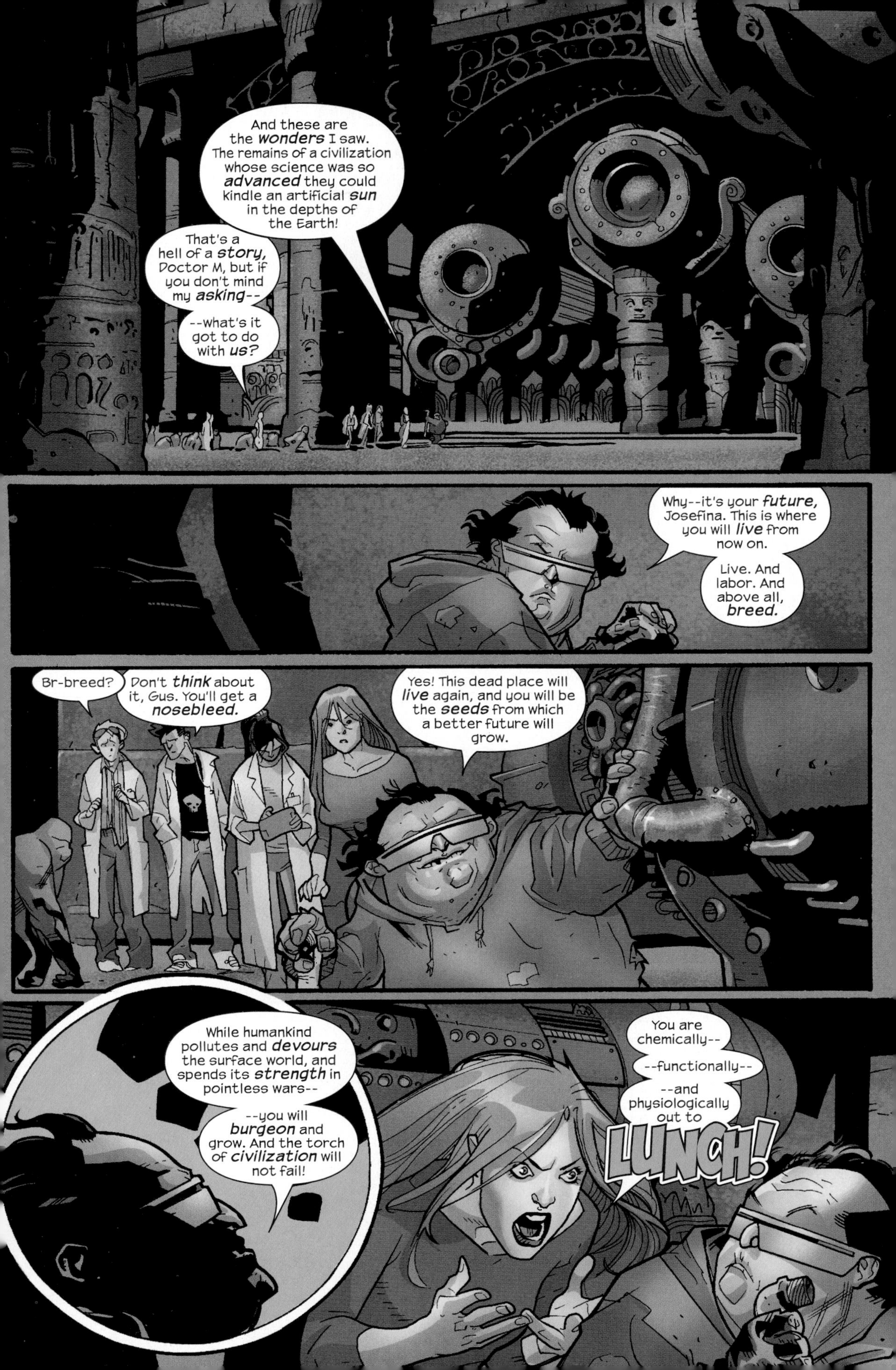
And these are the wonders I saw. The remains of a civilization whose science was so advanced they could kindle an artificial sun in the depths of the Earth!
That's a hell of a story, Doctor M, but if you don't mind my asking--
--what's it got to do with us?
Why--it's your future, Josefina. This is where you will live from now on.
Live. And labor. And above all, breed.
Br-breed?
Don't think about it, Gus. You'll get a nosebleed.
Yes! This dead place will live again, and you will be the seeds from which a better future will grow.
While humankind pollutes and devours the surface world, and spends its strength in pointless wars--
--you will burgeon and grow. And the torch of civilization will not fail!
You are chemically--
--functionally--
--and physiologically out to
LUNCH!

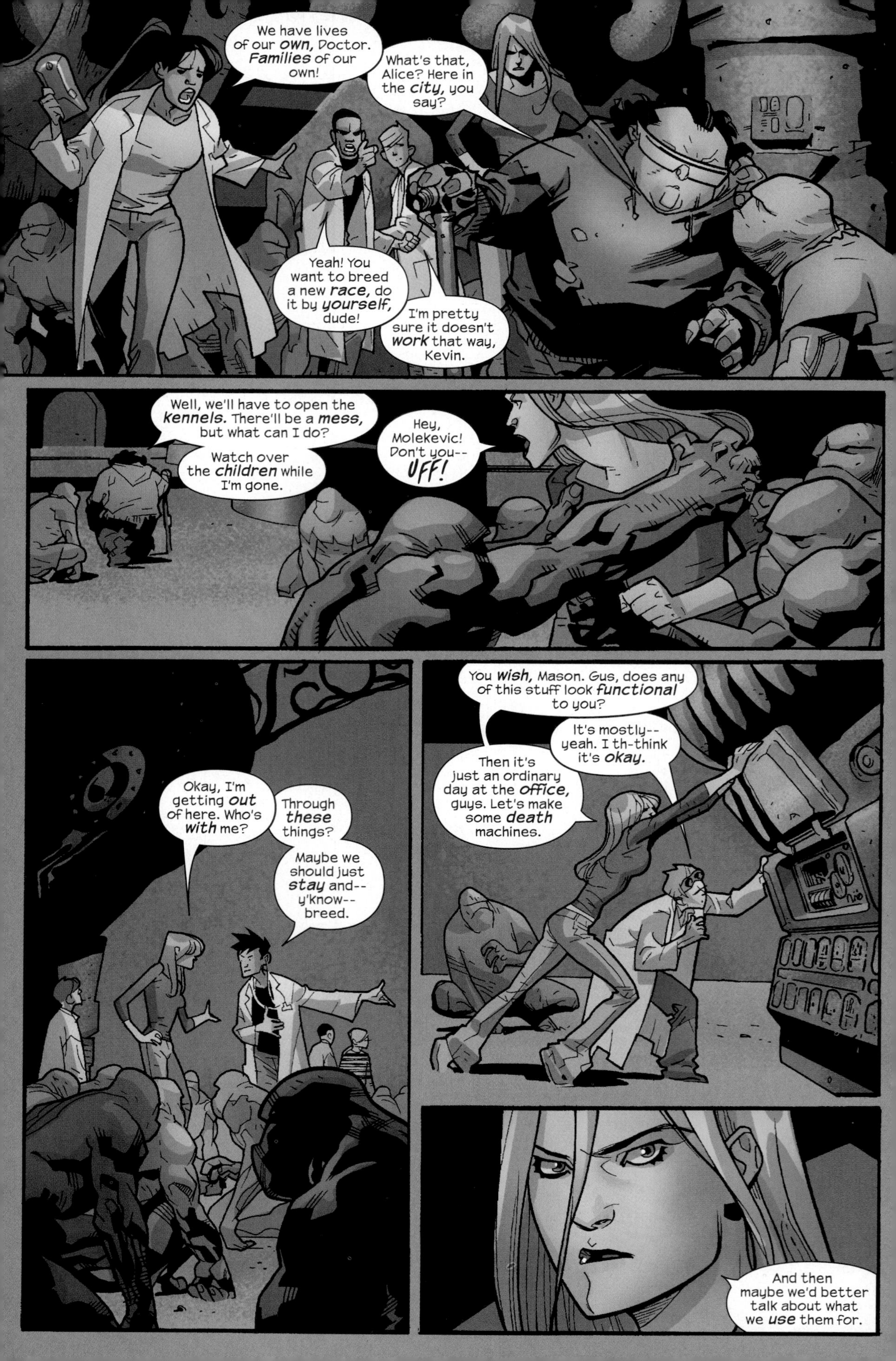
We have lives of our own, Doctor. Families of our own!
What's that, Alice? Here in the city, you say?
Yeah! You want to breed a new race, do it by yourself, dude!
I'm pretty sure it doesn't work that way, Kevin.
Well, we'll have to open the kennels. There'll be a mess, but what can I do?
Watch over the children while I'm gone.
Hey, Molekevic! Don't you-- UFF!
Okay, I'm getting out of here. Who's with me?
Through these things?
Maybe we should just stay and-- y'know-- breed.
You wish, Mason. Gus, does any of this stuff look functional to you?
It's mostly-- yeah. I th-think it's okay.
Then it's just an ordinary day at the office, guys. Let's make some death machines.
And then maybe we'd better talk about what we use them for.

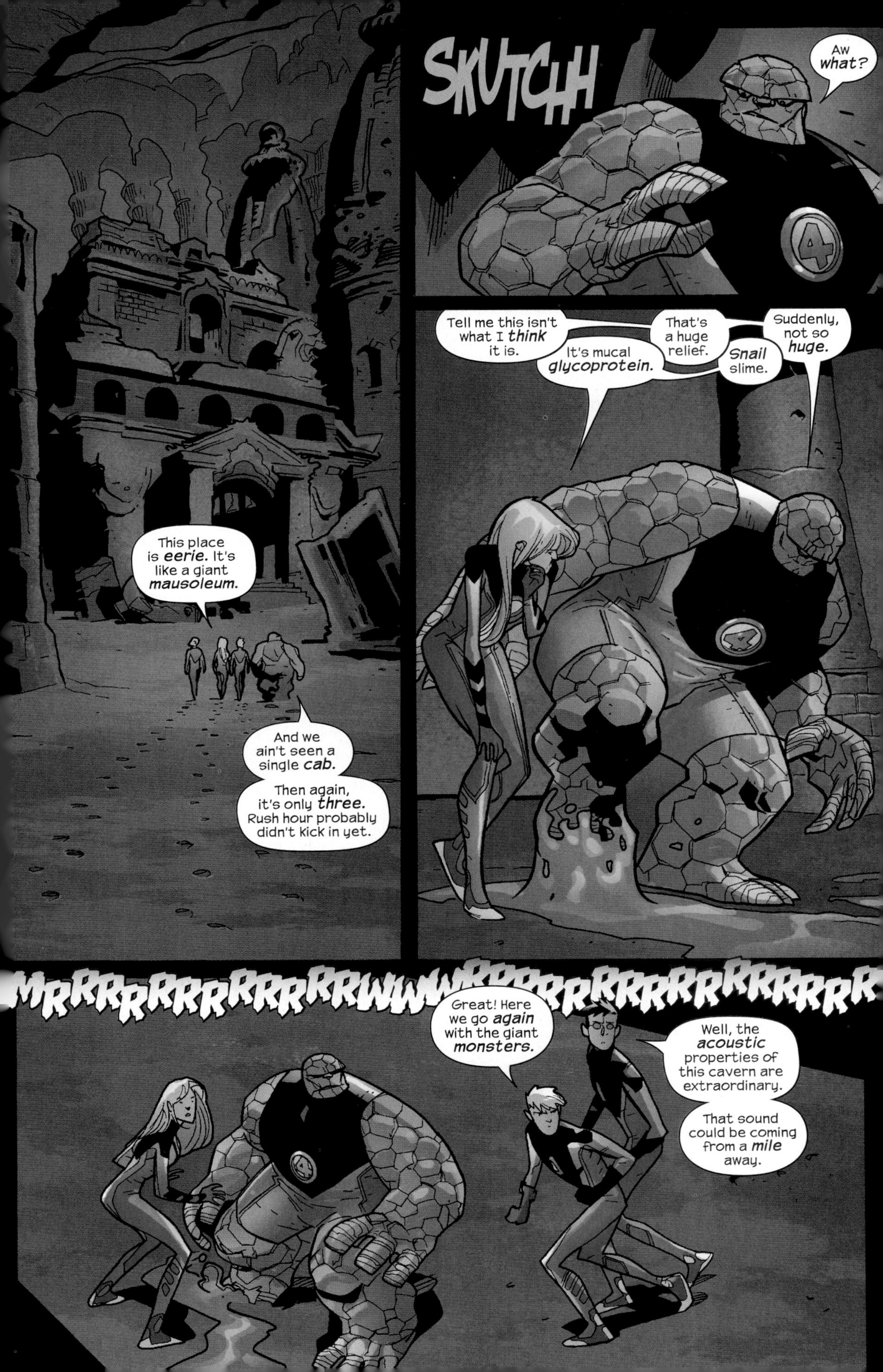
This place is eerie. It's like a giant mausoleum.
And we ain't seen a single cab.
Then again, it's only three. Rush hour probably didn't kick in yet.
SKUTCHH
Aw what?
Tell me this isn't what I think it is.
It's mucal glycoprotein.
That's a huge relief.
Snail slime.
Suddenly, not so huge.
MRRRRRRRRRRRRWWWRRRRRRRRRRRRRRR
Great! Here we go again with the giant monsters.
Well, the acoustic properties of this cavern are extraordinary.
That sound could be coming from a mile away.

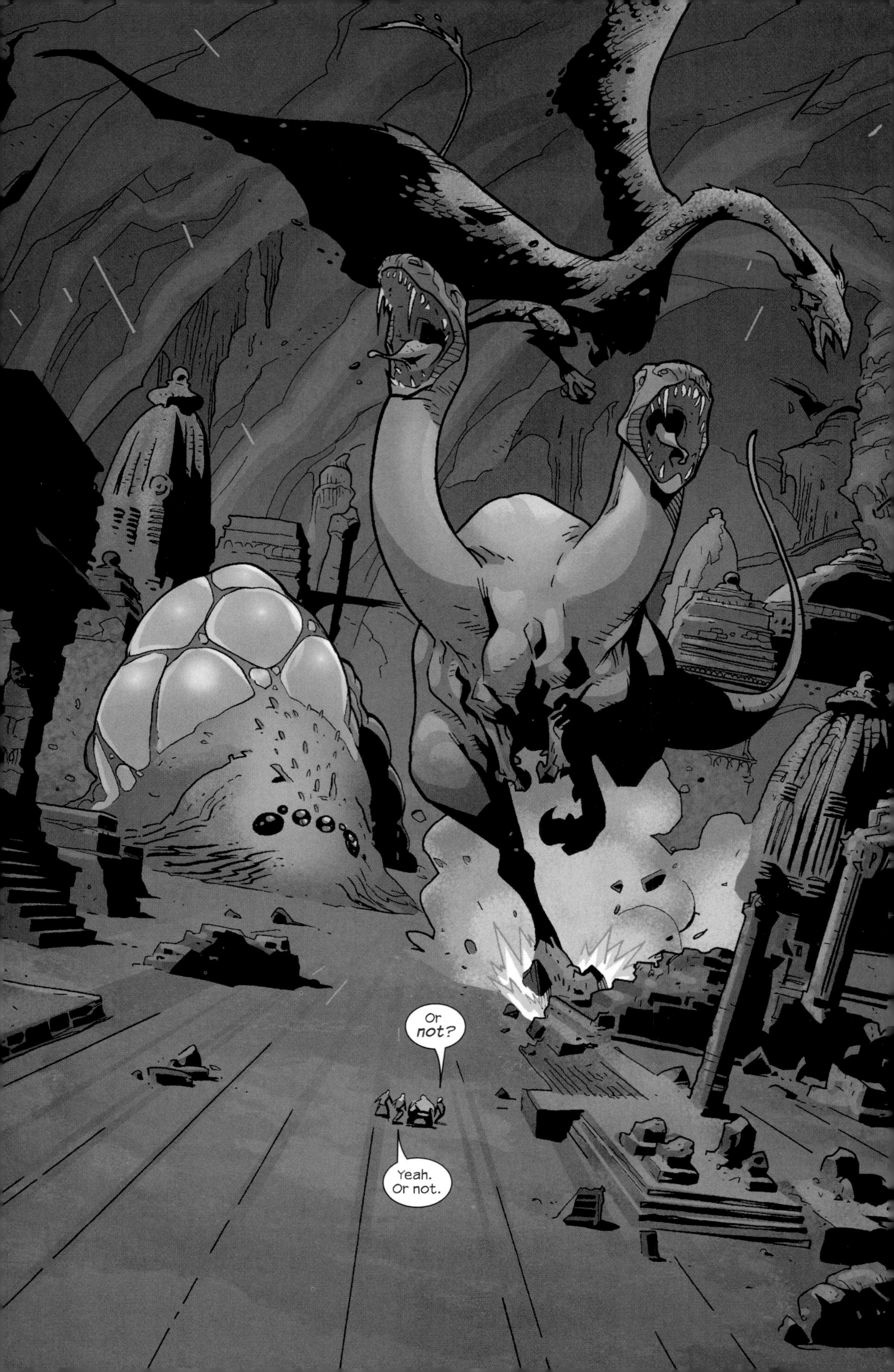
Or not?
Yeah. Or not.

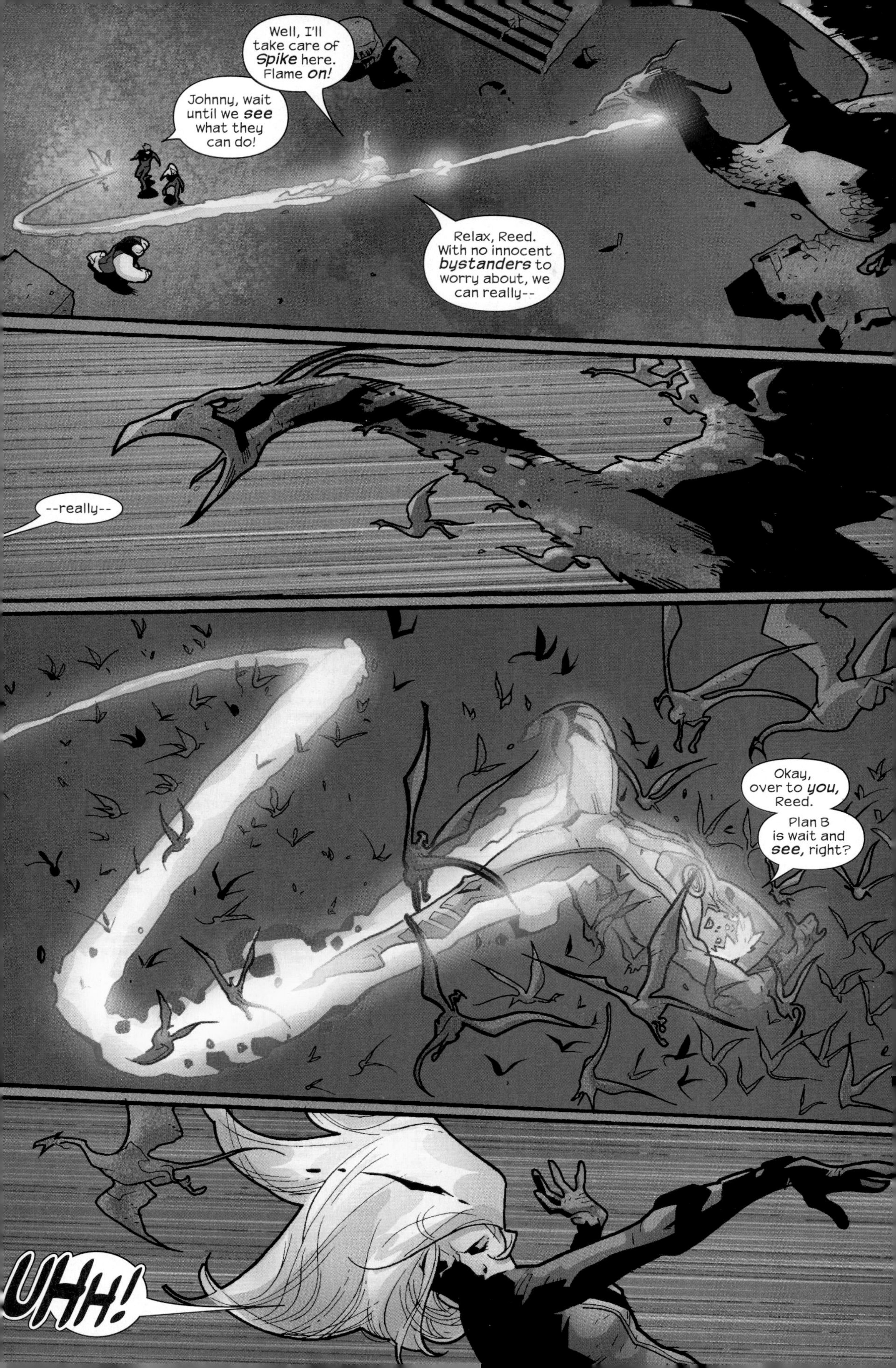

Well, I'll take care of Spike here. Flame on!
Johnny, wait until we see what they can do!
Relax, Reed. With no innocent bystanders to worry about, we can really--
--really--
Okay, over to you, Reed. Plan B is wait and see, right?
UHH!

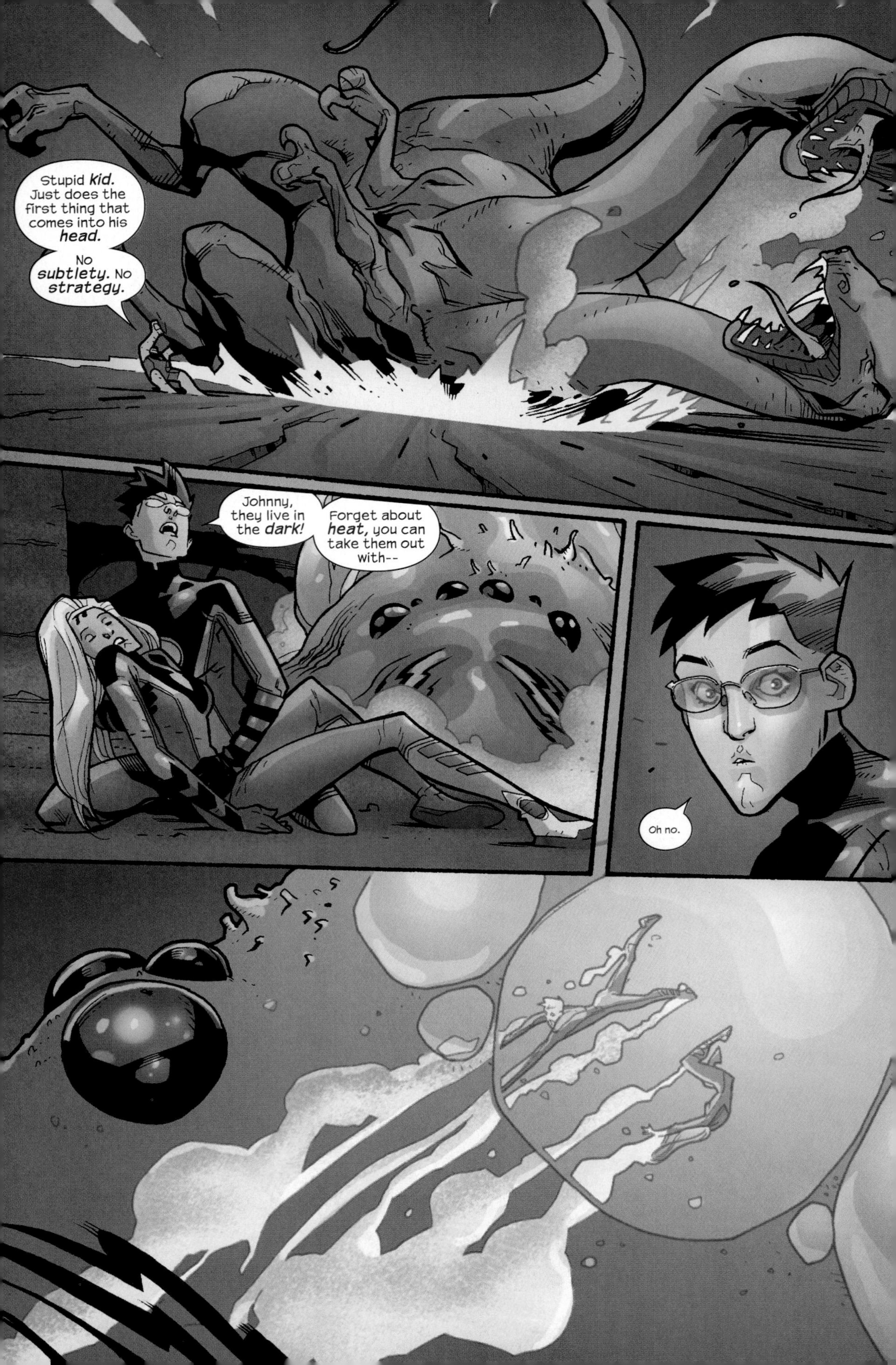
Stupid kid. Just does the first thing that comes into his head.
No subtlety. No strategy.
Johnny, they live in the dark!
Forget about heat, you can take them out with--
Oh no.

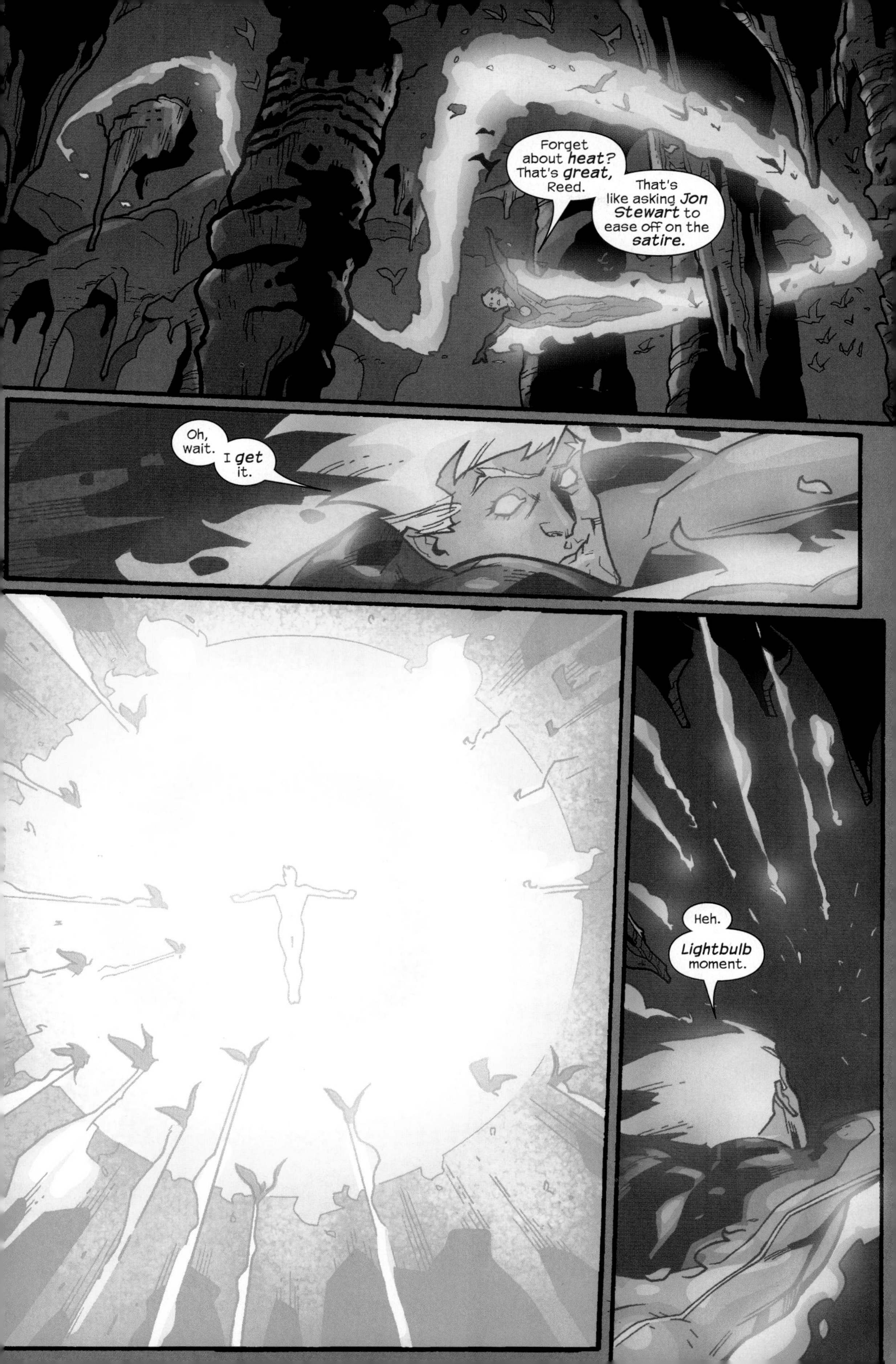
Forget about heat? That's great, Reed.
That's like asking Jon Stewart to ease off on the satire.
Oh, wait.
I get it.
Heh.
Lightbulb moment.

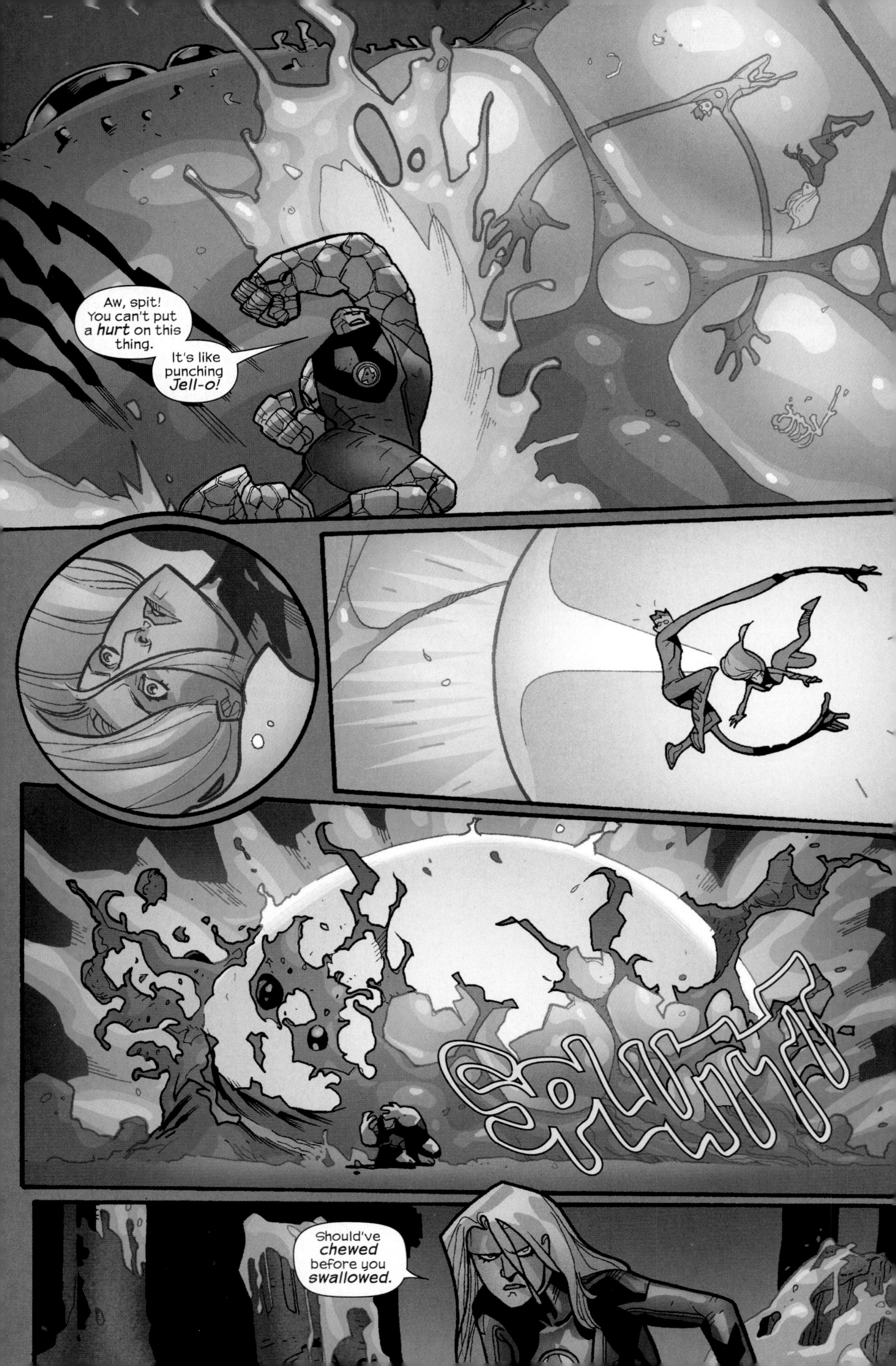
Aw, spit! You can't put a hurt on this thing.
It's like punching Jell-o!
SPLUNT
Should've chewed before you swallowed.

"Not so **fast**," I cried.

And their heads snapped **round** as my voice cut the **air** like a piano wire through ripe **Brie**.

Brie. B-R-I-E. It's a kind of *cheese*.

Mild and *creamy*. Somewhat *soft* in texture. Please, Alice, just *write*.

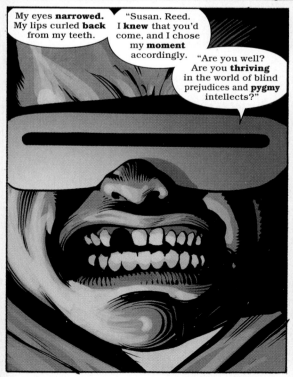

My eyes **narrowed**. My lips curled **back** from my teeth.

"Susan. Reed. I **knew** that you'd come, and I chose my **moment** accordingly.

"Are you well? Are you **thriving** in the world of blind prejudices and **pygmy** intellects?"

Personally, *I'm* happy anyplace where I don't have to wear exploded *slug*.

Doctor Molekevic, you *know* why we're here.

You've taken **hostages**. We want them *back*.

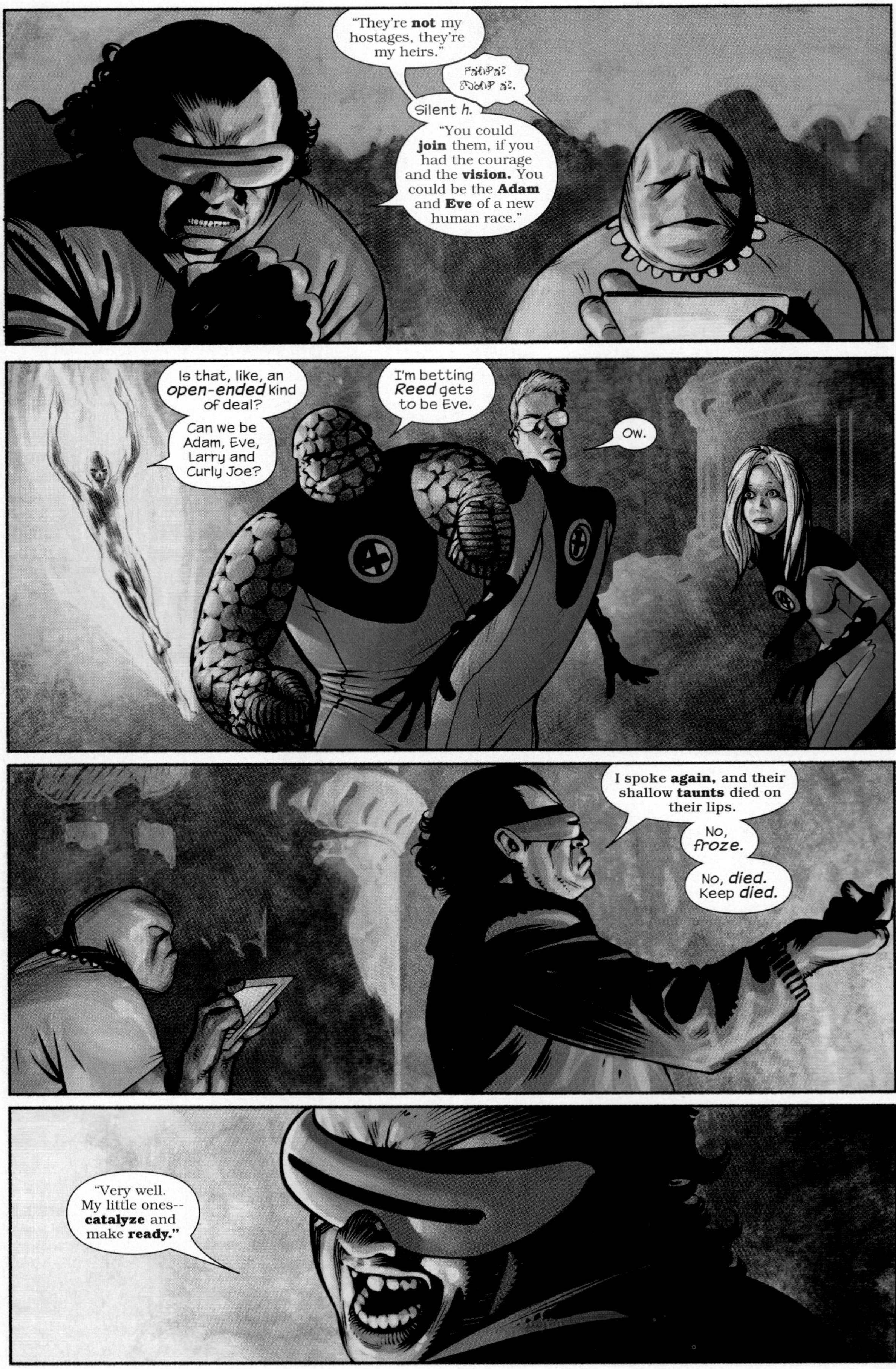
"They're **not** my hostages, they're my heirs."
Silent *h.*
"You could **join** them, if you had the courage and the **vision.** You could be the **Adam** and **Eve** of a new human race."
Is that, like, an *open-ended* kind of deal?
Can we be Adam, Eve, Larry and Curly Joe?
I'm betting *Reed* gets to be Eve.
Ow.
I spoke **again,** and their shallow **taunts** died on their lips.
No, *froze.*
No, *died.* Keep *died.*
"Very well. My little ones-- **catalyze** and make **ready.**"

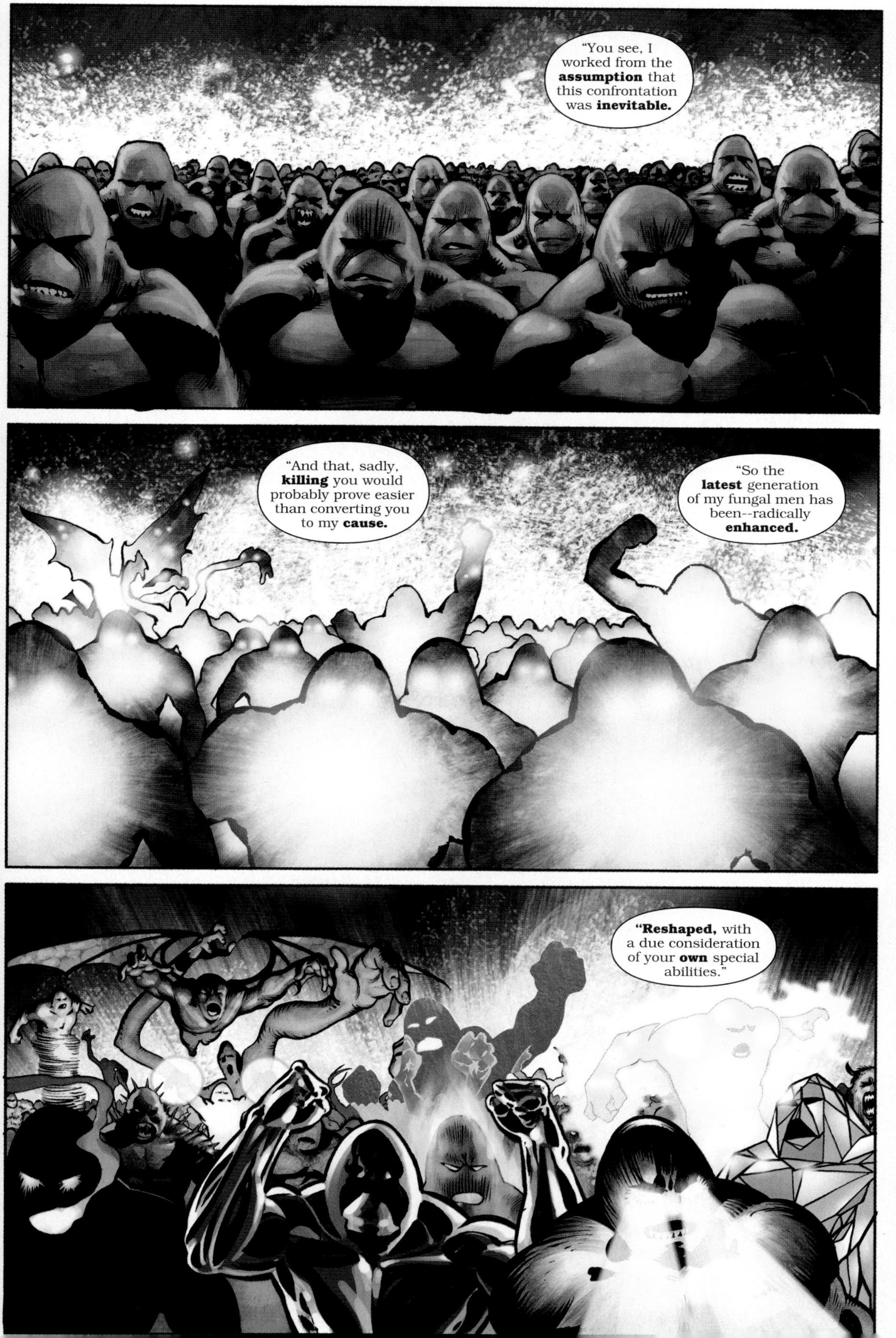
"You see, I worked from the **assumption** that this confrontation was **inevitable.**
"And that, sadly, **killing** you would probably prove easier than converting you to my **cause.**
"So the **latest** generation of my fungal men has been--radically **enhanced.**
"**Reshaped,** with a due consideration of your **own** special abilities."

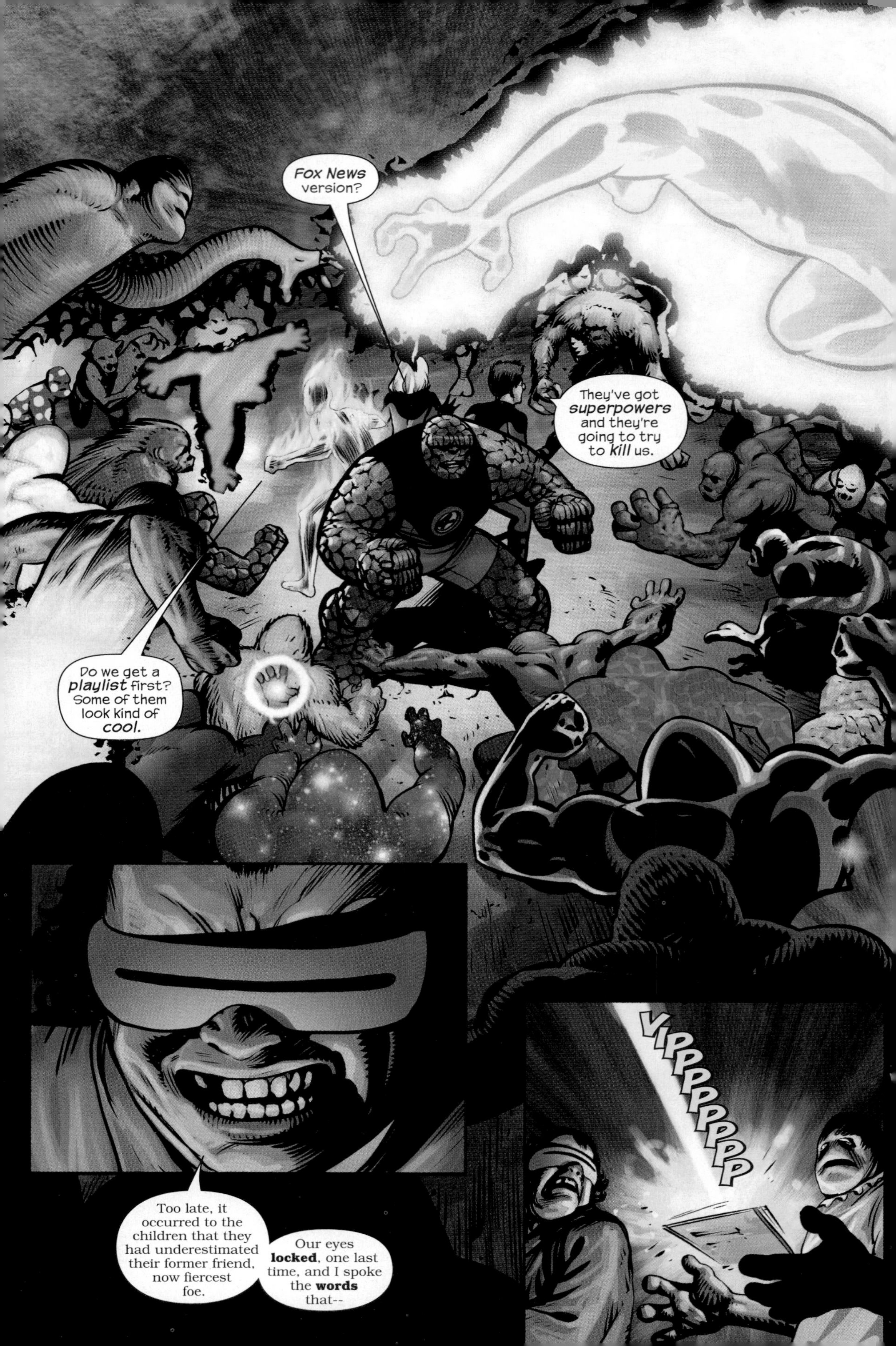
Fox News version?
They've got superpowers and they're going to try to kill us.
Do we get a playlist first? Some of them look kind of cool.
Too late, it occurred to the children that they had underestimated their former friend, now fiercest foe.
Our eyes locked, one last time, and I spoke the words that--
VIPPPPPPP

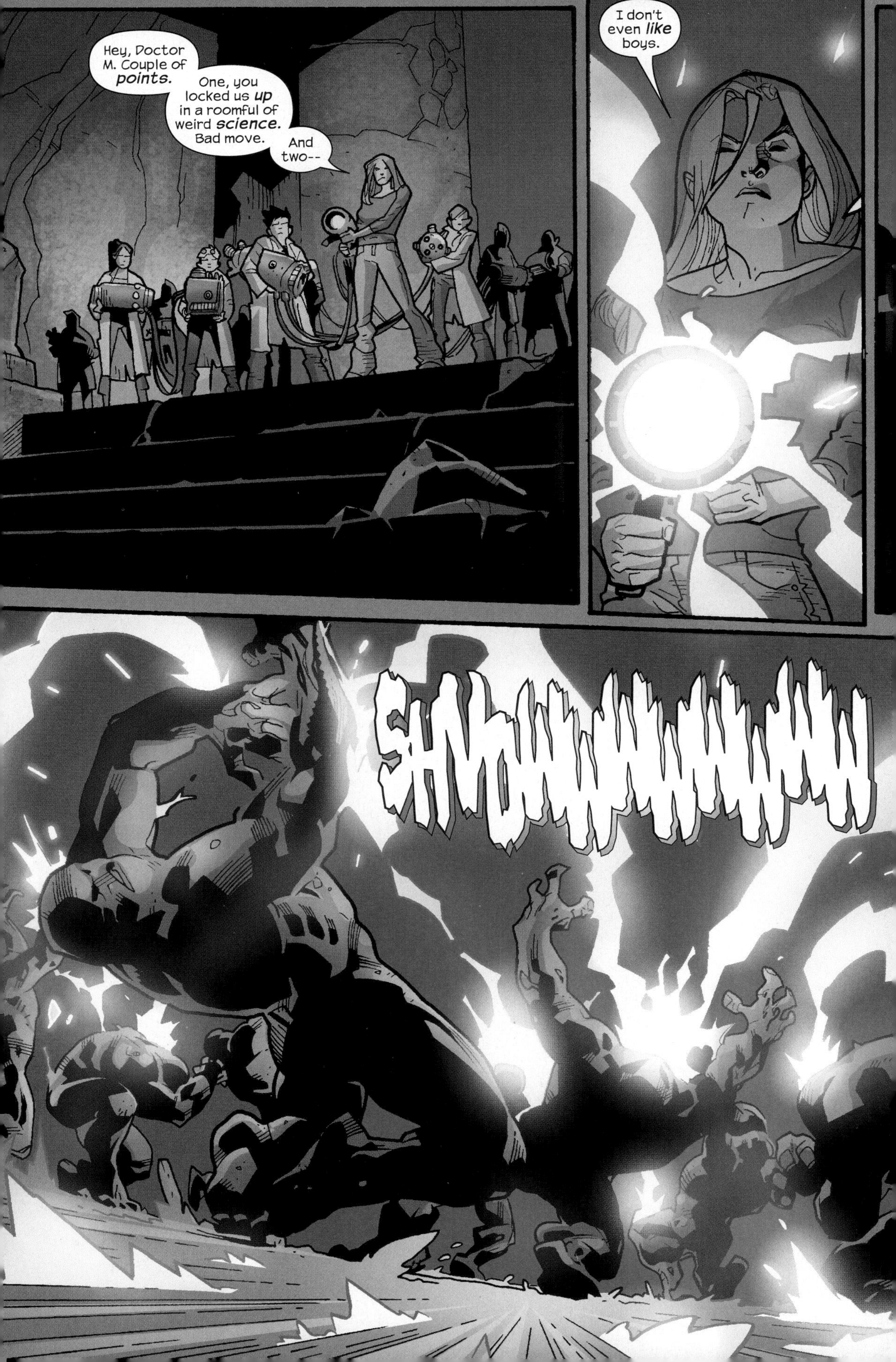

Hey, Doctor M. Couple of points.
One, you locked us up in a roomful of weird science. Bad move.
And two--
I don't even like boys.
SHHOWWWWWWWW

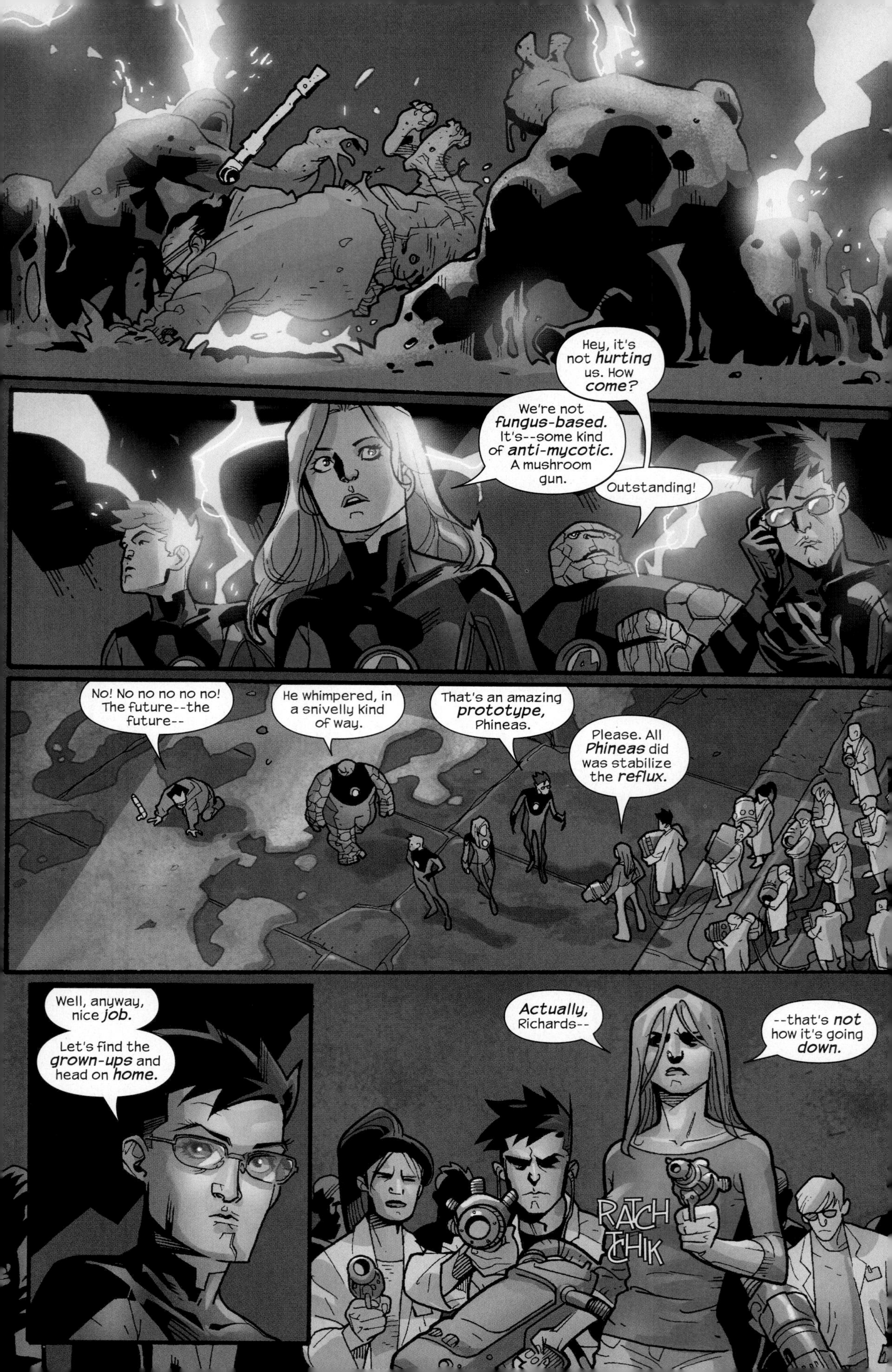

Hey, it's not hurting us. How come?
We're not fungus-based. It's--some kind of anti-mycotic. A mushroom gun.
Outstanding!
No! No no no no no! The future--the future--
He whimpered, in a snivelly kind of way.
That's an amazing prototype, Phineas.
Please. All Phineas did was stabilize the reflux.
Well, anyway, nice job.
Let's find the grown-ups and head on home.
Actually, Richards--
--that's not how it's going down.
RATCH CHIK

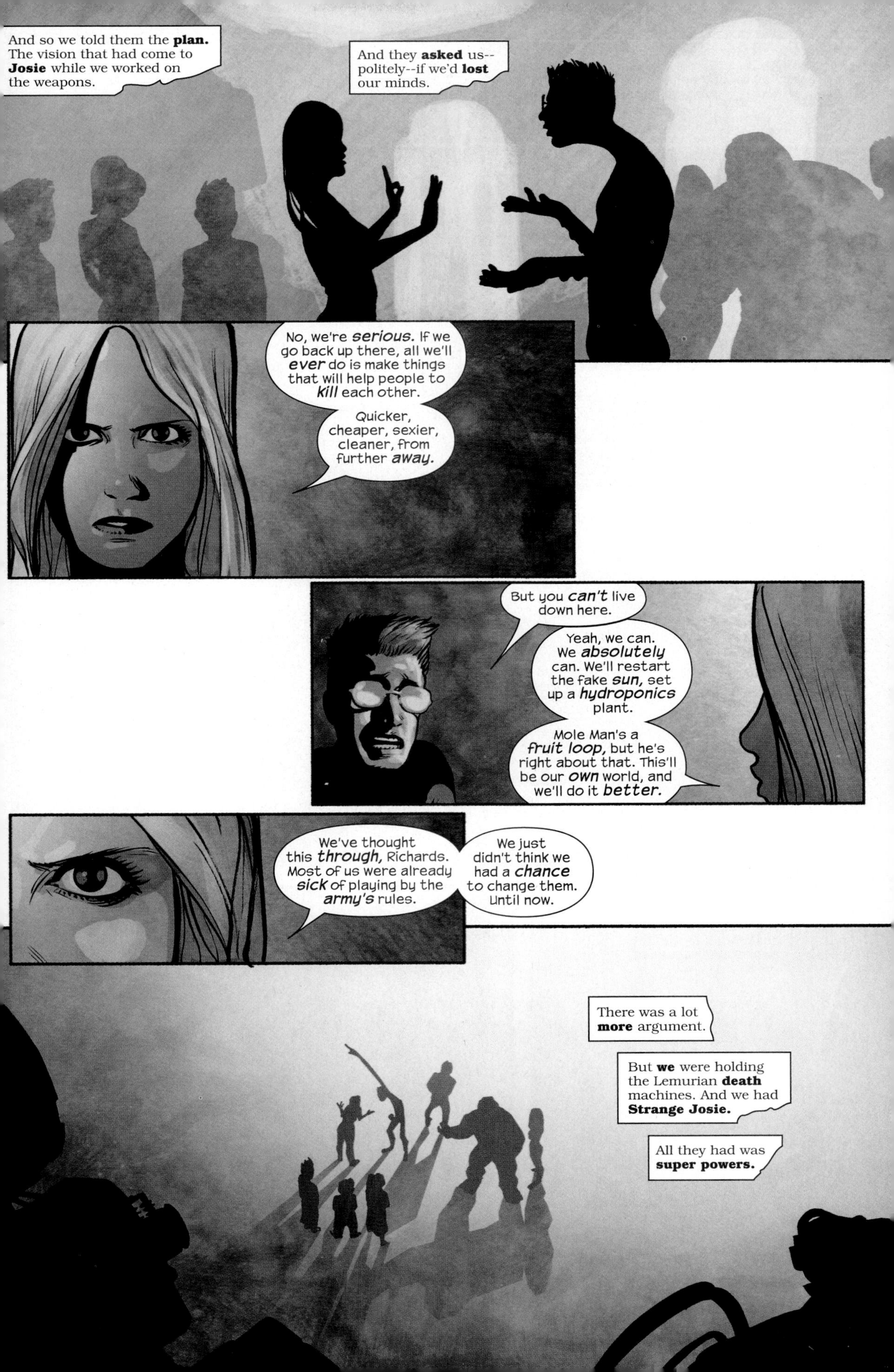

And so we told them the **plan.** The vision that had come to **Josie** while we worked on the weapons.
And they **asked** us--politely--if we'd **lost** our minds.
No, we're *serious.* If we go back up there, all we'll *ever* do is make things that will help people to *kill* each other.
Quicker, cheaper, sexier, cleaner, from further *away.*
But you *can't* live down here.
Yeah, we can. We *absolutely* can. We'll restart the fake *sun,* set up a *hydroponics* plant.
Mole Man's a *fruit loop,* but he's right about that. This'll be our *own* world, and we'll do it *better.*
We've thought this *through,* Richards. Most of us were already *sick* of playing by the *army's* rules.
We just didn't think we had a *chance* to change them. Until now.
There was a lot **more** argument.
But **we** were holding the Lemurian **death** machines. And we had **Strange Josie.**
All they had was **super powers.**

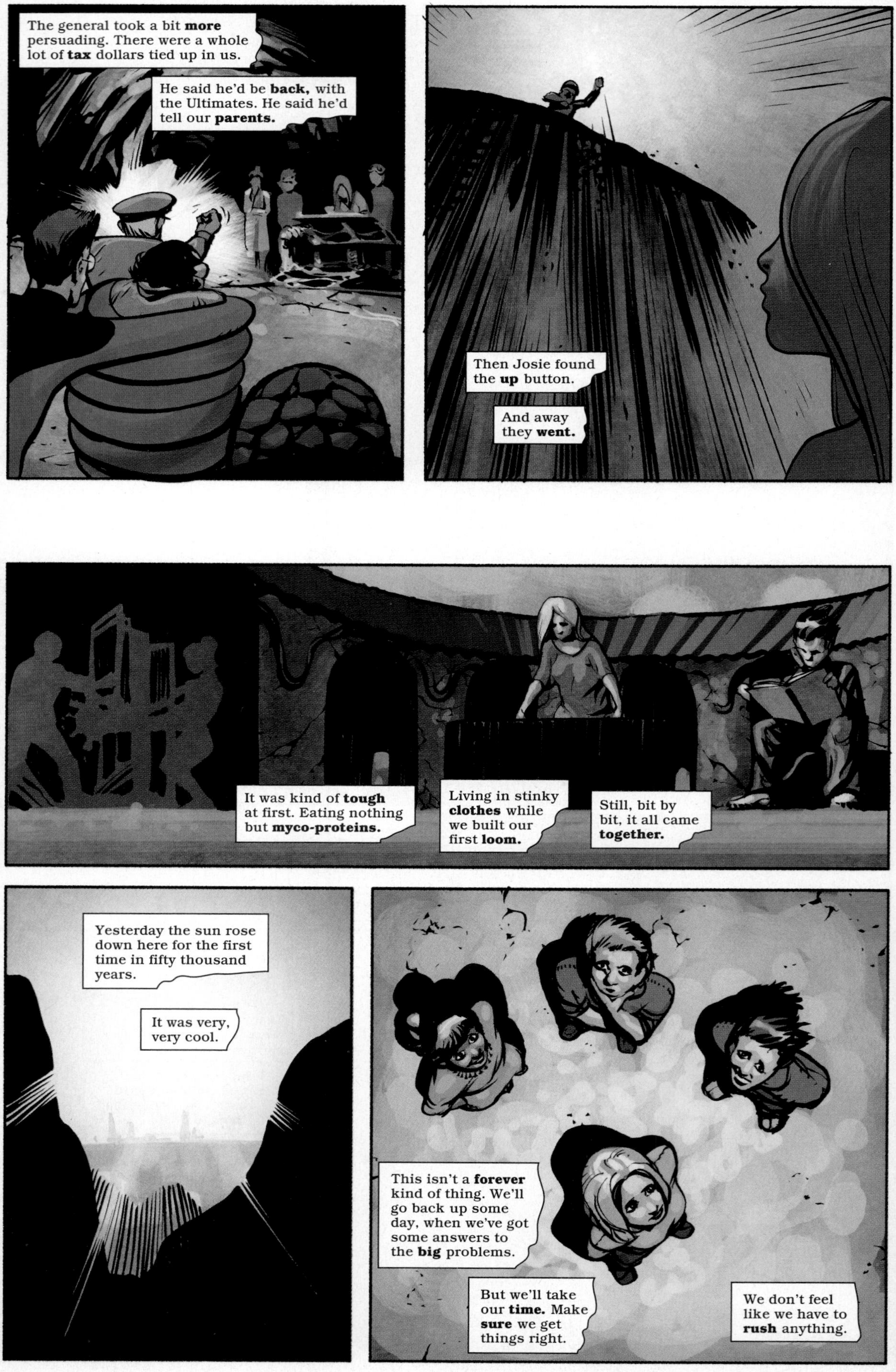
The general took a bit **more** persuading. There were a whole lot of **tax** dollars tied up in us.
He said he'd be **back,** with the Ultimates. He said he'd tell our **parents.**
Then Josie found the **up** button.
And away they **went.**
It was kind of **tough** at first. Eating nothing but **myco-proteins.**
Living in stinky **clothes** while we built our first **loom.**
Still, bit by bit, it all came **together.**
Yesterday the sun rose down here for the first time in fifty thousand years.
It was very, very cool.
This isn't a **forever** kind of thing. We'll go back up some day, when we've got some answers to the **big** problems.
But we'll take our **time.** Make **sure** we get things right.
We don't feel like we have to **rush** anything.

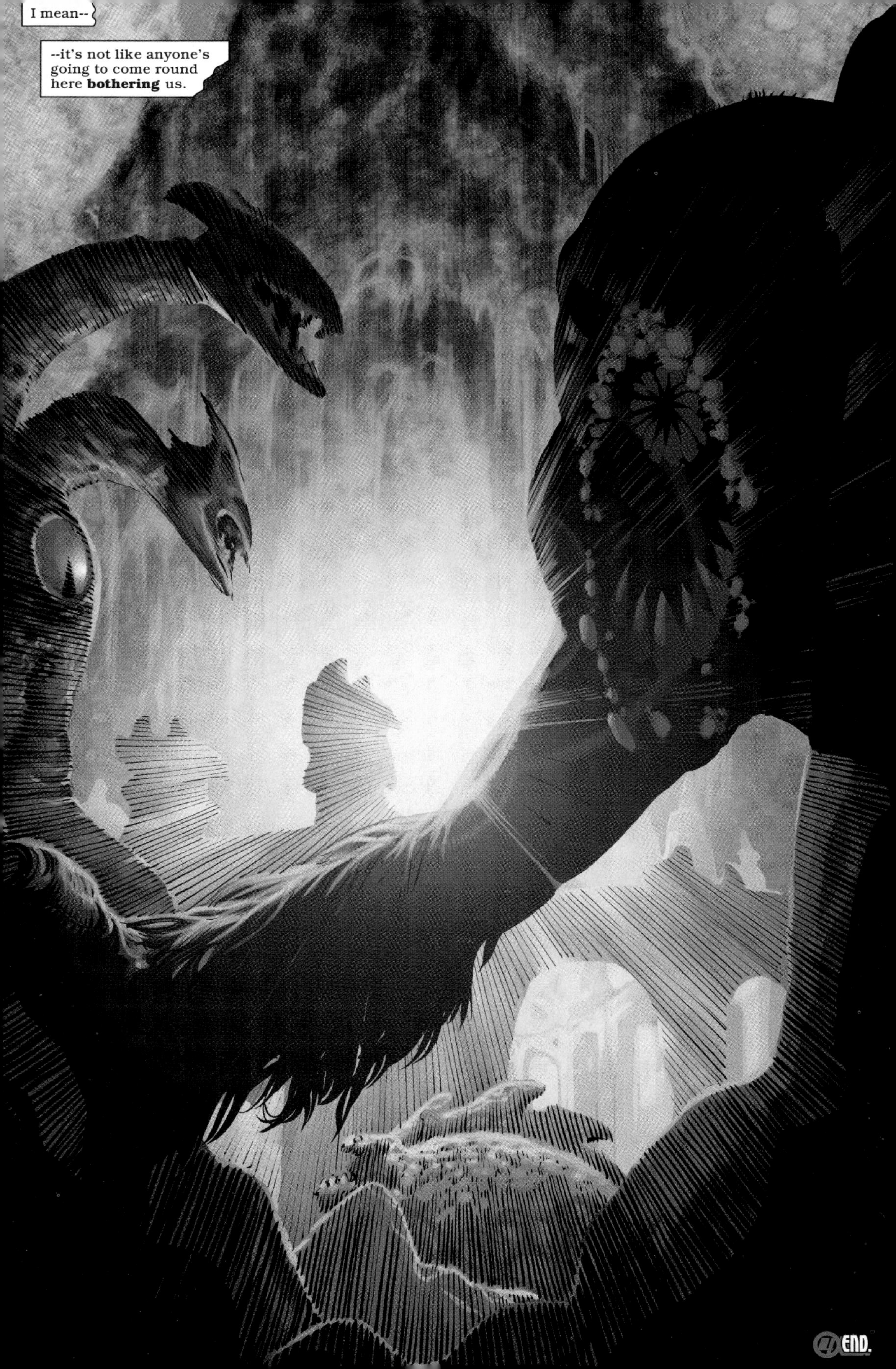
I mean--
--it's not like anyone's going to come round here **bothering** us.
END.

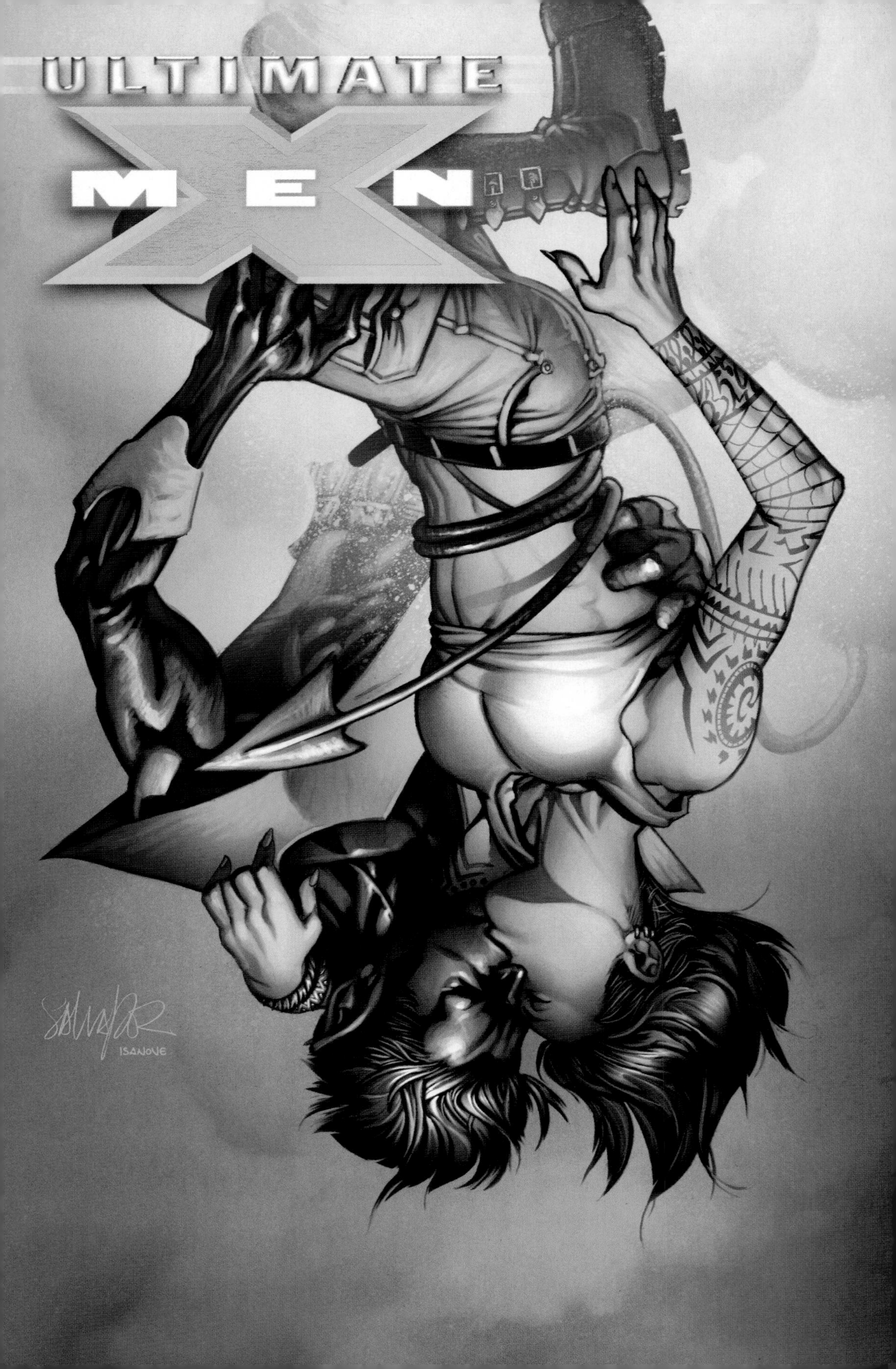
ULTIMATE
X MEN
ISANOVE

PREVIOUSLY IN ULTIMATE X-MEN:

Born with strange and amazing abilities, the X-Men are young mutant heroes, sworn to protect a world that fears and hates them.

One member of the team—Alison Blaire, better known as the punk singer, Dazzler—has been in a coma for the past several weeks, after she was injured in battle.

Her teammate, Nightcrawler, has been acting unusually since Dazzler's injury, frequently holding vigil in her hospital room.

Before joining the X-Men, Nightcrawler had been forced into working as an agent for the black-ops unit called Weapon X, which tortured mutants and turned them into killers...

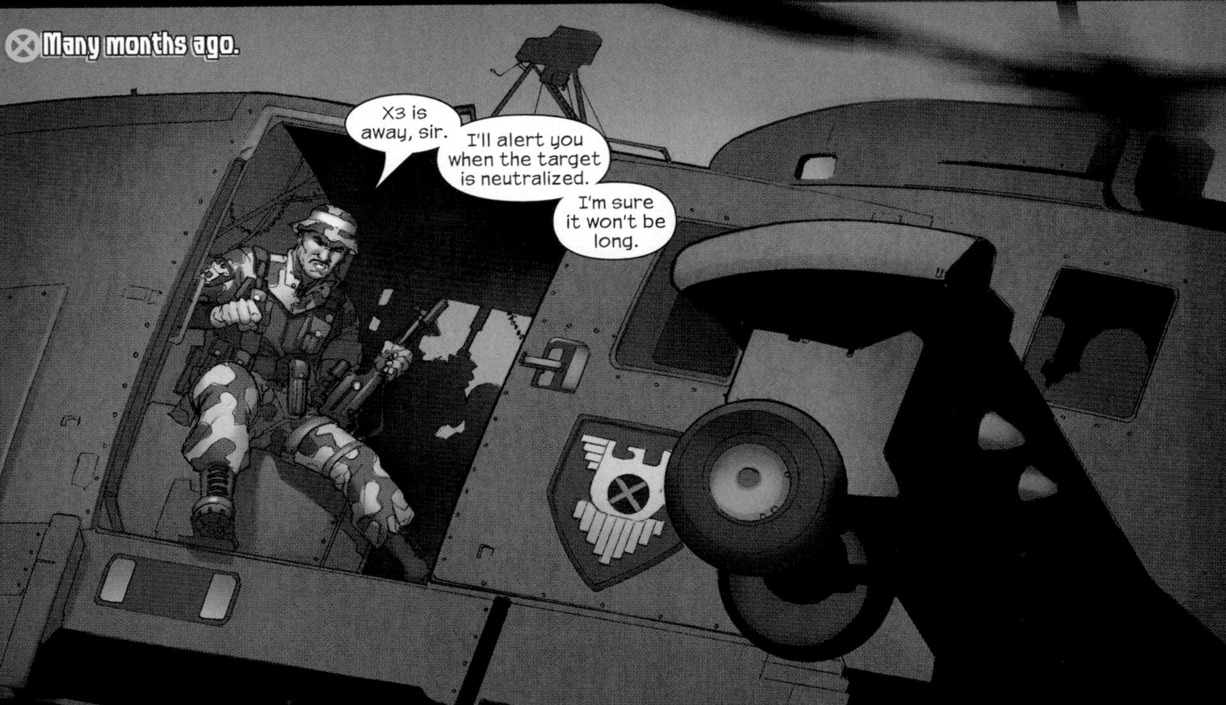
Many months ago.
X3 is away, sir.
I'll alert you when the target is neutralized.
I'm sure it won't be long.

BREAKING POINT

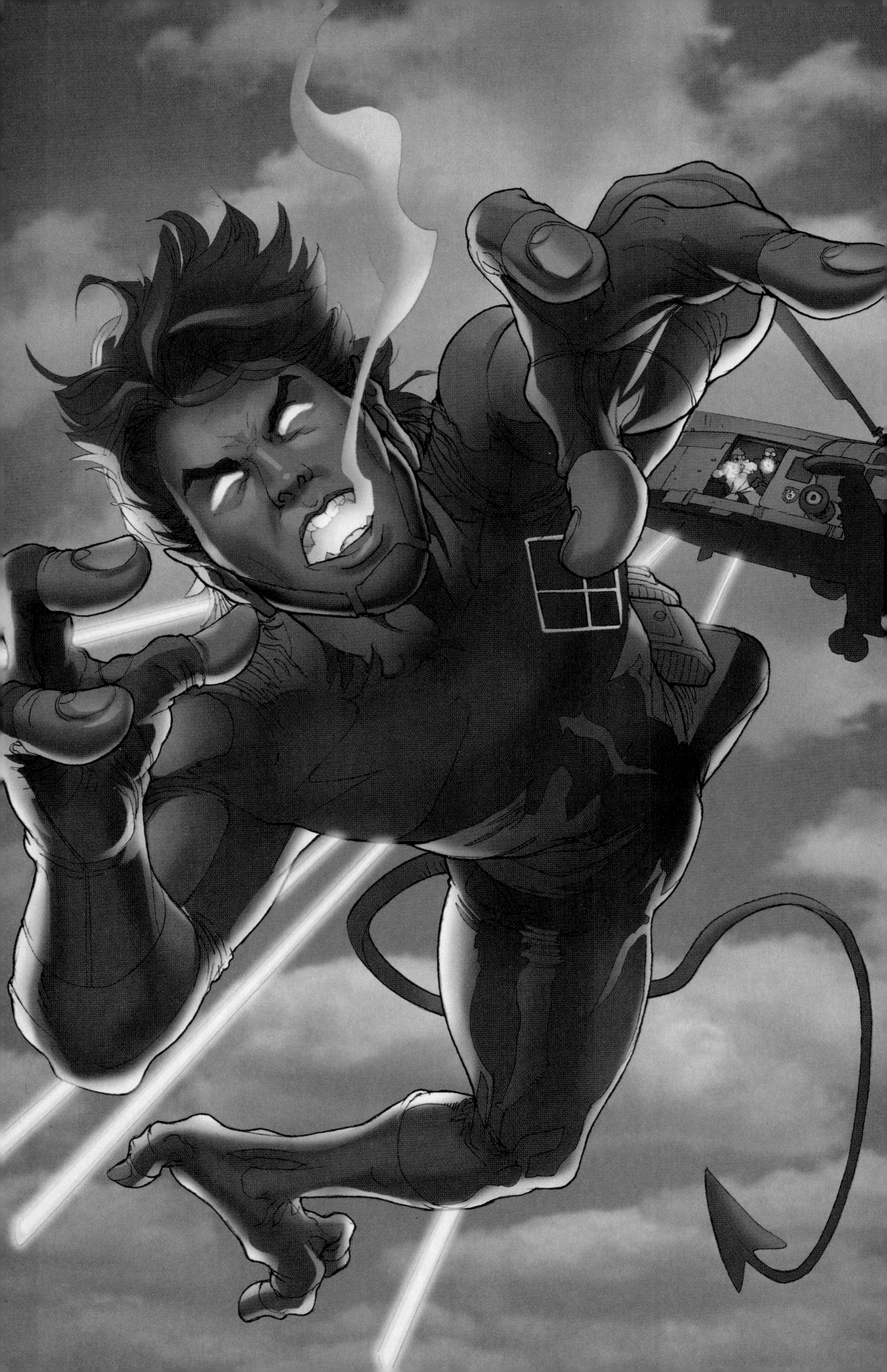

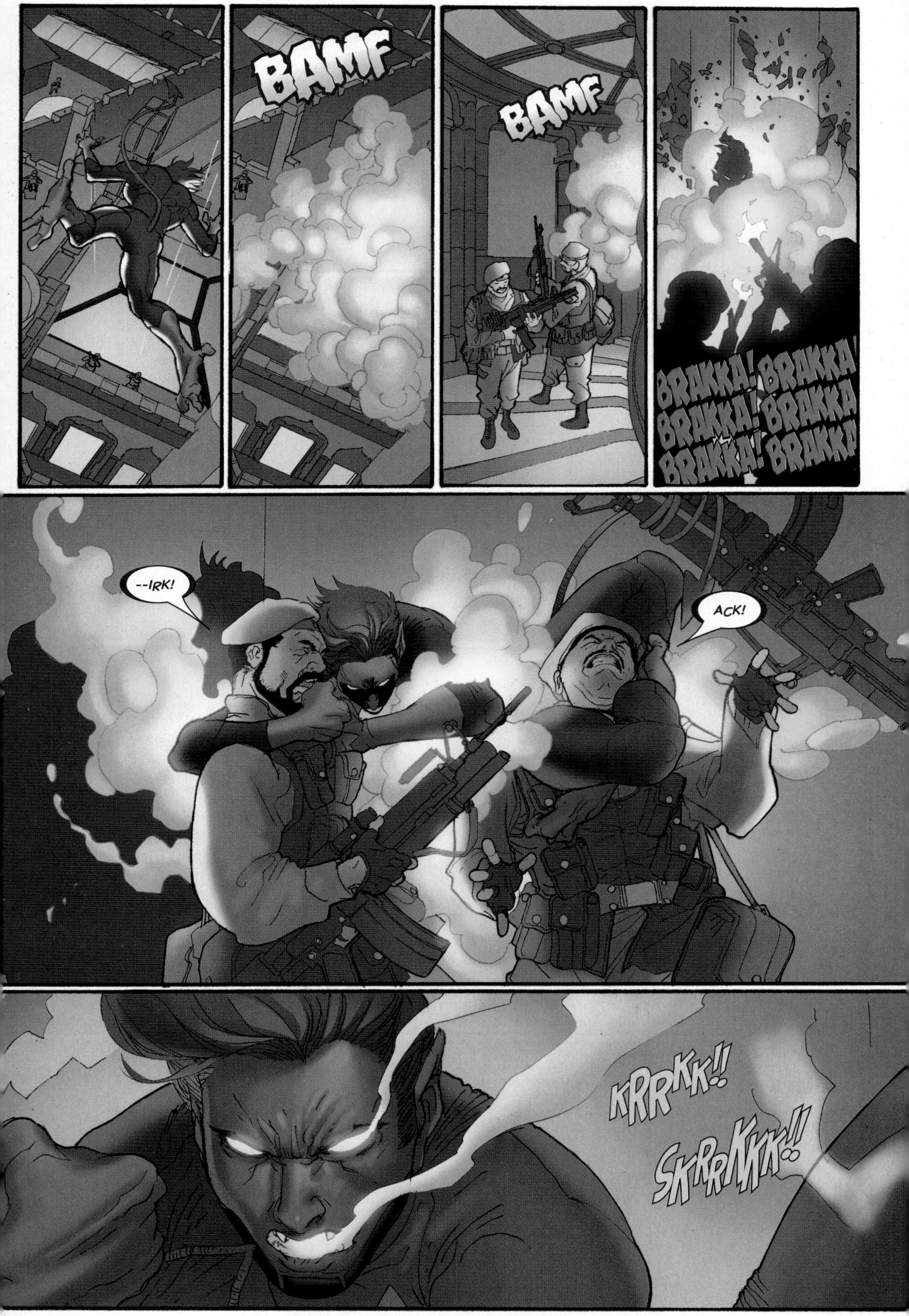
BAMF
BAMF
BRAKKA! BRAKKA! BRAKKA! BRAKKA! BRAKKA! BRAKKA!
--IRK!
ACK!
KRRKK!!
SKRRKKK!!

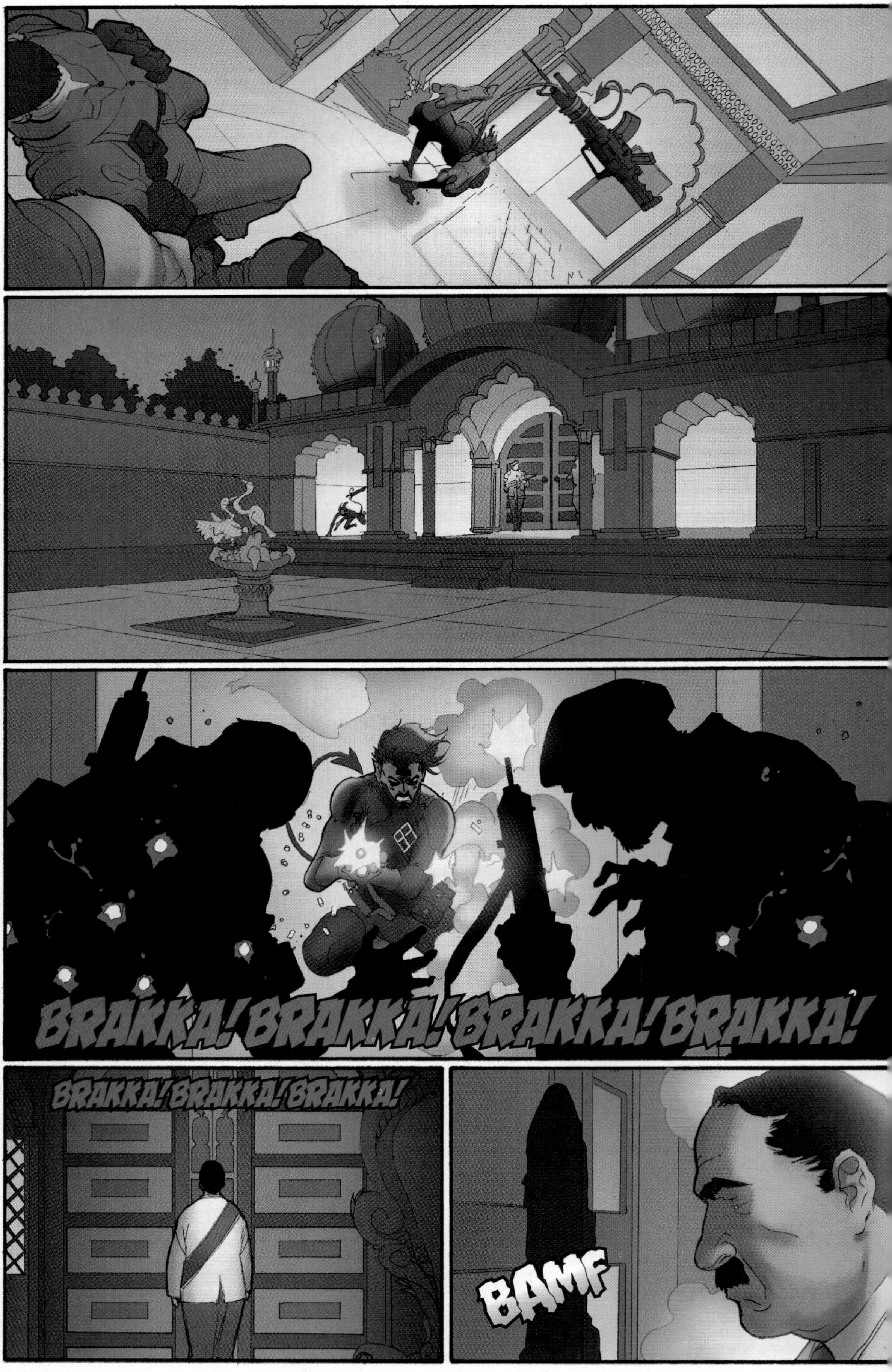
BRAKKA! BRAKKA! BRAKKA! BRAKKA!
BRAKKA! BRAKKA! BRAKKA!
BAMF

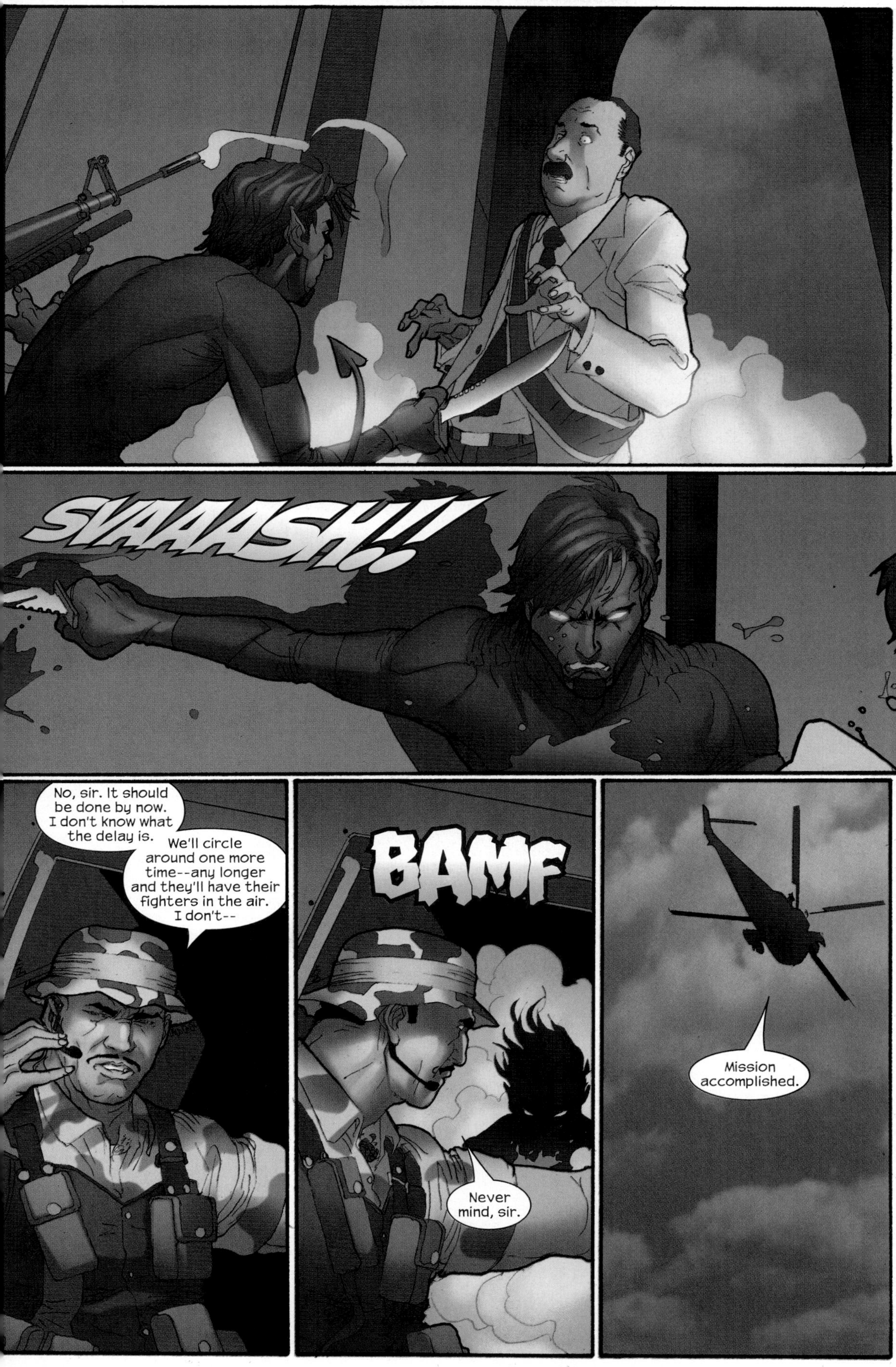
SVAAASH!!
No, sir. It should be done by now. I don't know what the delay is.
We'll circle around one more time--any longer and they'll have their fighters in the air. I don't--
BAMF
Never mind, sir.
Mission accomplished.

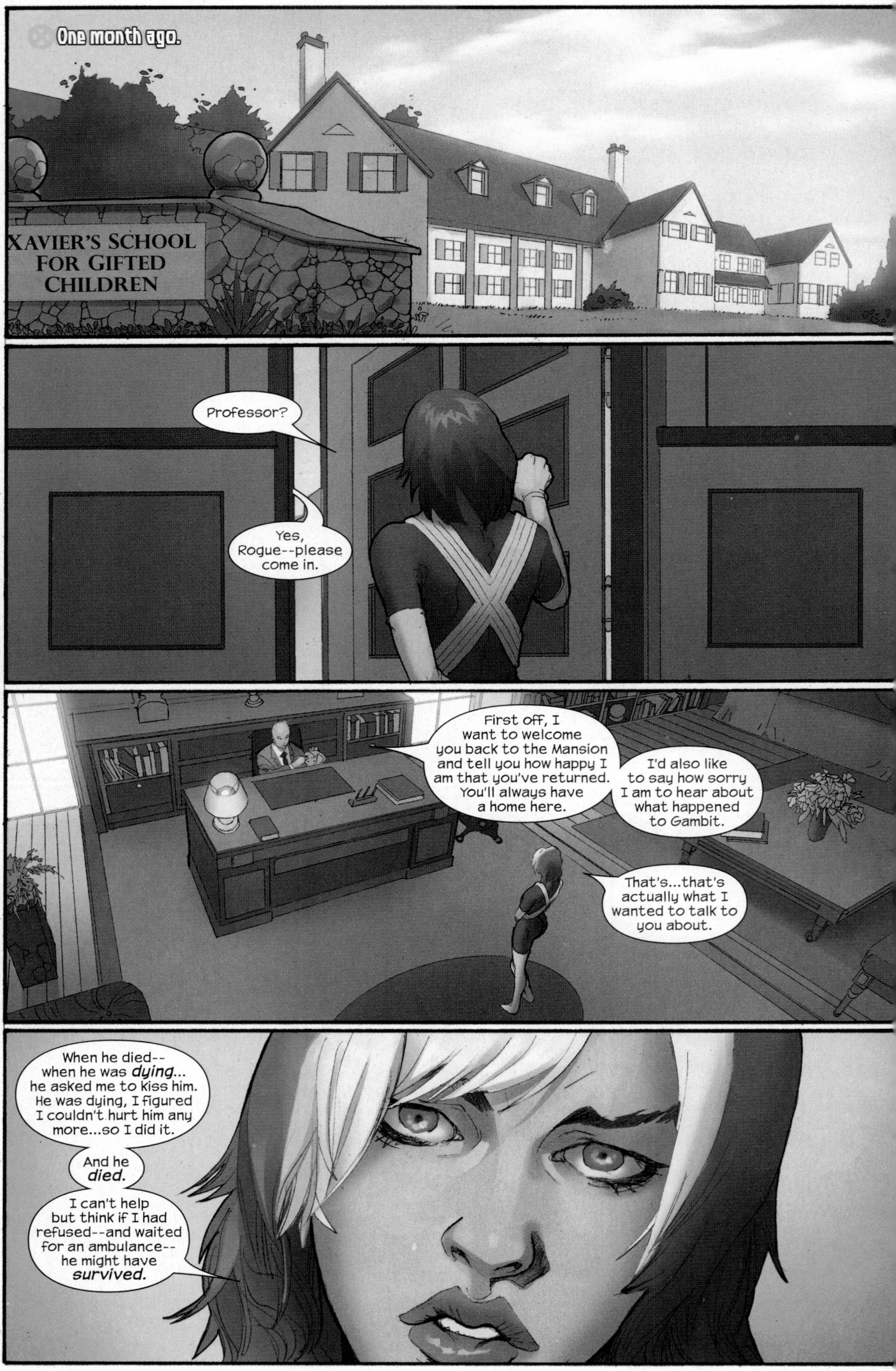

One month ago.
XAVIER'S SCHOOL FOR GIFTED CHILDREN
Professor?
Yes, Rogue--please come in.
First off, I want to welcome you back to the Mansion and tell you how happy I am that you've returned. You'll always have a home here.
I'd also like to say how sorry I am to hear about what happened to Gambit.
That's...that's actually what I wanted to talk to you about.
When he died-- when he was *dying*... he asked me to kiss him. He was dying, I figured I couldn't hurt him any more...so I did it.
And he *died.*
I can't help but think if I had refused--and waited for an ambulance-- he might have *survived.*

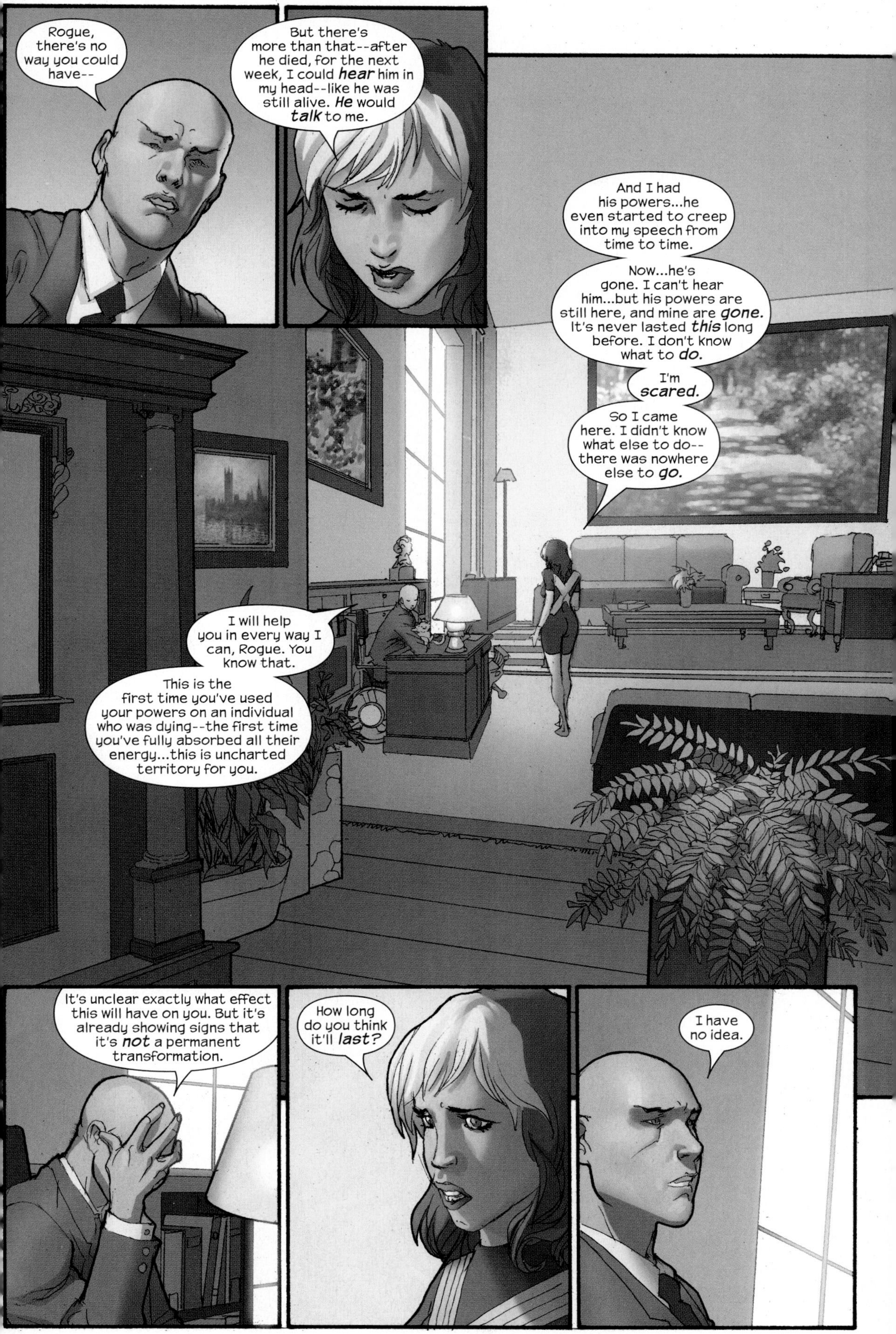

Rogue, there's no way you could have--
But there's more than that--after he died, for the next week, I could *hear* him in my head--like he was still alive. *He* would *talk* to me.
And I had his powers...he even started to creep into my speech from time to time.
Now...he's gone. I can't hear him...but his powers are still here, and mine are *gone.* It's never lasted *this* long before. I don't know what to *do.*
I'm *scared.*
So I came here. I didn't know what else to do--there was nowhere else to *go.*
I will help you in every way I can, Rogue. You know that.
This is the first time you've used your powers on an individual who was dying--the first time you've fully absorbed all their energy...this is uncharted territory for you.
It's unclear exactly what effect this will have on you. But it's already showing signs that it's *not* a permanent transformation.
How long do you think it'll *last?*
I have no idea.

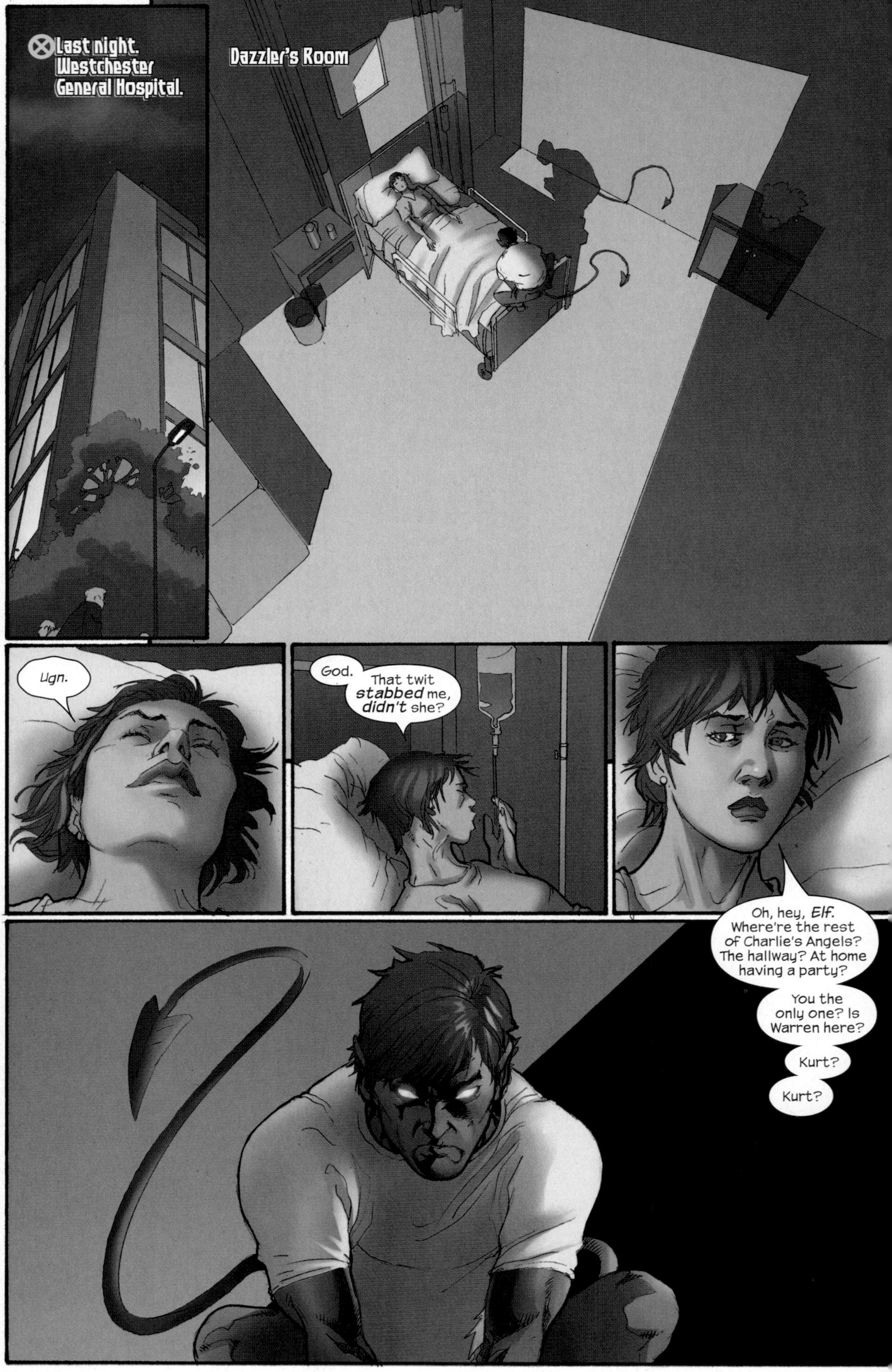
Last night. Westchester General Hospital.
Dazzler's Room
Ugn.
God.
That twit *stabbed* me, *didn't* she?
Oh, hey, *Elf*. Where're the rest of Charlie's Angels? The hallway? At home having a party?
You the only one? Is Warren here?
Kurt?
Kurt?

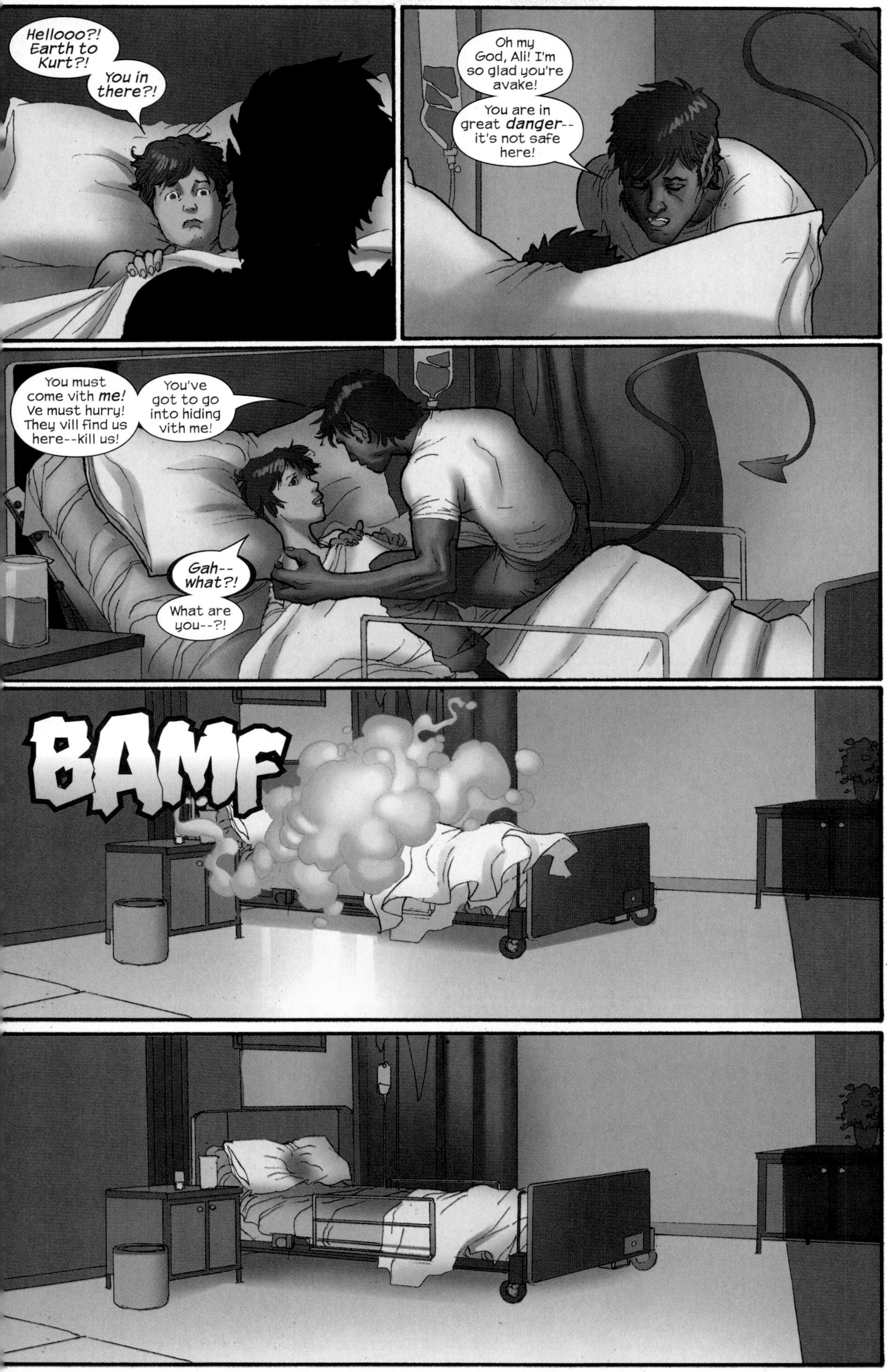
Hellooo?! Earth to Kurt?!
You in there?!
Oh my God, Ali! I'm so glad you're avake!
You are in great danger-- it's not safe here!
You must come vith me! Ve must hurry! They vill find us here--kill us!
You've got to go into hiding vith me!
Gah-- what?!
What are you--?!
BAMF

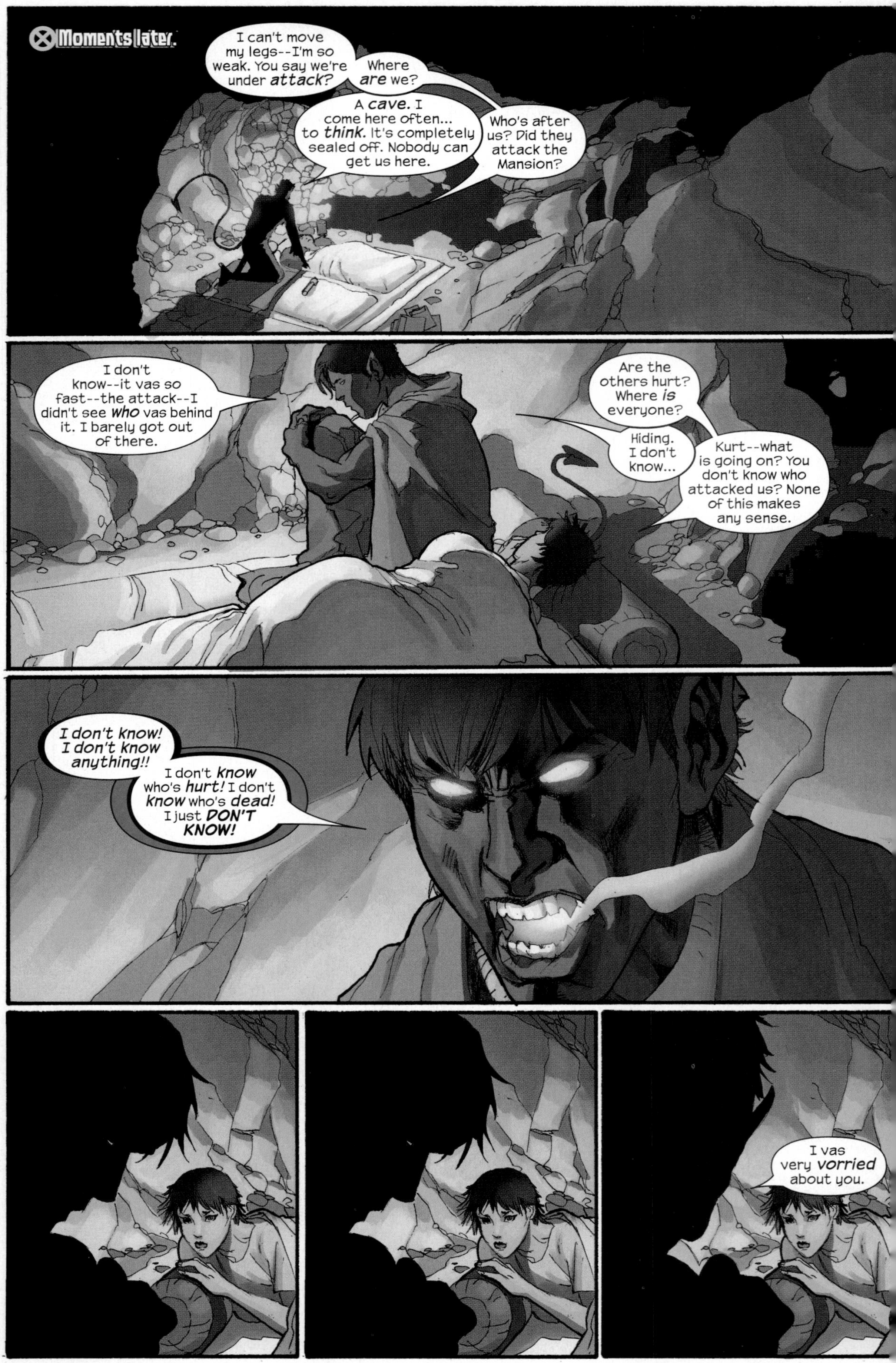
Moments later.
I can't move my legs--I'm so weak. You say we're under attack?
Where are we?
A cave. I come here often... to think. It's completely sealed off. Nobody can get us here.
Who's after us? Did they attack the Mansion?
I don't know--it vas so fast--the attack--I didn't see who vas behind it. I barely got out of there.
Are the others hurt? Where is everyone?
Hiding. I don't know...
Kurt--what is going on? You don't know who attacked us? None of this makes any sense.
I don't know! I don't know anything!!
I don't know who's hurt! I don't know who's dead! I just DON'T KNOW!
I vas very vorried about you.

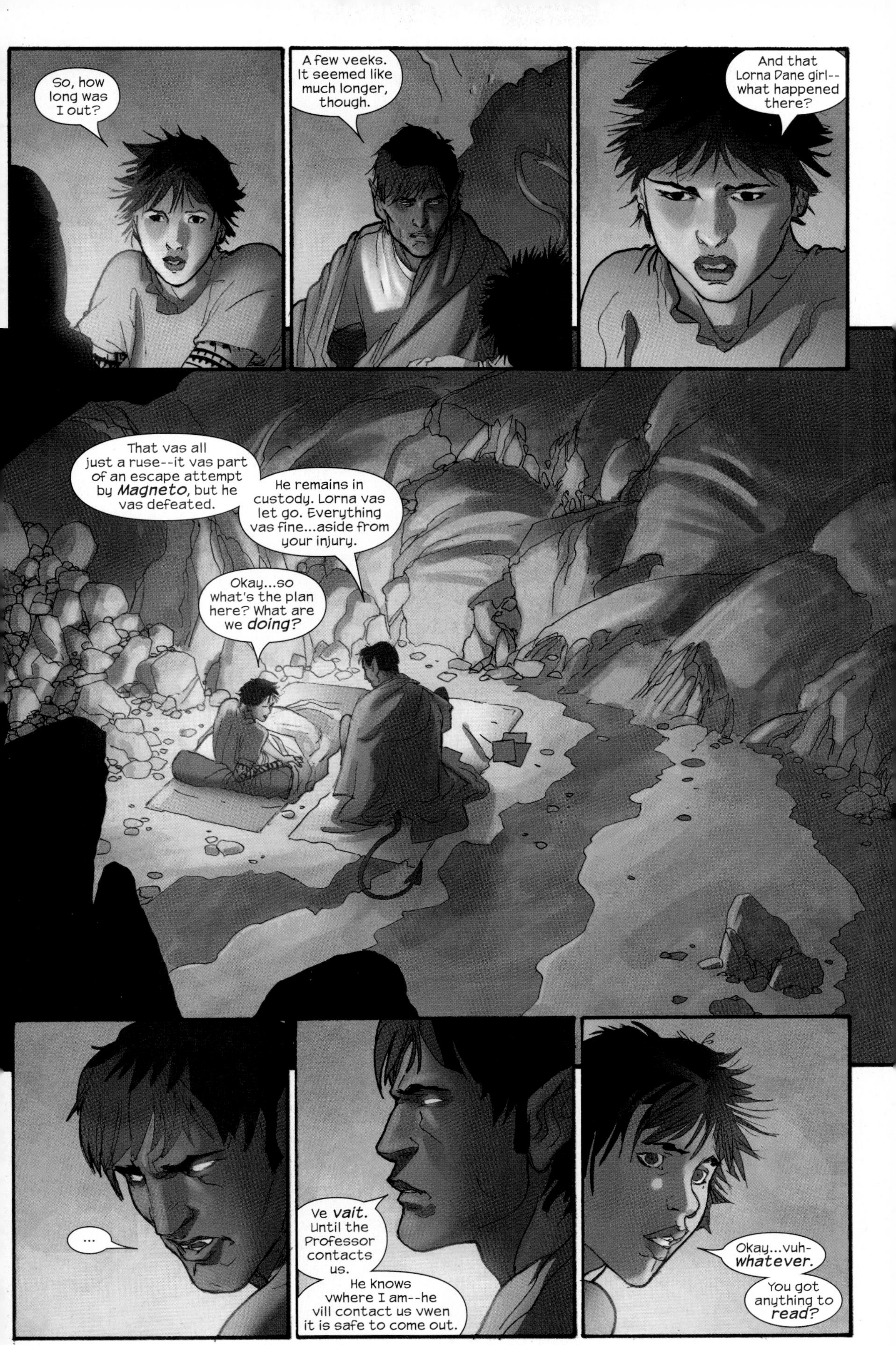
So, how long was I out?
A few veeks. It seemed like much longer, though.
And that Lorna Dane girl--what happened there?
That vas all just a ruse--it vas part of an escape attempt by *Magneto*, but he vas defeated.
He remains in custody. Lorna vas let go. Everything vas fine...aside from your injury.
Okay...so what's the plan here? What are we *doing?*
...
Ve *vait.* Until the Professor contacts us.
He knows vwhere I am--he vill contact us vwen it is safe to come out.
Okay...vuh-*whatever.*
You got anything to *read?*

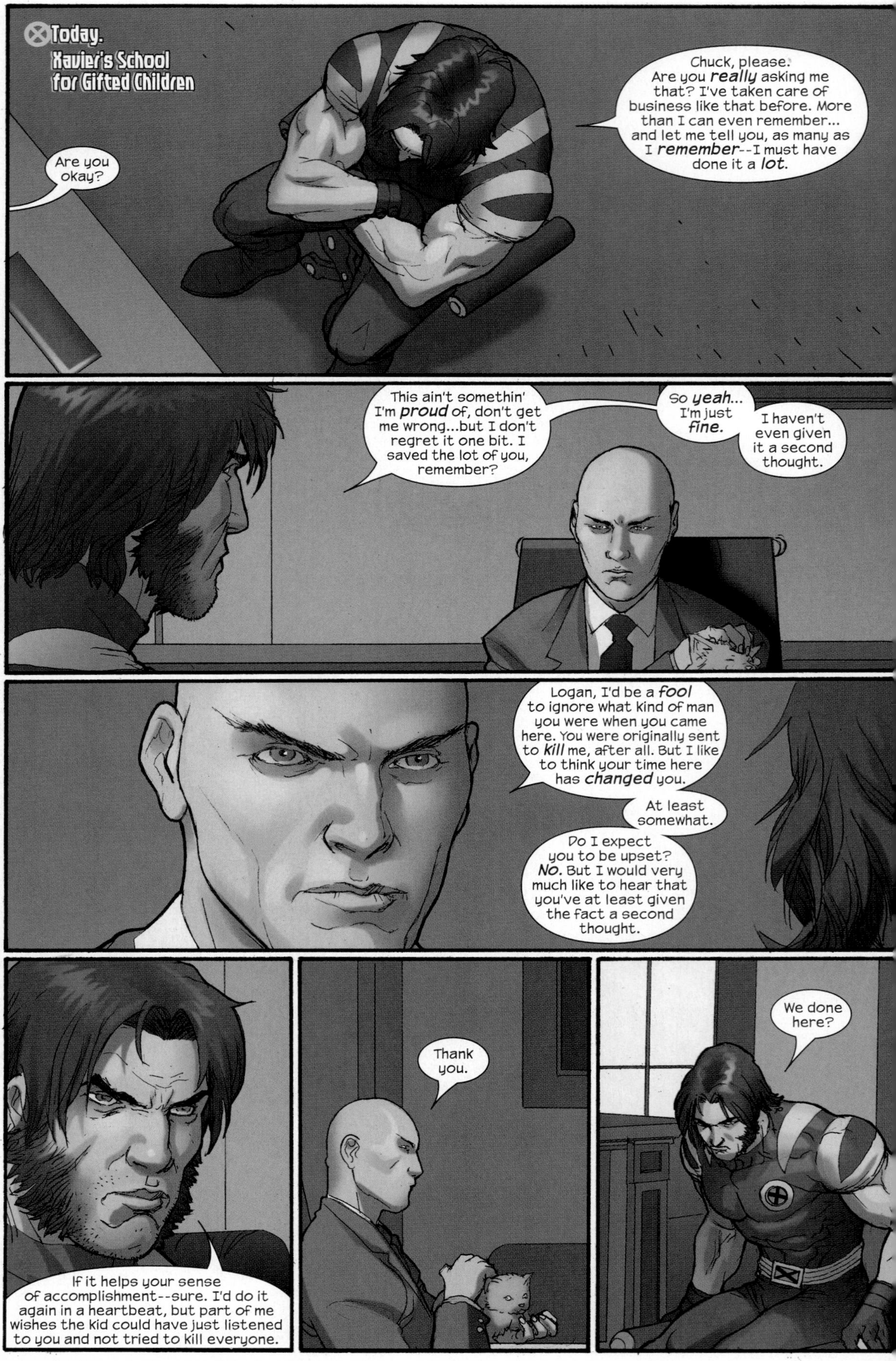
Today.
Xavier's School for Gifted Children
Are you okay?
Chuck, please. Are you really asking me that? I've taken care of business like that before. More than I can even remember... and let me tell you, as many as I remember--I must have done it a lot.
This ain't somethin' I'm proud of, don't get me wrong...but I don't regret it one bit. I saved the lot of you, remember?
So yeah... I'm just fine.
I haven't even given it a second thought.
Logan, I'd be a fool to ignore what kind of man you were when you came here. You were originally sent to kill me, after all. But I like to think your time here has changed you.
At least somewhat.
Do I expect you to be upset? No. But I would very much like to hear that you've at least given the fact a second thought.
If it helps your sense of accomplishment--sure. I'd do it again in a heartbeat, but part of me wishes the kid could have just listened to you and not tried to kill everyone.
Thank you.
We done here?

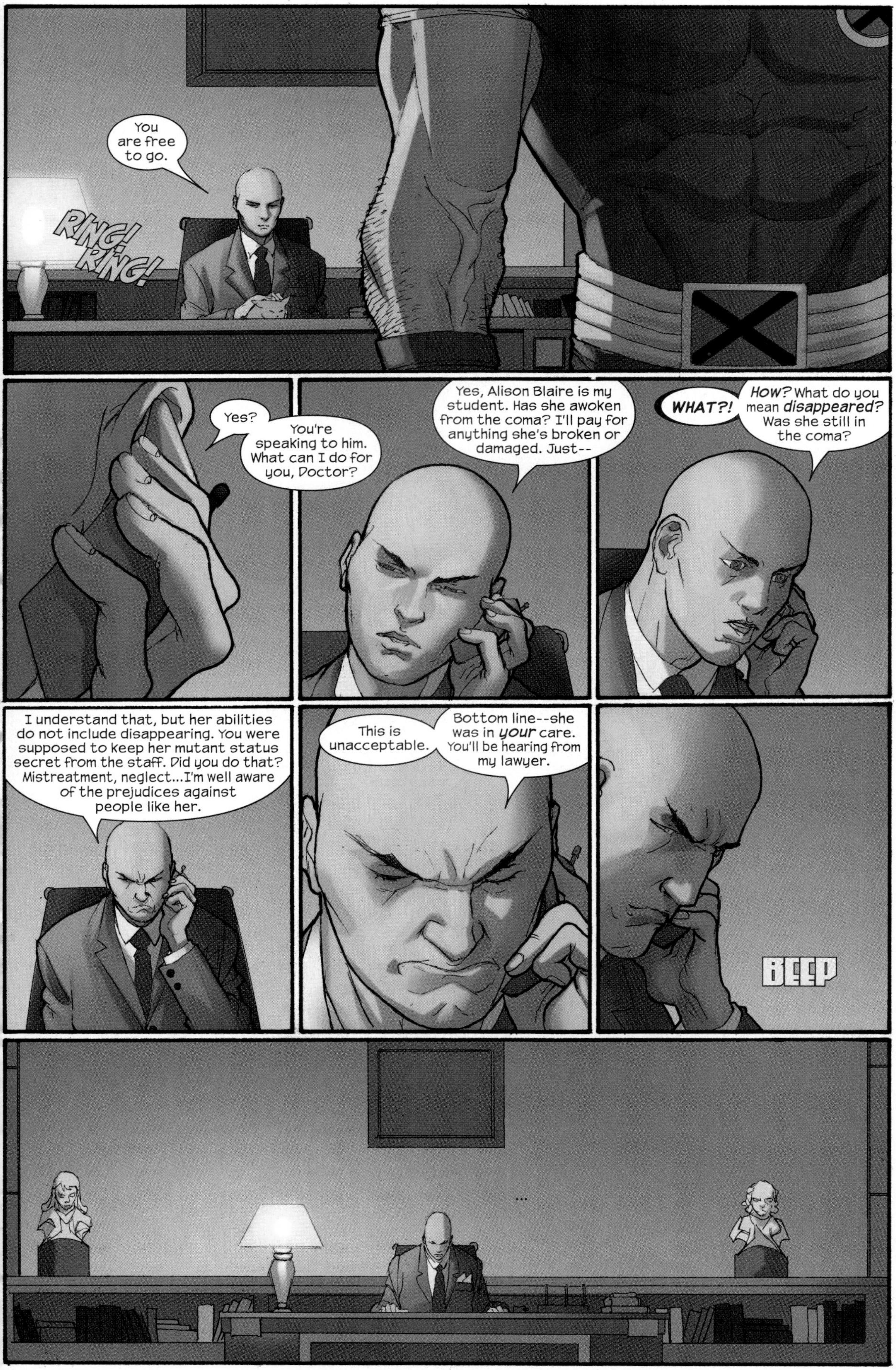
You are free to go.
RING! RING!
Yes?
You're speaking to him. What can I do for you, Doctor?
Yes, Alison Blaire is my student. Has she awoken from the coma? I'll pay for anything she's broken or damaged. Just--
WHAT?!
HOW? What do you mean disappeared? Was she still in the coma?
I understand that, but her abilities do not include disappearing. You were supposed to keep her mutant status secret from the staff. Did you do that? Mistreatment, neglect...I'm well aware of the prejudices against people like her.
This is unacceptable.
Bottom line--she was in your care. You'll be hearing from my lawyer.
BEEP
...

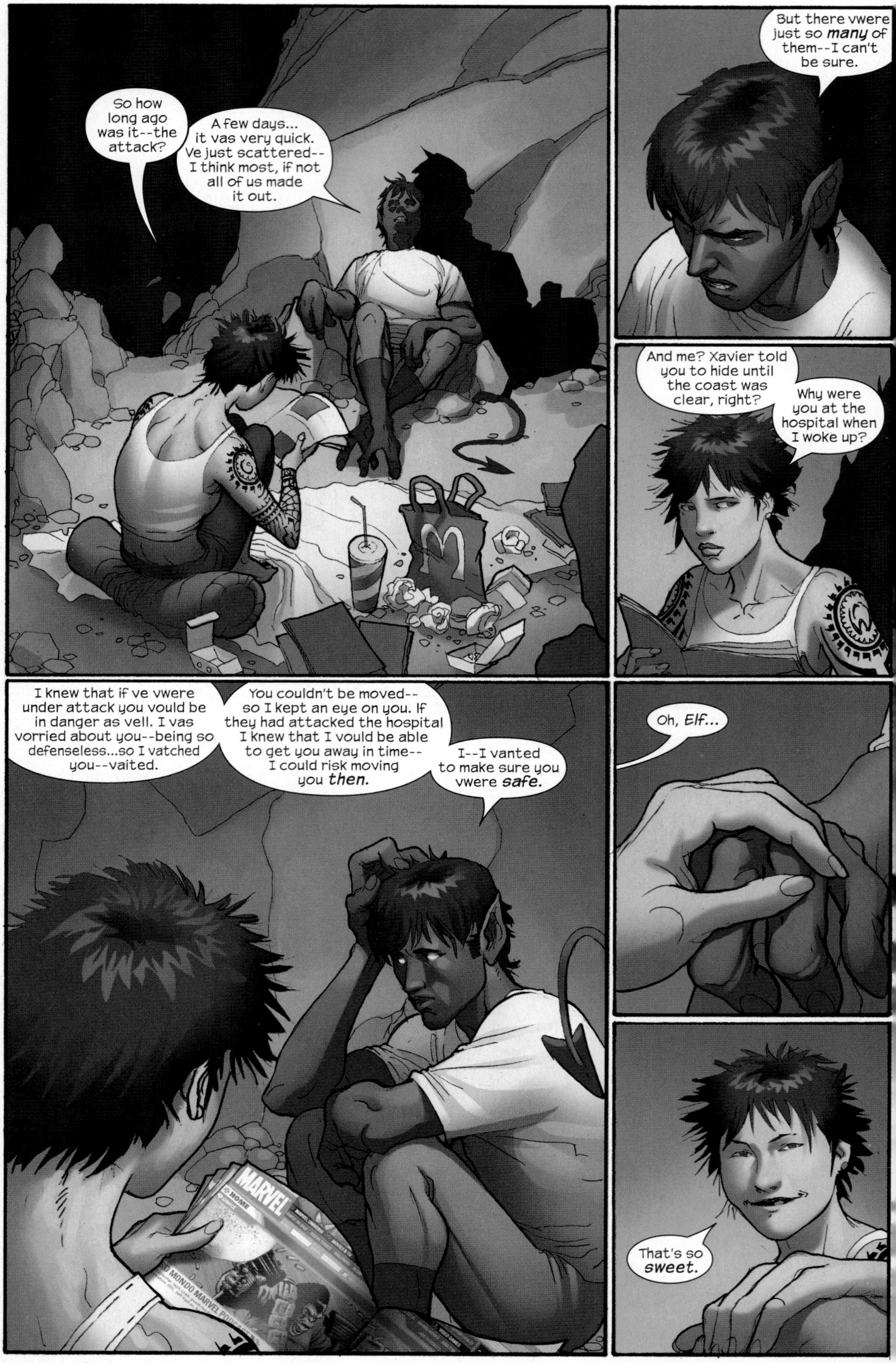
So how long ago was it--the attack?
A few days... it vas very quick. Ve just scattered-- I think most, if not all of us made it out.
But there vwere just so *many* of them--I can't be sure.
And me? Xavier told you to hide until the coast was clear, right?
Why were you at the hospital when I woke up?
I knew that if ve vwere under attack you vould be in danger as vell. I vas vorried about you--being so defenseless...so I vatched you--vaited.
You couldn't be moved-- so I kept an eye on you. If they had attacked the hospital I knew that I vould be able to get you away in time-- I could risk moving you *then.*
I--I vanted to make sure you vwere *safe.*
Oh, *Elf...*
That's so *sweet.*

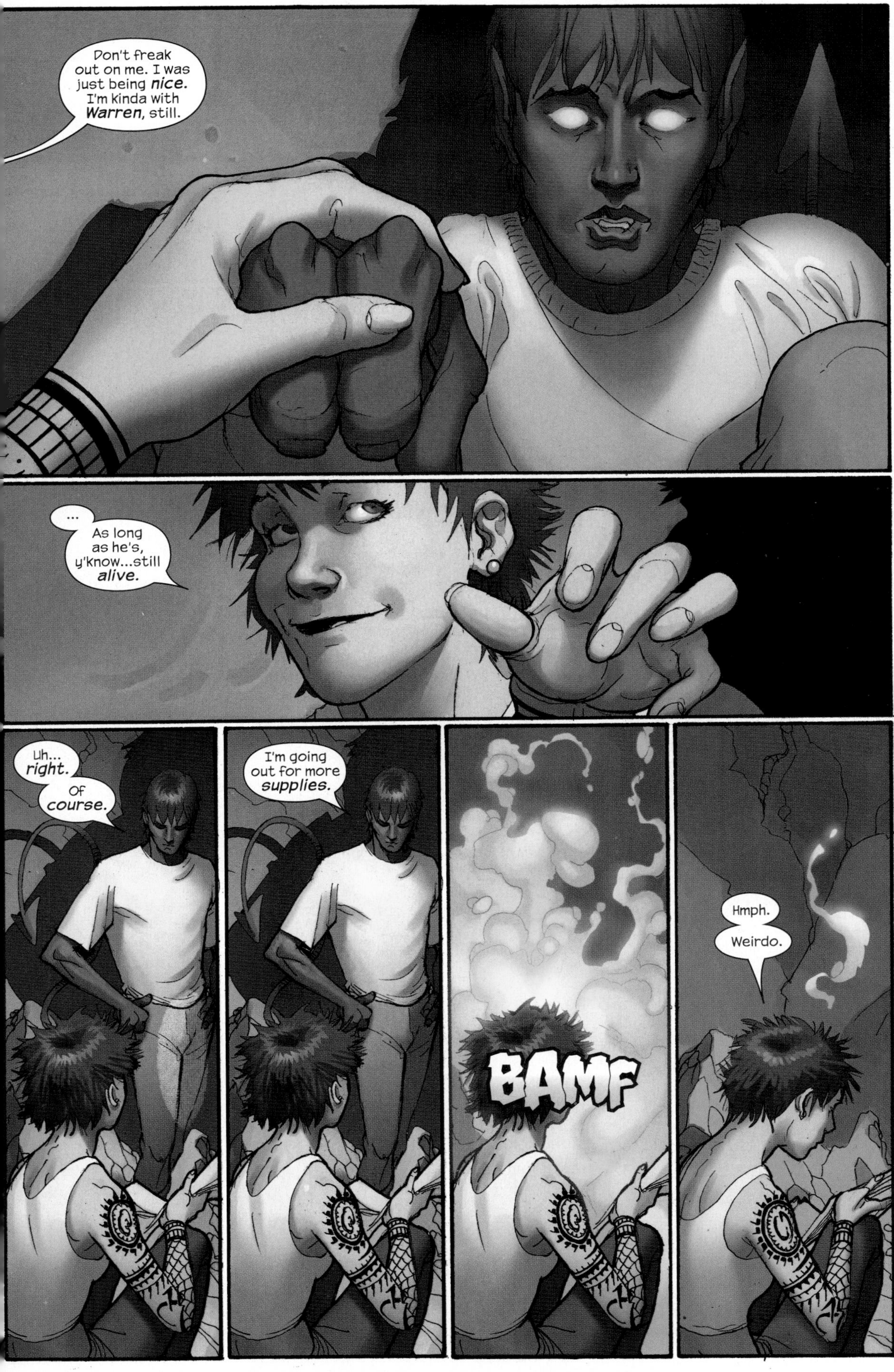
Don't freak out on me. I was just being nice. I'm kinda with Warren, still.
...
As long as he's, y'know...still alive.
Uh... right.
Of course.
I'm going out for more supplies.
BAMF
Hmph.
Weirdo.

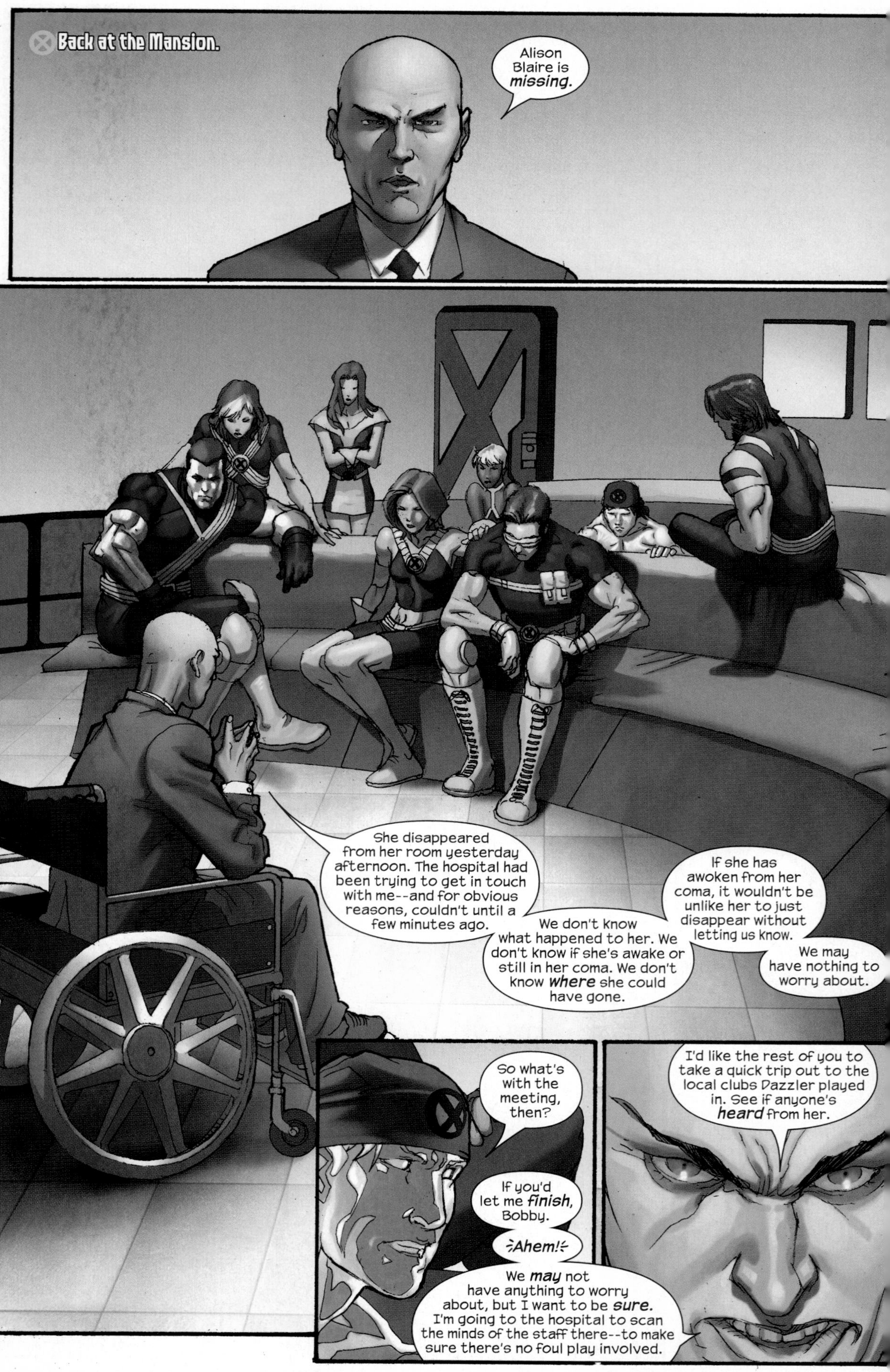
Back at the Mansion.
Alison Blaire is *missing.*
She disappeared from her room yesterday afternoon. The hospital had been trying to get in touch with me--and for obvious reasons, couldn't until a few minutes ago.
We don't know what happened to her. We don't know if she's awake or still in her coma. We don't know *where* she could have gone.
If she has awoken from her coma, it wouldn't be unlike her to just disappear without letting us know.
We may have nothing to worry about.
So what's with the meeting, then?
If you'd let me *finish*, Bobby.
Ahem!
We *may* not have anything to worry about, but I want to be *sure.* I'm going to the hospital to scan the minds of the staff there--to make sure there's no foul play involved.
I'd like the rest of you to take a quick trip out to the local clubs Dazzler played in. See if anyone's *heard* from her.

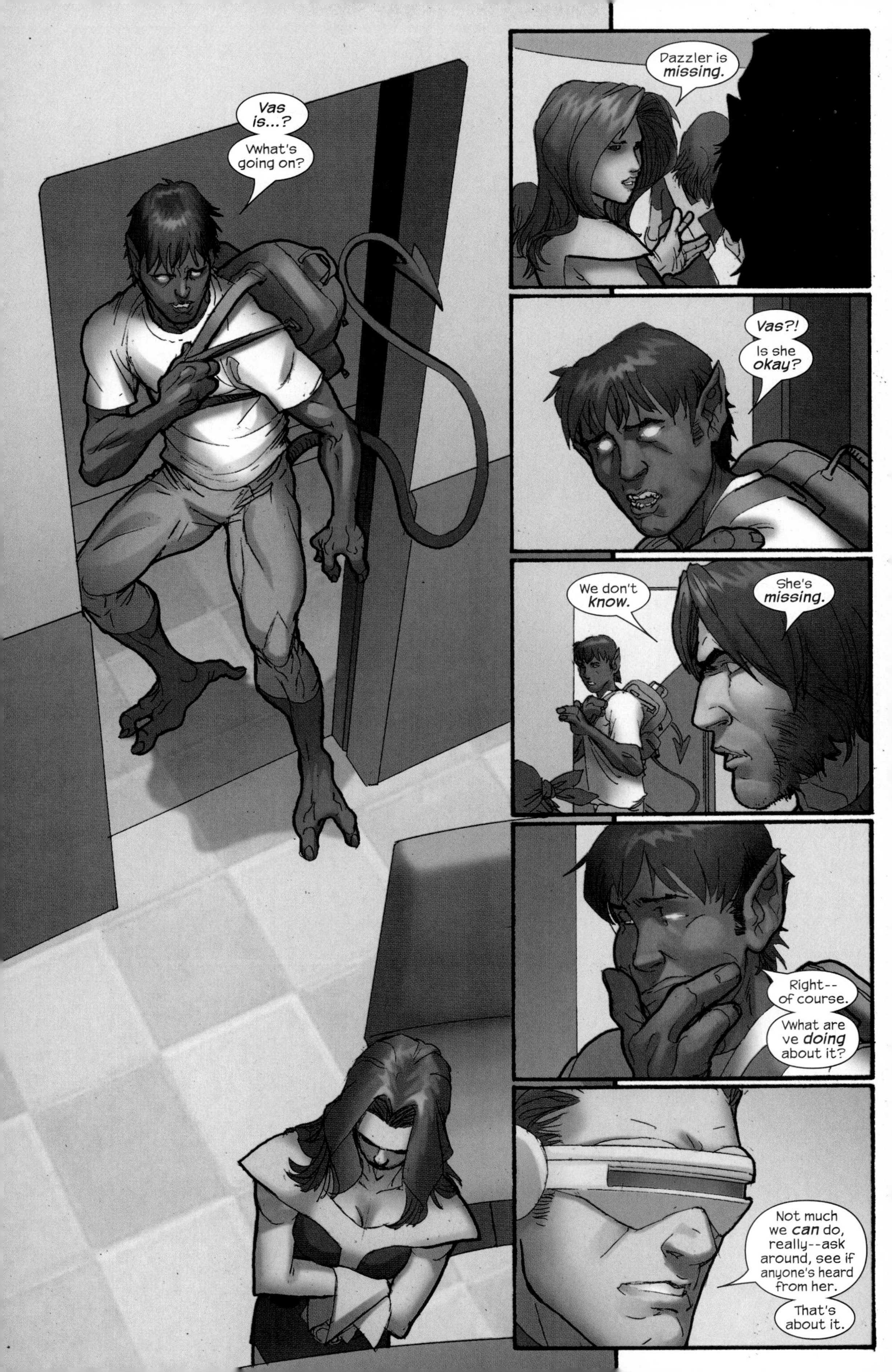

Vas is...?
What's going on?
Dazzler is missing.
Vas?!
Is she okay?
We don't know.
She's missing.
Right-- of course.
What are ve doing about it?
Not much we can do, really--ask around, see if anyone's heard from her.
That's about it.

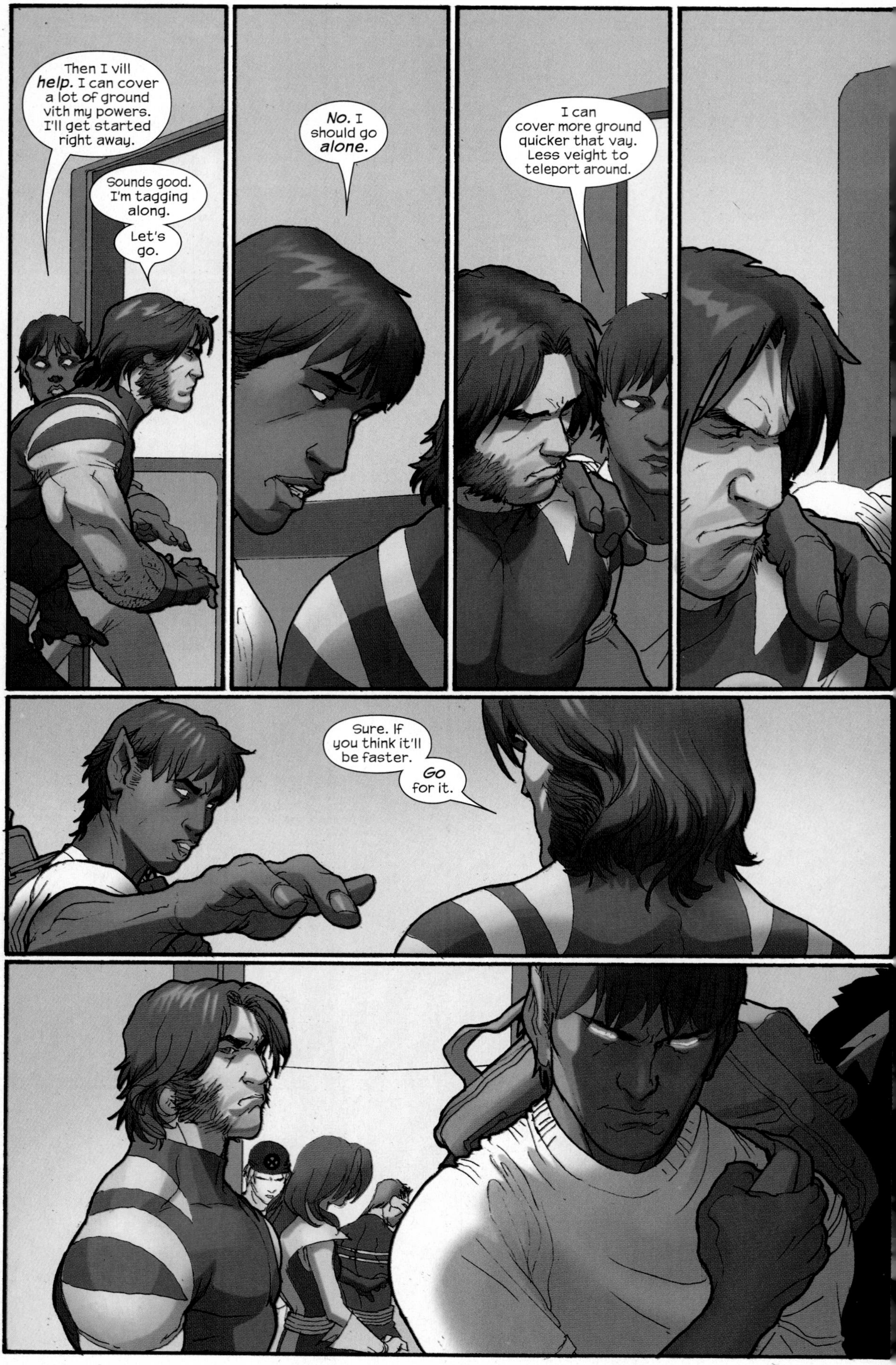
Then I vill help. I can cover a lot of ground vith my powers. I'll get started right away.
Sounds good. I'm tagging along.
Let's go.
No. I should go alone.
I can cover more ground quicker that vay. Less veight to teleport around.
Sure. If you think it'll be faster.
Go for it.

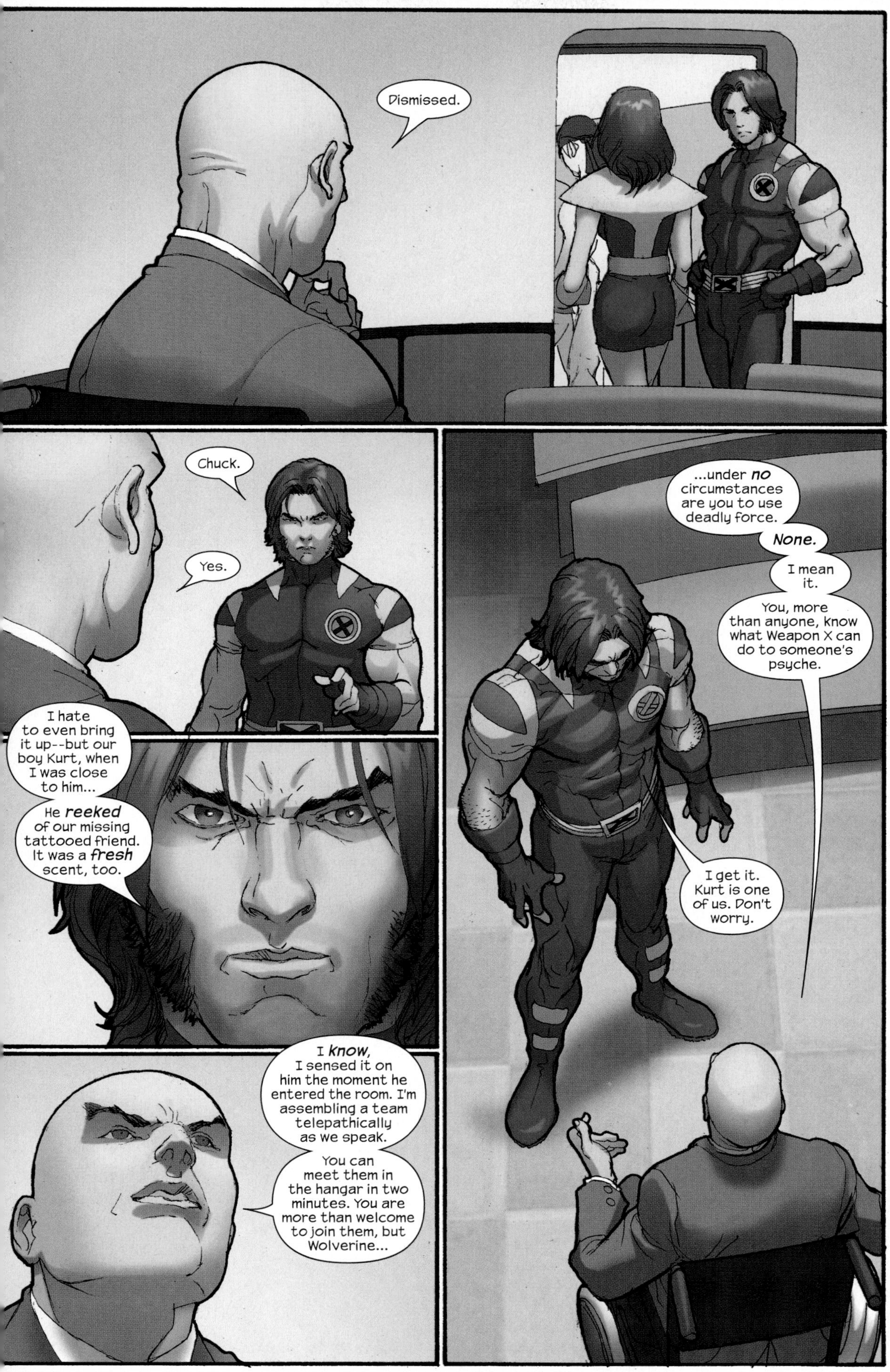
Dismissed.
Chuck.
Yes.
I hate to even bring it up--but our boy Kurt, when I was close to him...
He reeked of our missing tattooed friend. It was a fresh scent, too.
I know, I sensed it on him the moment he entered the room. I'm assembling a team telepathically as we speak.
You can meet them in the hangar in two minutes. You are more than welcome to join them, but Wolverine...
...under no circumstances are you to use deadly force.
None.
I mean it.
You, more than anyone, know what Weapon X can do to someone's psyche.
I get it. Kurt is one of us. Don't worry.

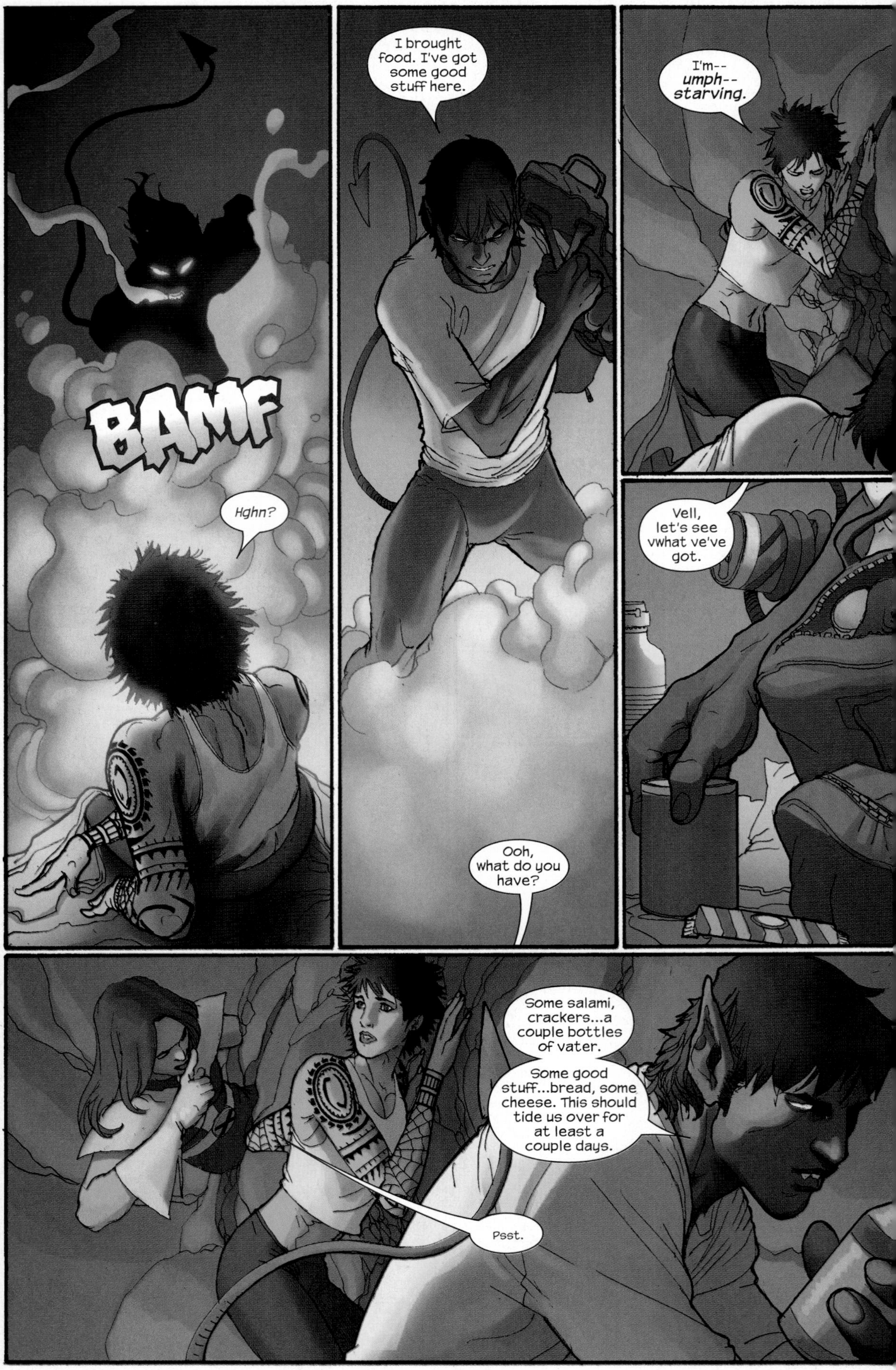
BAMF
Hghn?
I brought food. I've got some good stuff here.
Ooh, what do you have?
I'm-- umph-- starving.
Vell, let's see vwhat ve've got.
Some salami, crackers...a couple bottles of vater.
Some good stuff...bread, some cheese. This should tide us over for at least a couple days.
Psst.

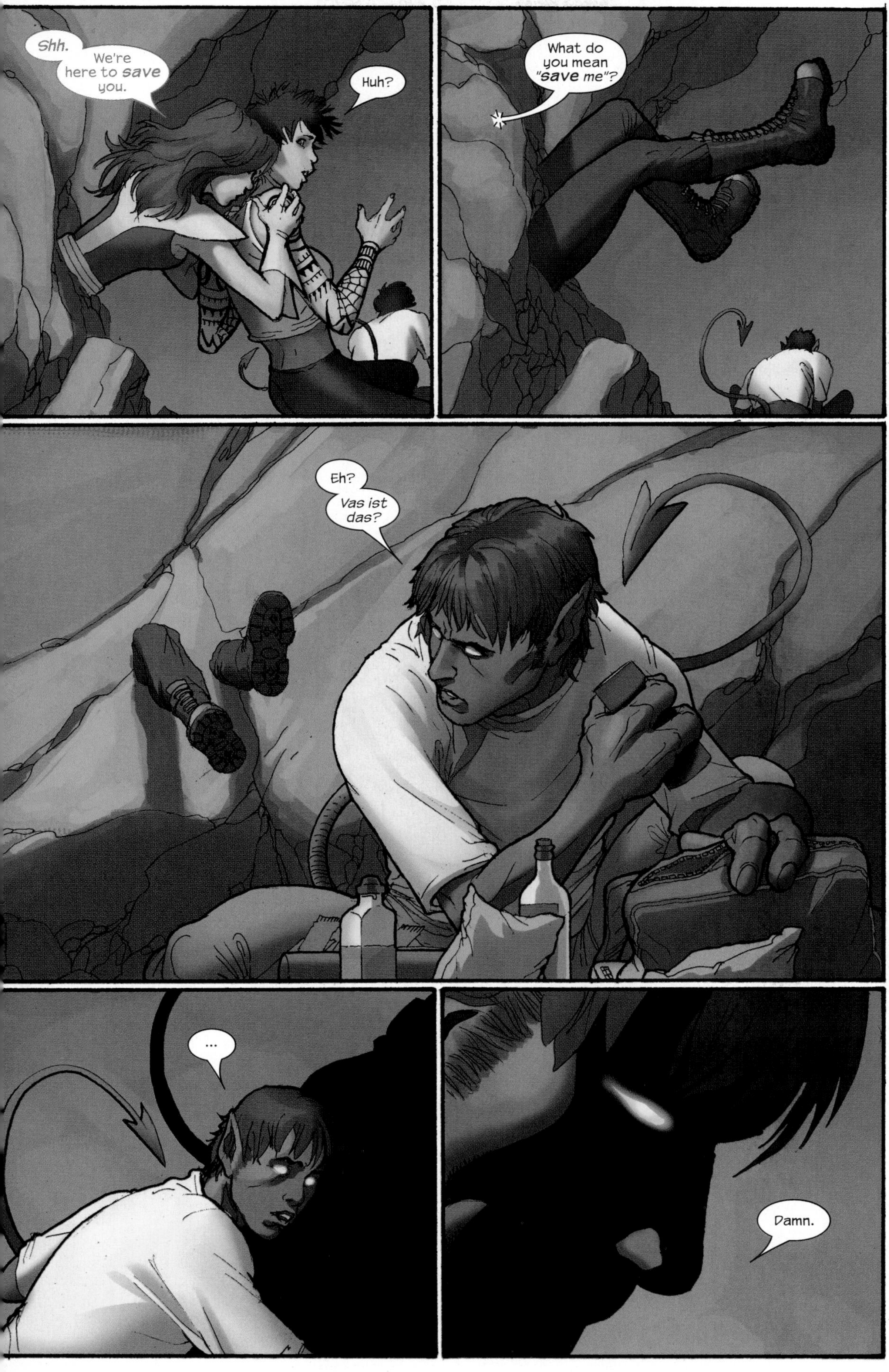
Shh.
We're here to save you.
Huh?
What do you mean "save me"?
Eh? Vas ist das?
...
Damn.

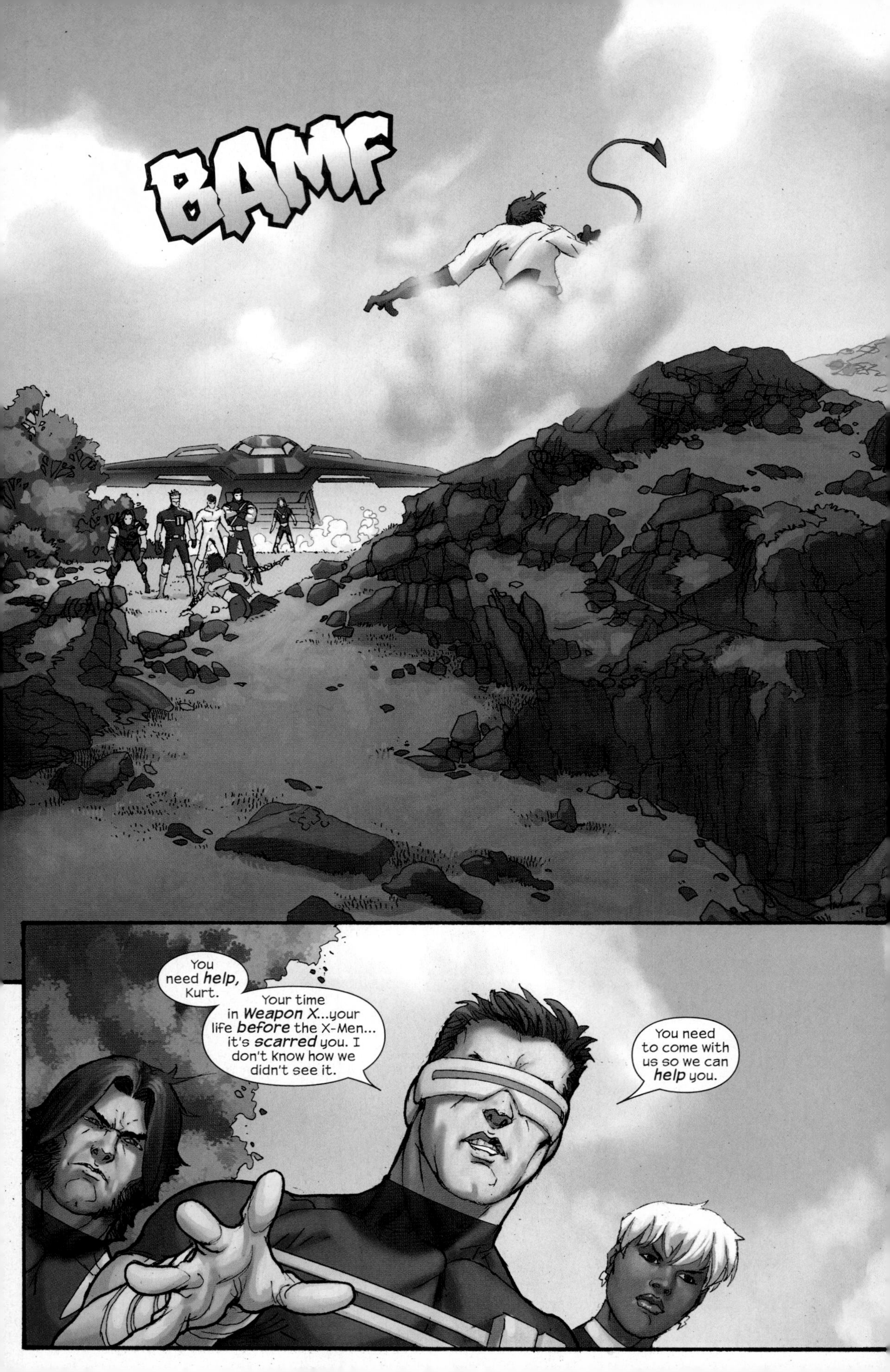
BAMF
You need *help,* Kurt.
Your time in *Weapon X*...your life *before* the X-Men... it's *scarred* you. I don't know how we didn't see it.
You need to come with us so we can *help* you.

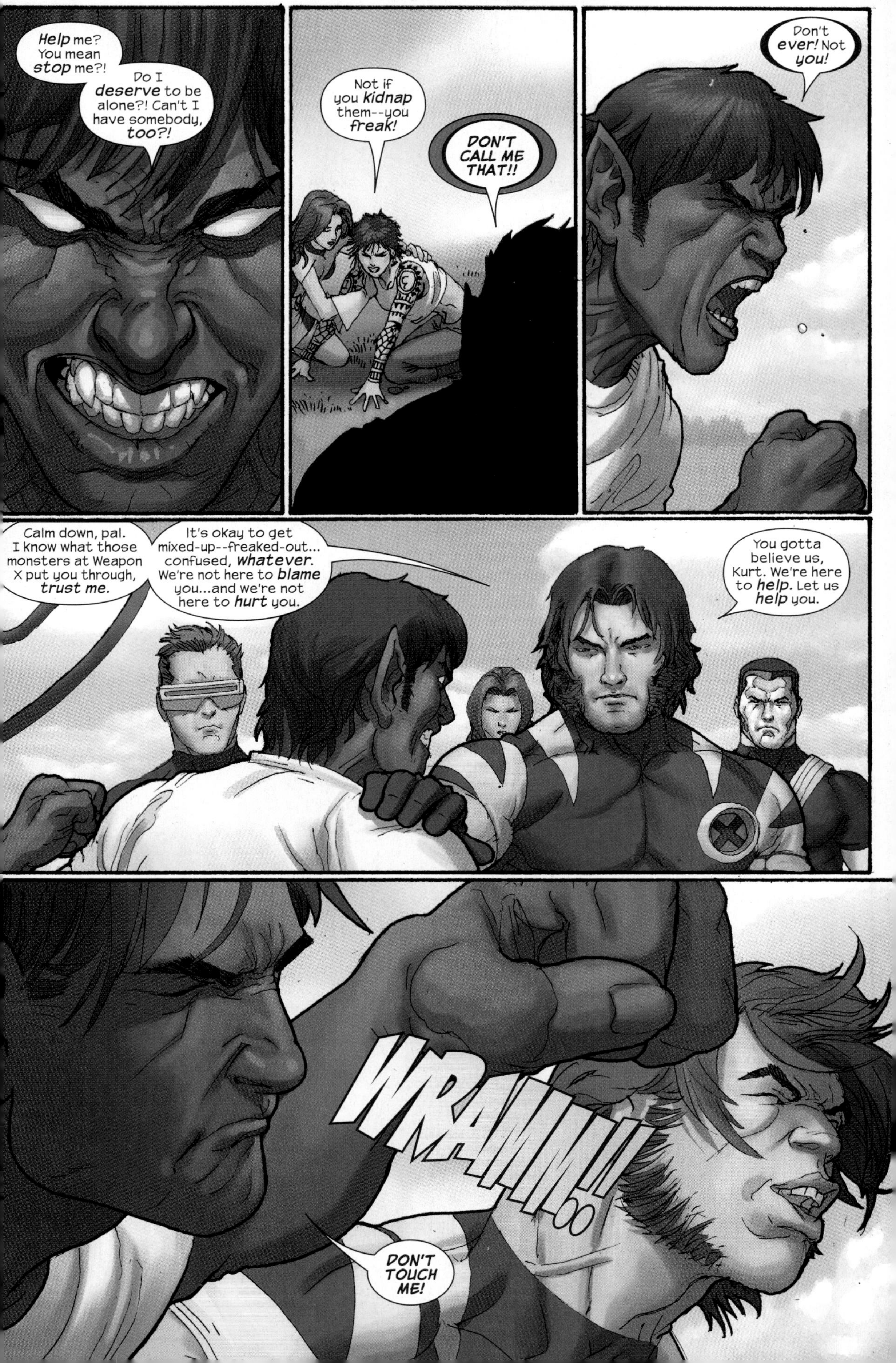
Help me? You mean stop me?!
Do I deserve to be alone?! Can't I have somebody, too?!
Not if you kidnap them--you freak!
DON'T CALL ME THAT!!
Don't ever! Not you!
Calm down, pal. I know what those monsters at Weapon X put you through, trust me.
It's okay to get mixed-up--freaked-out... confused, whatever. We're not here to blame you...and we're not here to hurt you.
You gotta believe us, Kurt. We're here to help. Let us help you.
WRAMM!!
DON'T TOUCH ME!

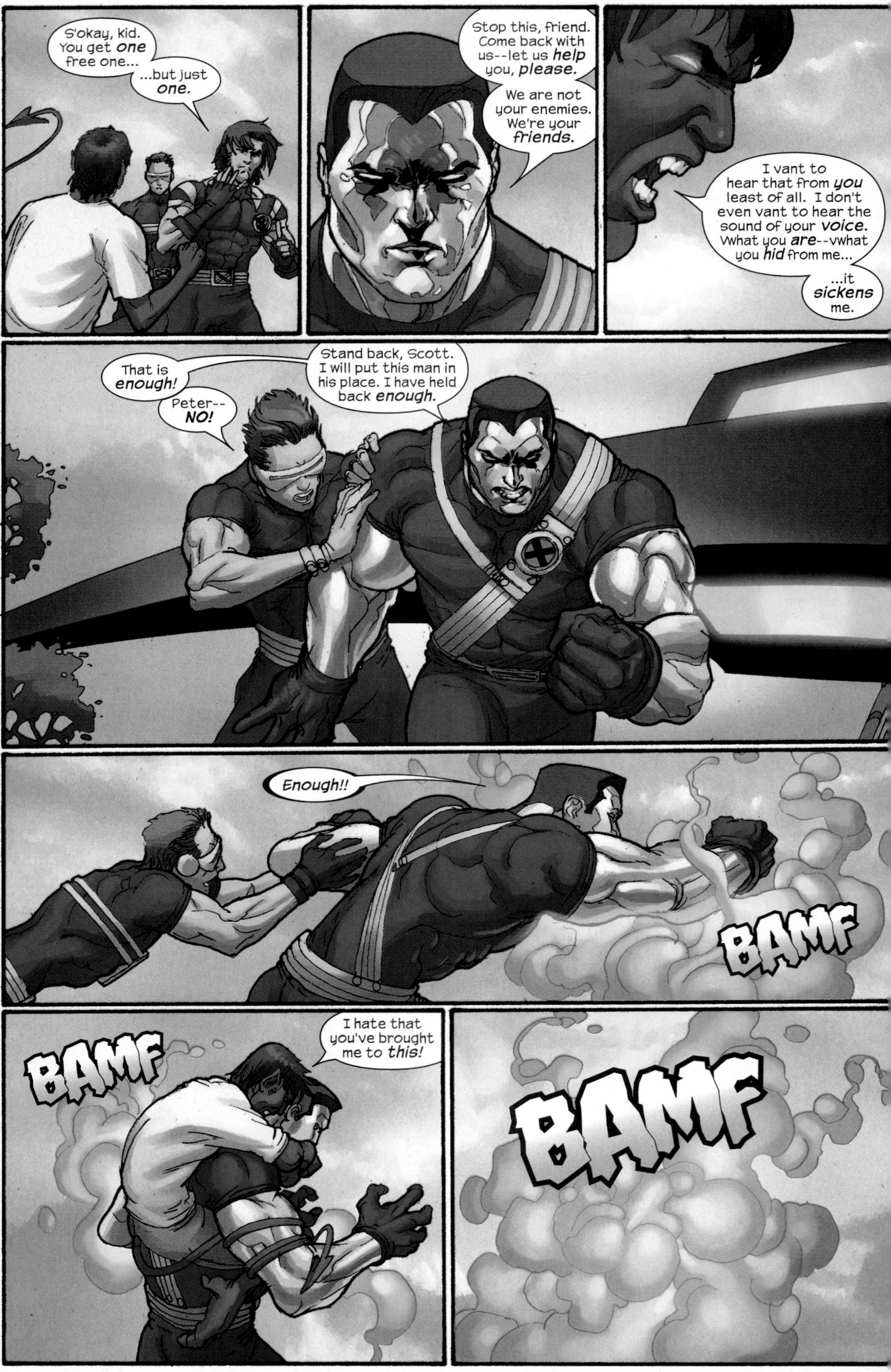
S'okay, kid. You get *one* free one...
...but just *one.*
Stop this, friend. Come back with us--let us *help* you, *please.*
We are not your enemies. We're your *friends.*
I vant to hear that from *you* least of all. I don't even vant to hear the sound of your *voice.* Vwhat you *are*--vwhat you *hid* from me...
...it *sickens* me.
That is *enough!*
Peter-- *NO!*
Stand back, Scott. I will put this man in his place. I have held back *enough.*
Enough!!
BAMF
BAMF
I hate that you've brought me to *this!*
BAMF

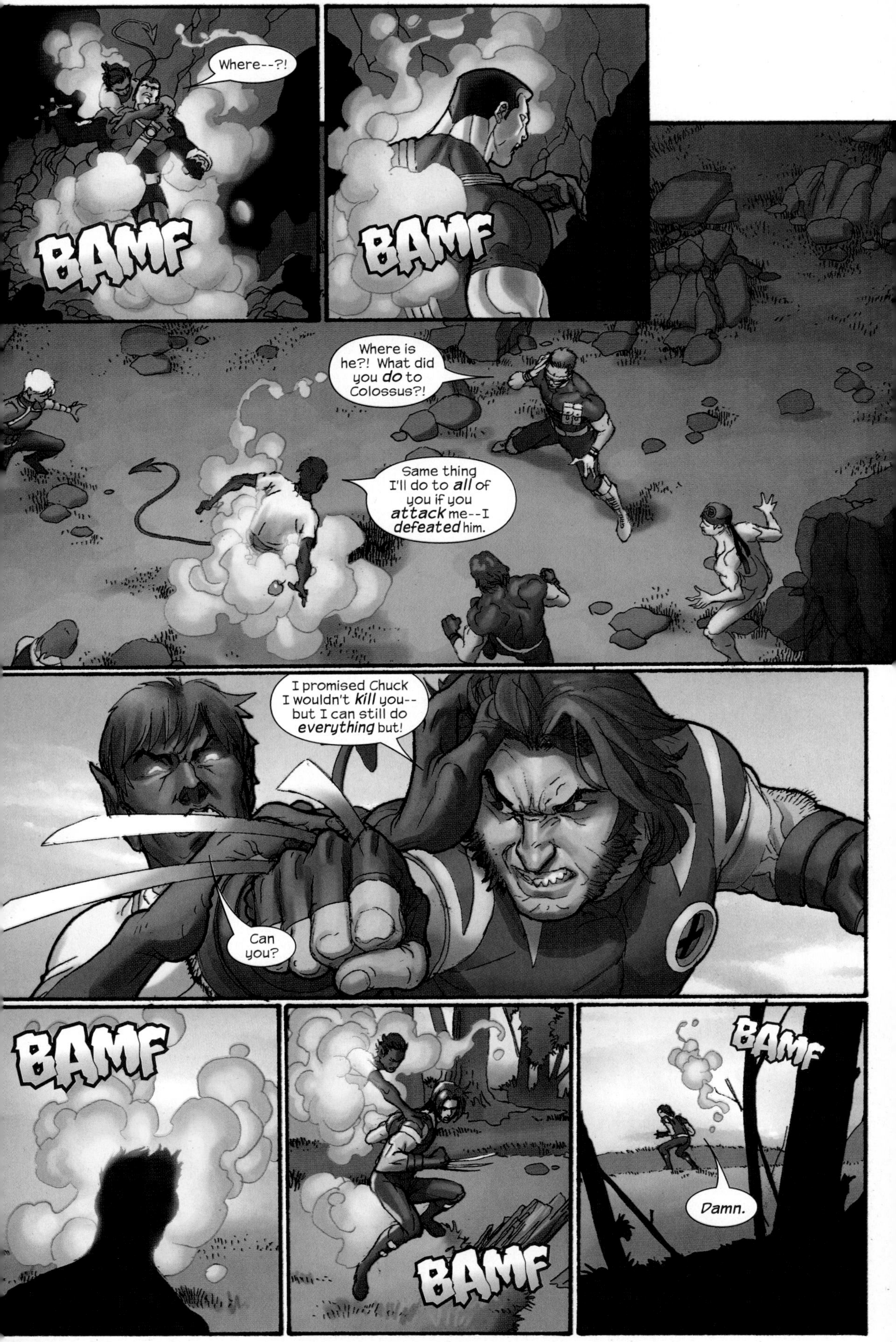
Where--?!
BAMF
BAMF
Where is he?! What did you *do* to Colossus?!
Same thing I'll do to *all* of you if you *attack* me--I *defeated* him.
I promised Chuck I wouldn't *kill* you--but I can still do *everything* but!
Can you?
BAMF
BAMF
BAMF
Damn.

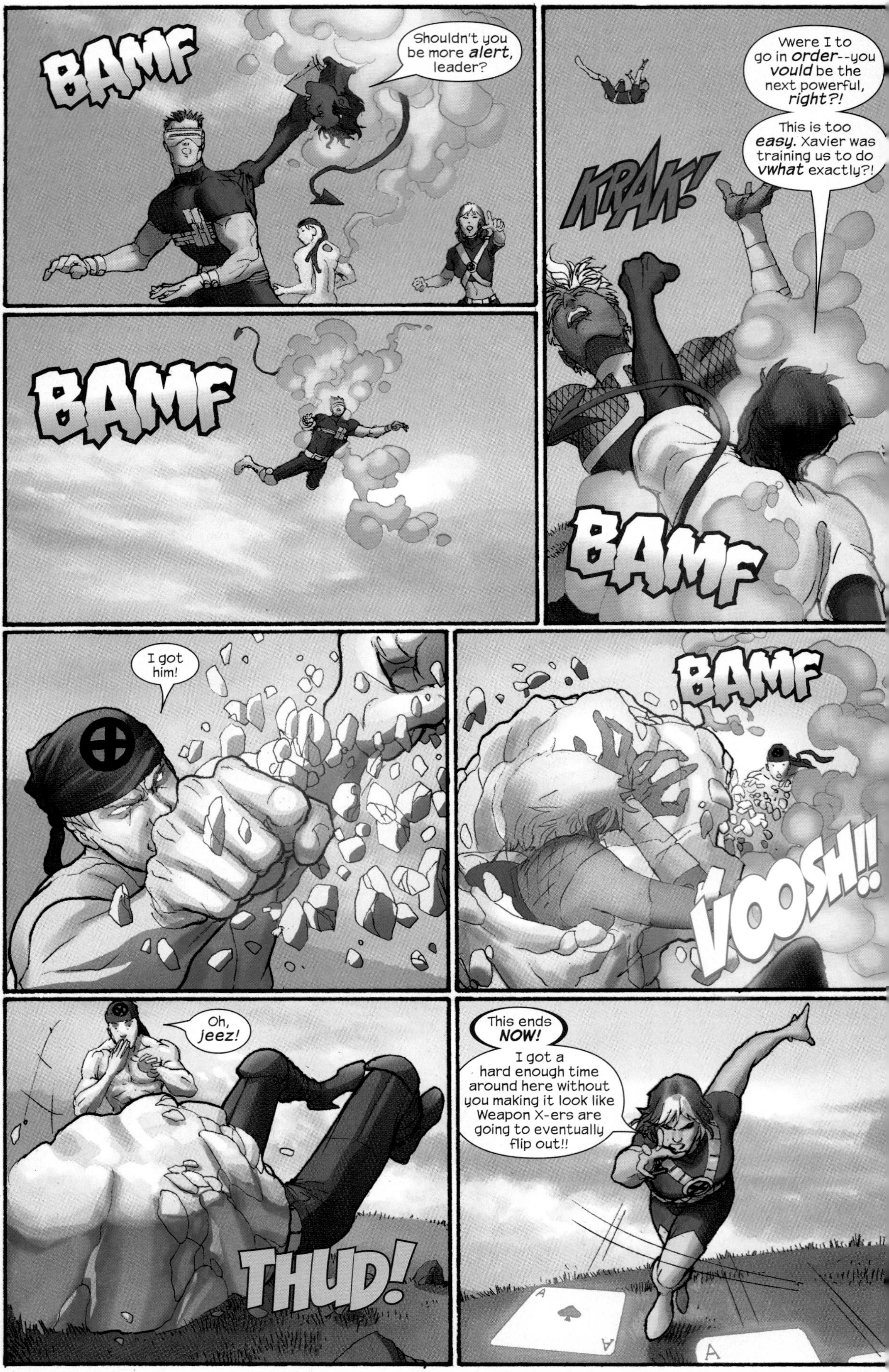
BAMF
Shouldn't you be more *alert*, leader?
Vwere I to go in *order*--you *vould* be the next powerful, *right?!*
This is too *easy*. Xavier was training us to do *vwhat* exactly?!
KRAK!
BAMF
BAMF
I got him!
BAMF
VOOSH!!
Oh, *jeez!*
THUD!
This ends *NOW!*
I got a hard enough time around here without you making it look like Weapon X-ers are going to eventually flip out!!

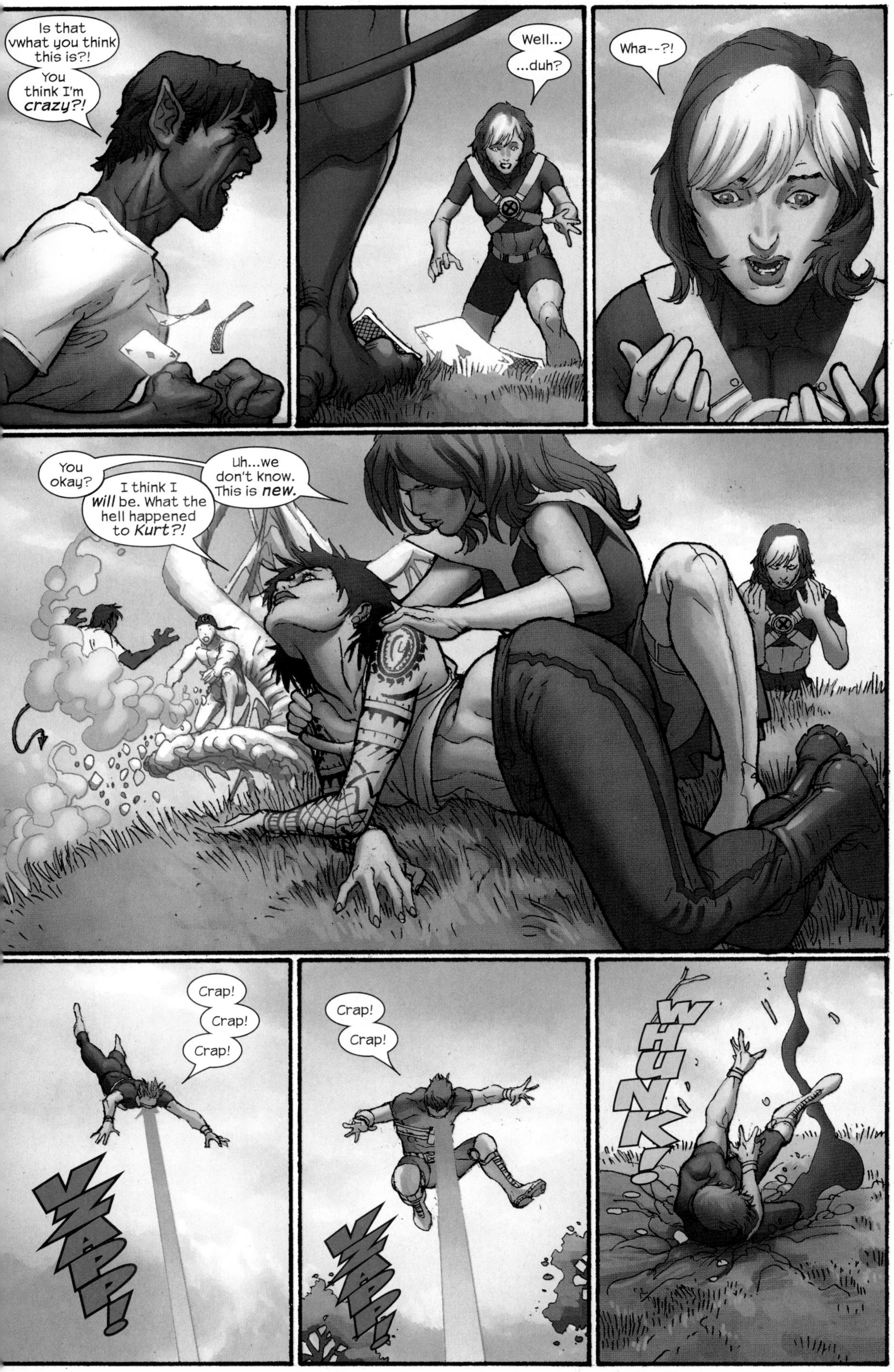
Is that vwhat you think this is?!
You think I'm *crazy?!*
Well... ...duh?
Wha--?!
You okay?
Uh...we don't know. This is *new.*
I think I *will* be. What the hell happened to *Kurt?!*
Crap! Crap! Crap!
VZAPP!
Crap! Crap!
VZAPP!
WHUNK!

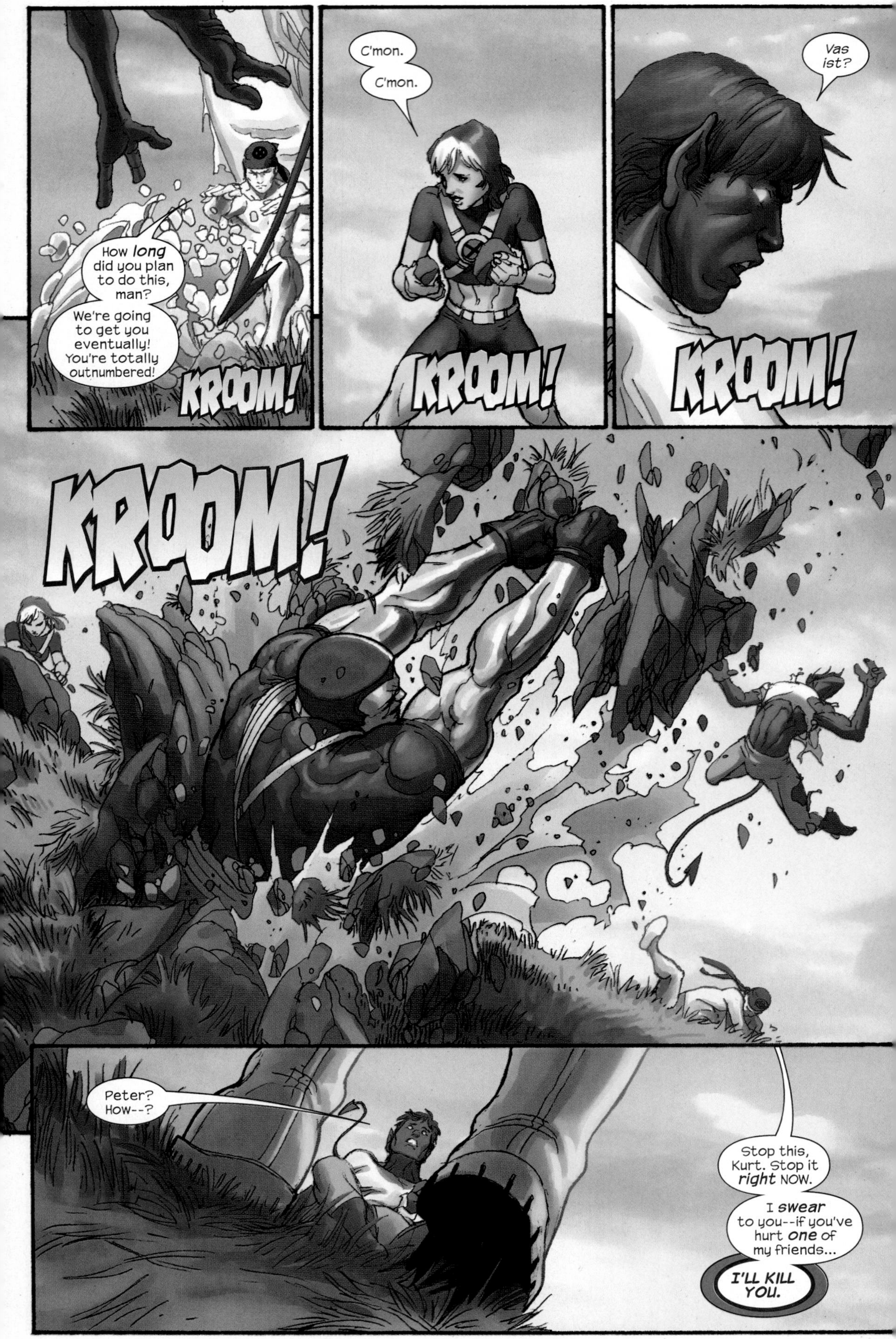
How *long* did you plan to do this, man?
We're going to get you eventually! You're totally outnumbered!
KROOM!
C'mon.
C'mon.
KROOM!
Vas ist?
KROOM!
KROOM!
Peter? How--?
Stop this, Kurt. Stop it *right* NOW.
I *swear* to you--if you've hurt *one* of my friends...
I'LL KILL YOU.

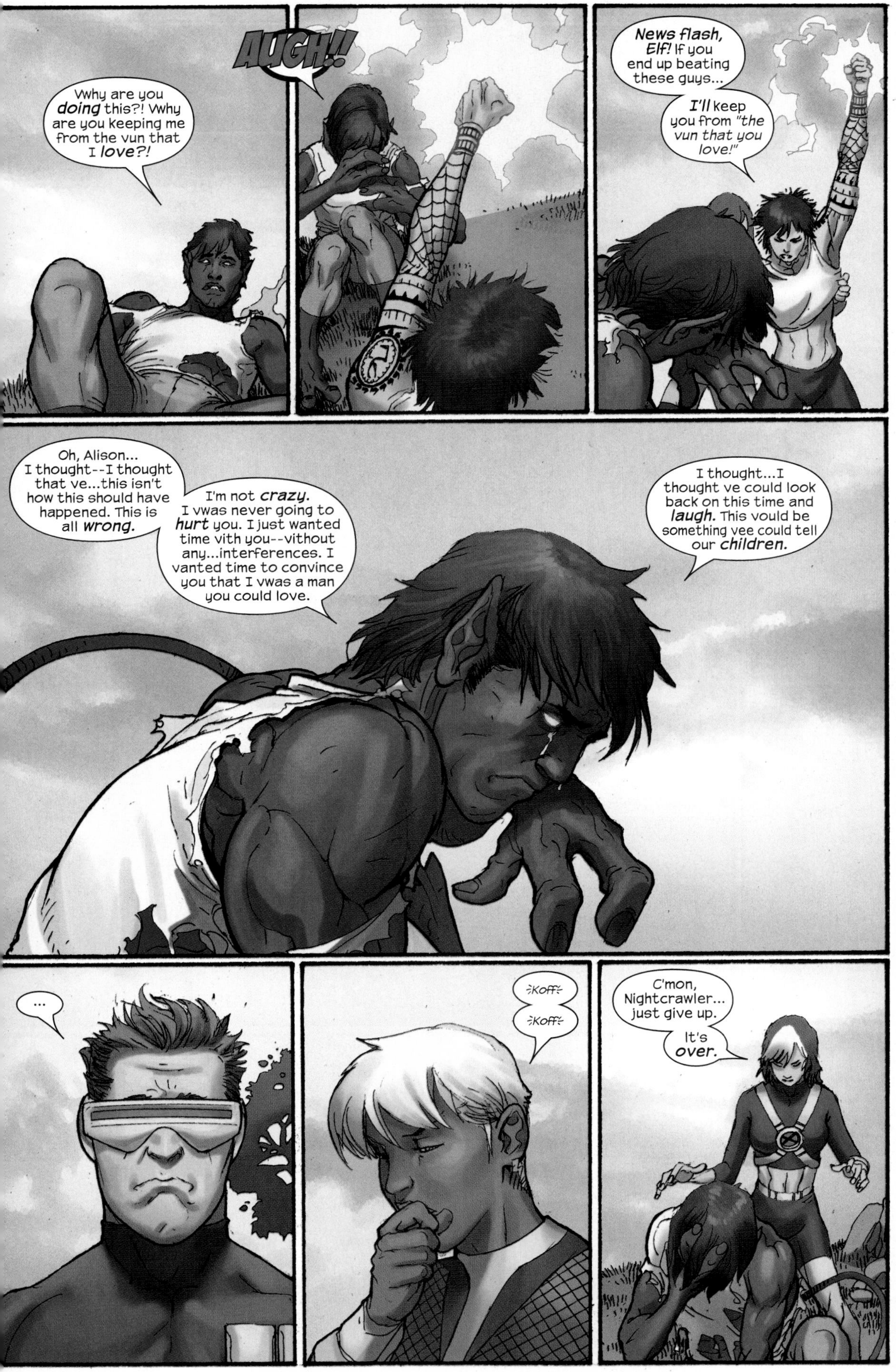
Vwhy are you doing this?! Vwhy are you keeping me from the vun that I love?!
AUGH!!
News flash, Elf! If you end up beating these guys...
I'll keep you from "the vun that you love!"
Oh, Alison... I thought--I thought that ve...this isn't how this should have happened. This is all wrong.
I'm not crazy. I vwas never going to hurt you. I just wanted time vith you--vithout any...interferences. I vanted time to convince you that I vwas a man you could love.
I thought...I thought ve could look back on this time and laugh. This vould be something vee could tell our children.
...
Koff
Koff
C'mon, Nightcrawler... just give up.
It's over.

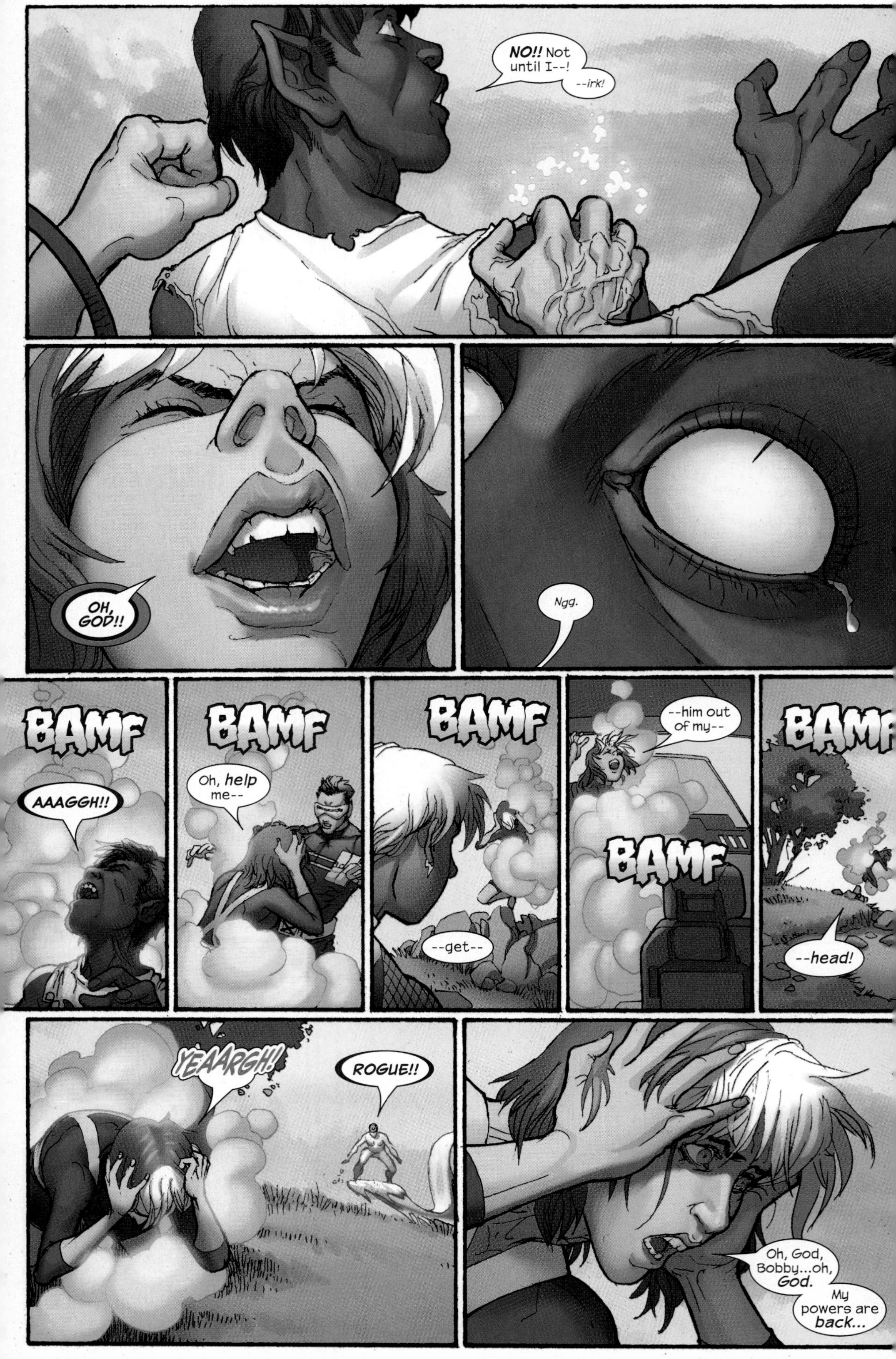

NO!! Not until I--!
--irk!
OH, GOD!!
Ngg.
BAMF
AAAGGH!!
BAMF
Oh, help me--
BAMF
--get--
--him out of my--
BAMF
BAMF
--head!
YEAARGH!
ROGUE!!
Oh, God, Bobby...oh, God.
My powers are back...

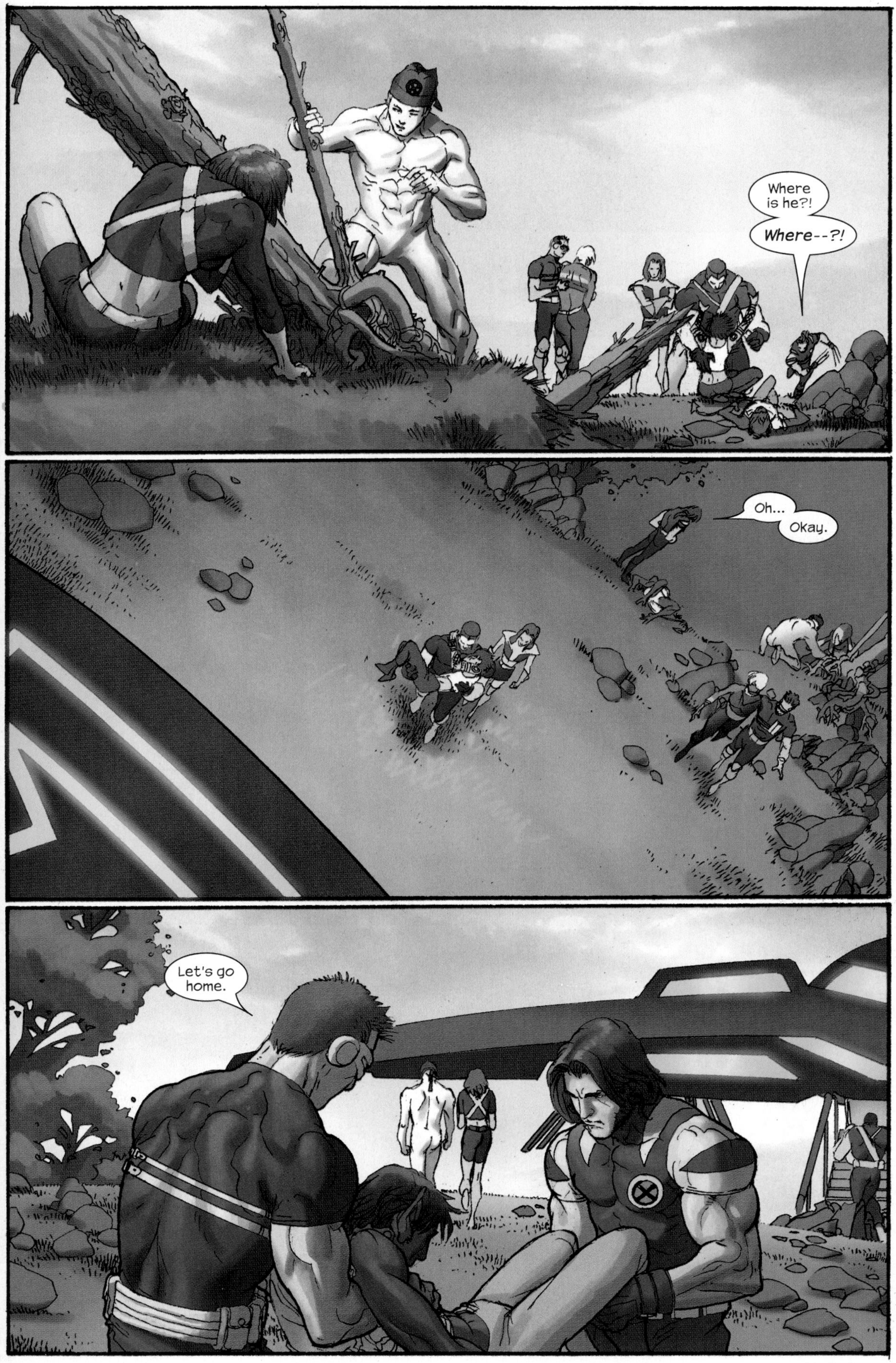
Where is he?!
Where--?!
Oh... Okay.
Let's go home.

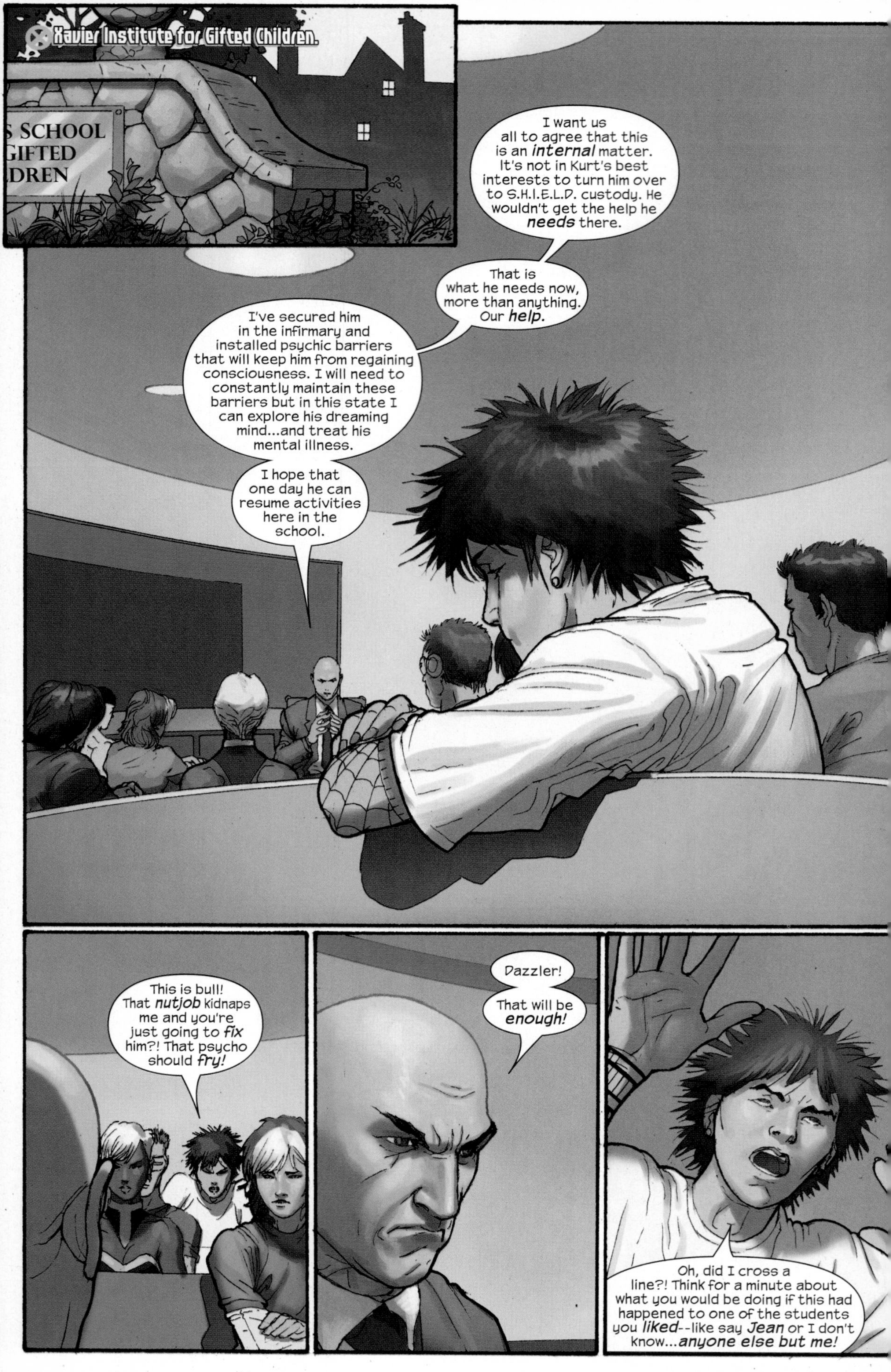
Xavier Institute for Gifted Children.
S SCHOOL
GIFTED
DREN
I want us all to agree that this is an internal matter. It's not in Kurt's best interests to turn him over to S.H.I.E.L.D. custody. He wouldn't get the help he needs there.
That is what he needs now, more than anything. Our help.
I've secured him in the infirmary and installed psychic barriers that will keep him from regaining consciousness. I will need to constantly maintain these barriers but in this state I can explore his dreaming mind...and treat his mental illness.
I hope that one day he can resume activities here in the school.
This is bull! That nutjob kidnaps me and you're just going to fix him?! That psycho should fry!
Dazzler!
That will be enough!
Oh, did I cross a line?! Think for a minute about what you would be doing if this had happened to one of the students you liked--like say Jean or I don't know...anyone else but me!

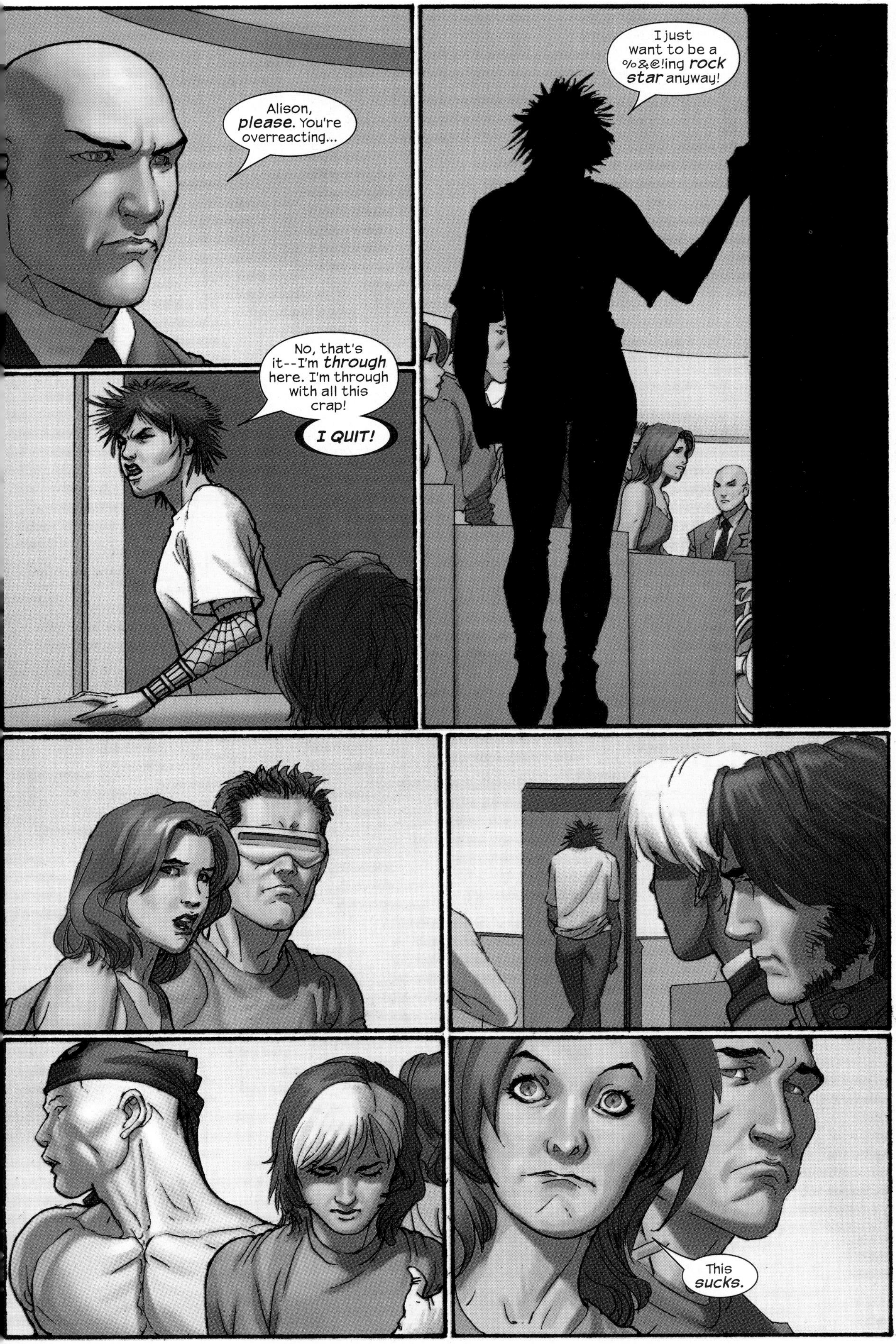
Alison, please. You're overreacting...
I just want to be a %&@!ing rock star anyway!
No, that's it--I'm through here. I'm through with all this crap!
I QUIT!
This sucks.

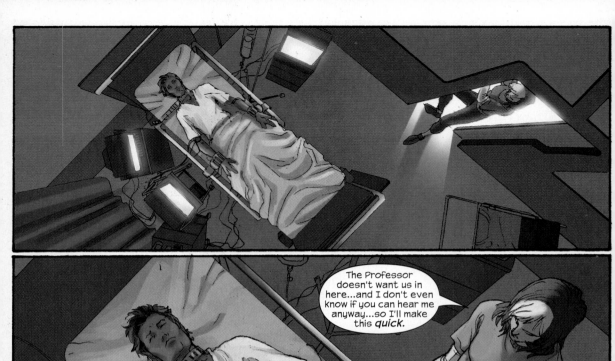

The Professor doesn't want us in here...and I don't even know if you can hear me anyway...so I'll make this *quick.*

I know what it's like to grow up being a mutant. To have people treat you a certain way just because you're different. I know about the ridicule, the isolation.

I know that it must be especially hard when you *look* different too. People who judged you just by the way you look...they probably thought you were a *monster.*

I just wanted to say that after being in your head... seeing what you *really* are...on the inside...

...I *know* you're a monster.

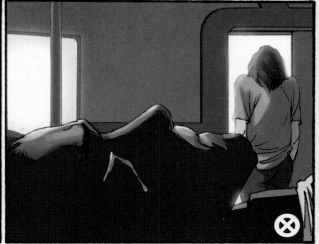

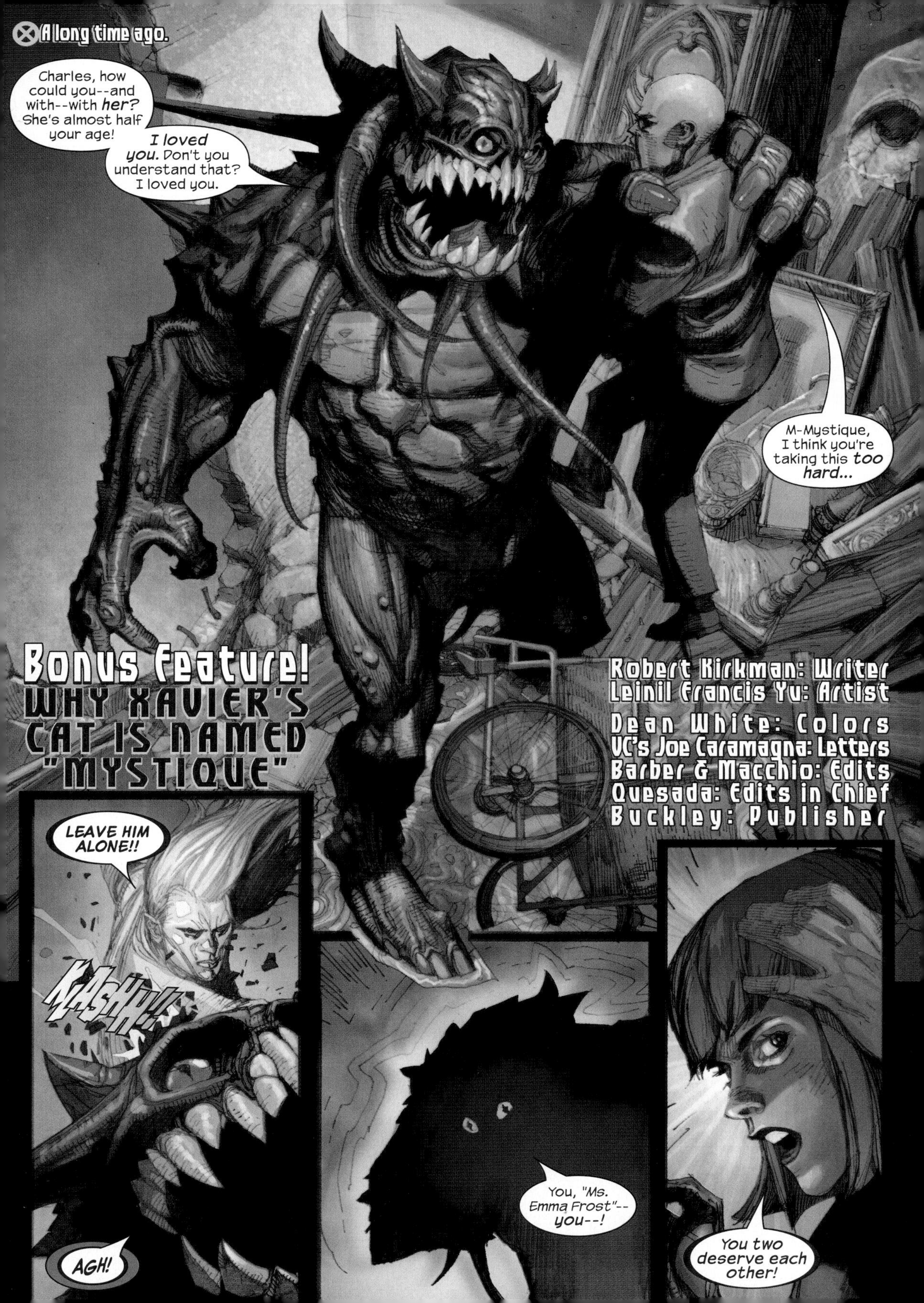
A long time ago.
Charles, how could you--and with--with *her*? She's almost half your age!
I loved you. Don't you understand that? I loved you.
M-Mystique, I think you're taking this *too hard*...
Bonus Feature!
WHY XAVIER'S CAT IS NAMED "MYSTIQUE"
Robert Kirkman: Writer
Leinil Francis Yu: Artist
Dean White: Colors
VC's Joe Caramagna: Letters
Barber & Macchio: Edits
Quesada: Edits in Chief
Buckley: Publisher
LEAVE HIM ALONE!!
KASHH!!
AGH!
You, "Ms. Emma Frost"-- *you*--!
You two deserve each other!

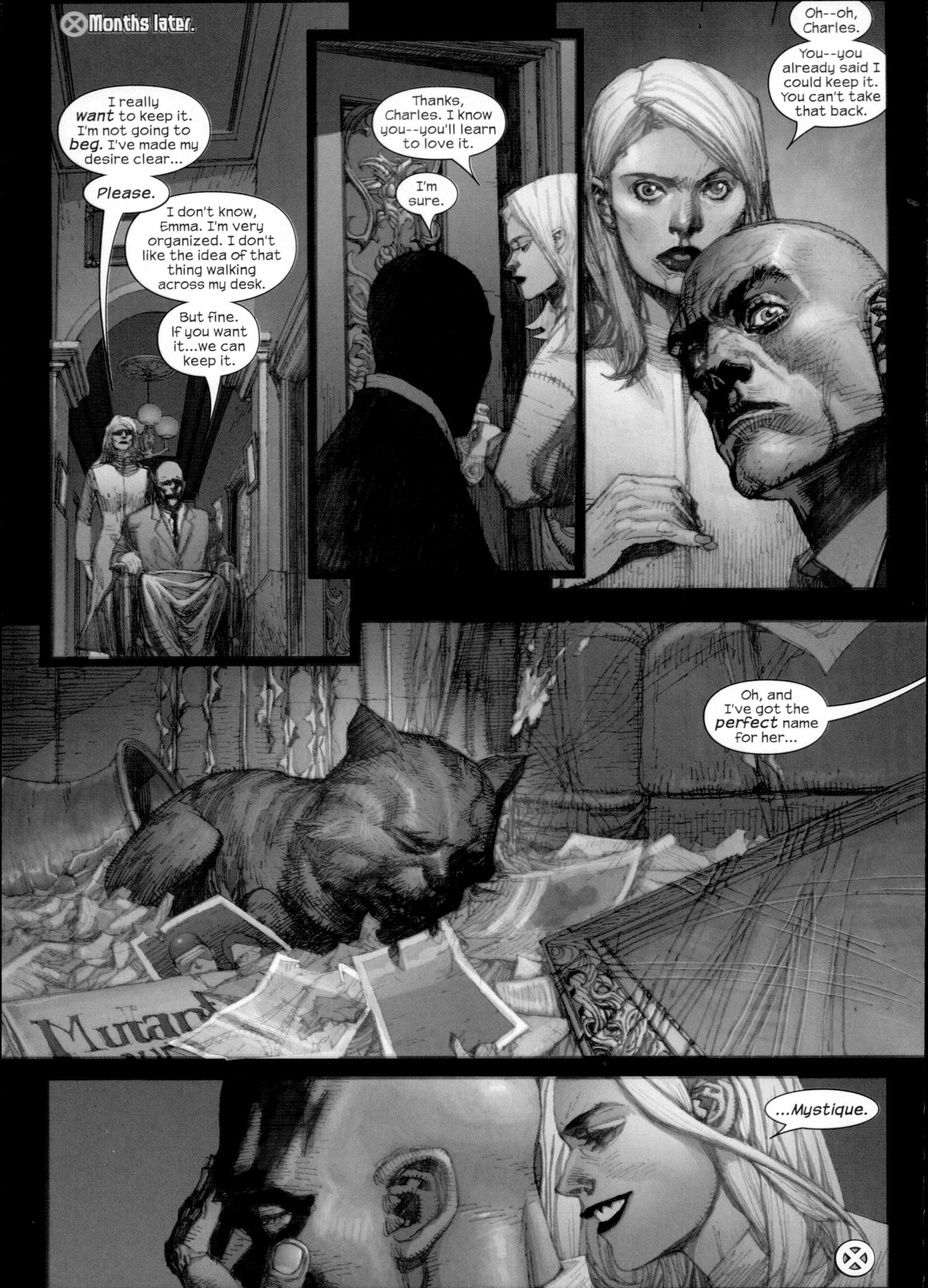
Months later.
I really want to keep it. I'm not going to beg. I've made my desire clear...
Please.
I don't know, Emma. I'm very organized. I don't like the idea of that thing walking across my desk.
But fine. If you want it...we can keep it.
Thanks, Charles. I know you--you'll learn to love it.
I'm sure.
Oh--oh, Charles.
You--you already said I could keep it. You can't take that back.
Oh, and I've got the perfect name for her...
...Mystique.

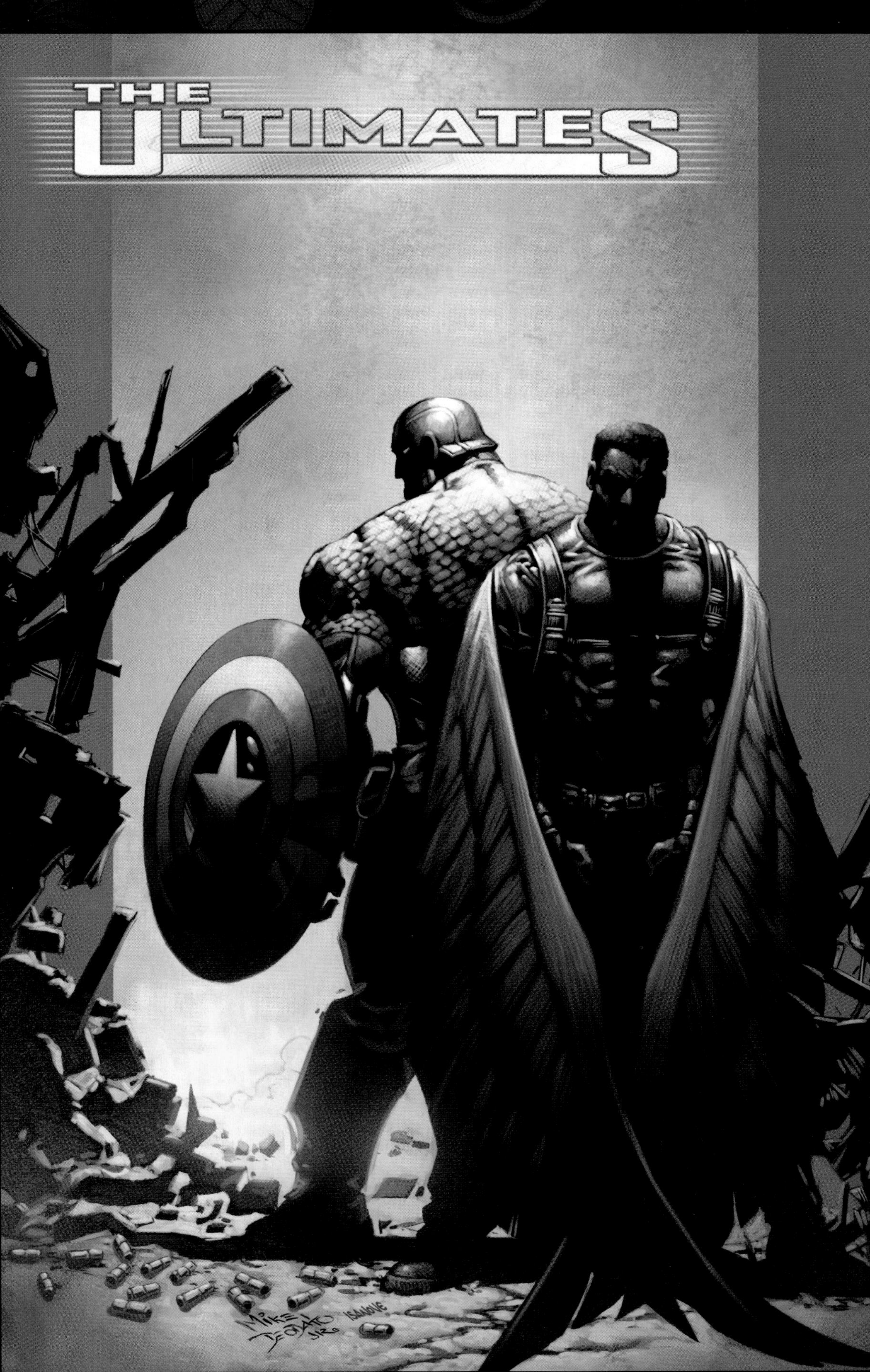
THE ULTIMATES

PREVIOUSLY IN THE ULTIMATES:

When faced with Nazi Germany's military advances, the U.S. government decided that the best weapon against them was a person, not a bomb. With this in mind, Steve Rogers volunteered for a covert military experiment that turned him into Captain America. After a few years of exemplary service, Captain America fell in battle—his body wasn't recovered.

Years passed and Captain America was found frozen in suspended animation. When he awoke, he was convinced to join Iron Man, The Wasp, Giant Man, Black Widow, Hawkeye, and Thor in forming the superhuman defense initiative run by Nick Fury, called the Ultimates.

Sam Wilson, a.k.a. the Falcon, is a scientist and field agent of Fury's elite espionage organization, S.H.I.E.L.D. Wilson teamed up with Captain America to combat the space-born threat called Gah Lak Tus.

More recently, America itself has been invaded by hostile foreign superhumans. The nation has been devastated, and Cap and the Falcon try to pick up the pieces...

THE ULTIMATES

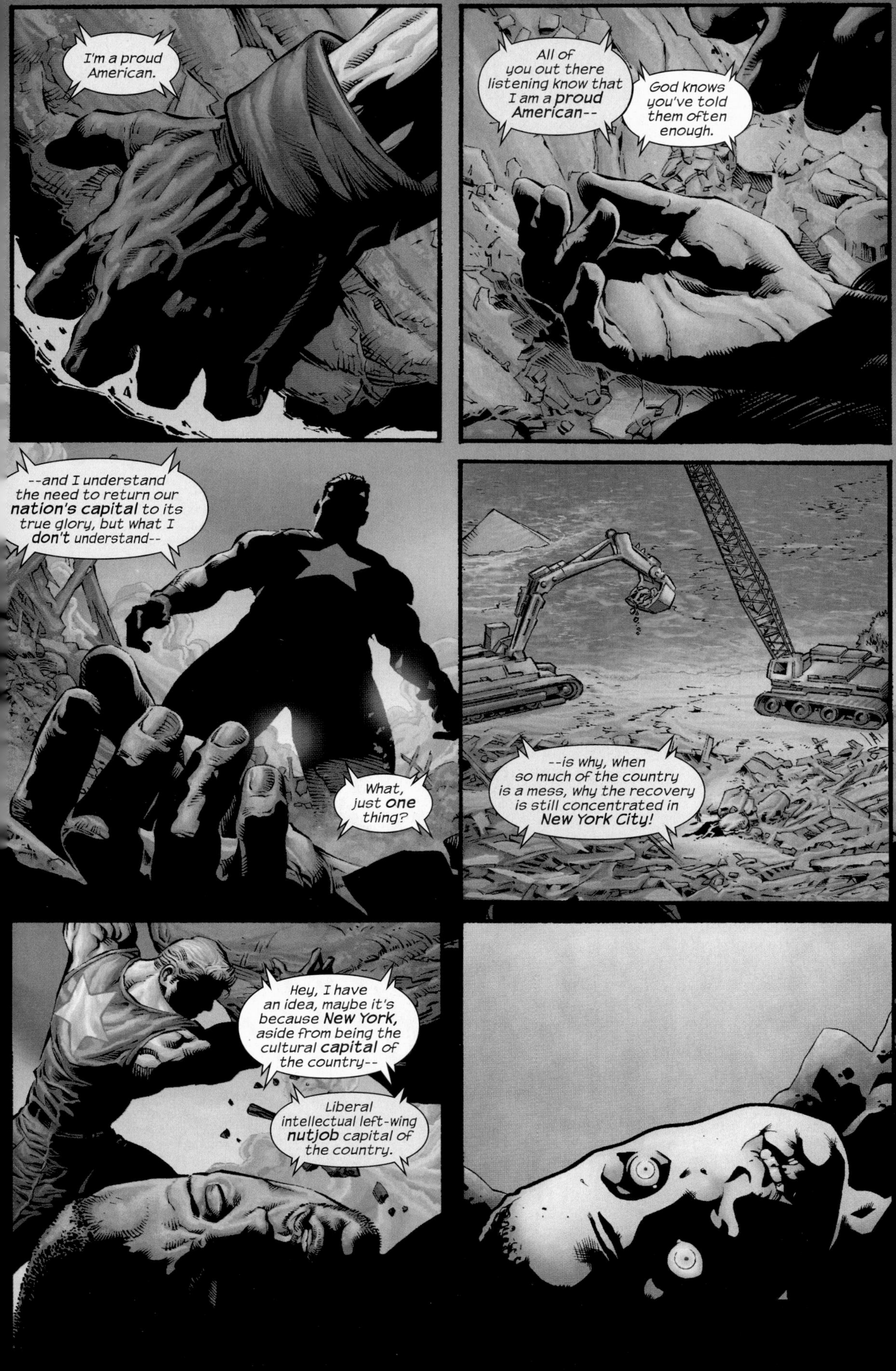
I'm a proud American.
All of you out there listening know that I am a proud American--
God knows you've told them often enough.
--and I understand the need to return our nation's capital to its true glory, but what I don't understand--
What, just one thing?
--is why, when so much of the country is a mess, why the recovery is still concentrated in New York City!
Hey, I have an idea, maybe it's because New York, aside from being the cultural capital of the country--
Liberal intellectual left-wing nutjob capital of the country.

--that it suffered the most extensive damage and loss of life during the occupation.

"Occupation"? "Occupation"? Is that what you people call a terrorist attack these days?

"Give you a hand?"

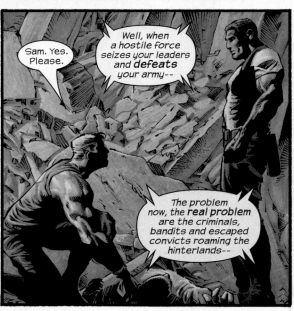

Sam. Yes. Please.

Well, when a hostile force seizes your leaders and defeats your army--

The problem now, the real problem are the criminals, bandits and escaped convicts roaming the hinterlands--

Hinterlands? Oh my God! You talk like it's the Dark Ages out there!

You know, Quicksilver says there's still a few survivors. He's calling in as he finds them.

I think there may be another one under this.

If we can roll this boulder all the way off and--

Cap, the dead can wait.

Let me read just the top of the ticker here--we got prison riots, military armories being looted, we got plague reports. Sounds like the Dark Ages to me.

Come on! Plague?

You're wrong.

These people, they came here to see something important. A symbol of what the world should be like.

And those animals pushed it down on their heads.

There are people better suited to the heavy lifting...

America's so-called "heroes" just don't--

I can't believe this, just a few days ago you were singing the praises of that band of fascists and now--

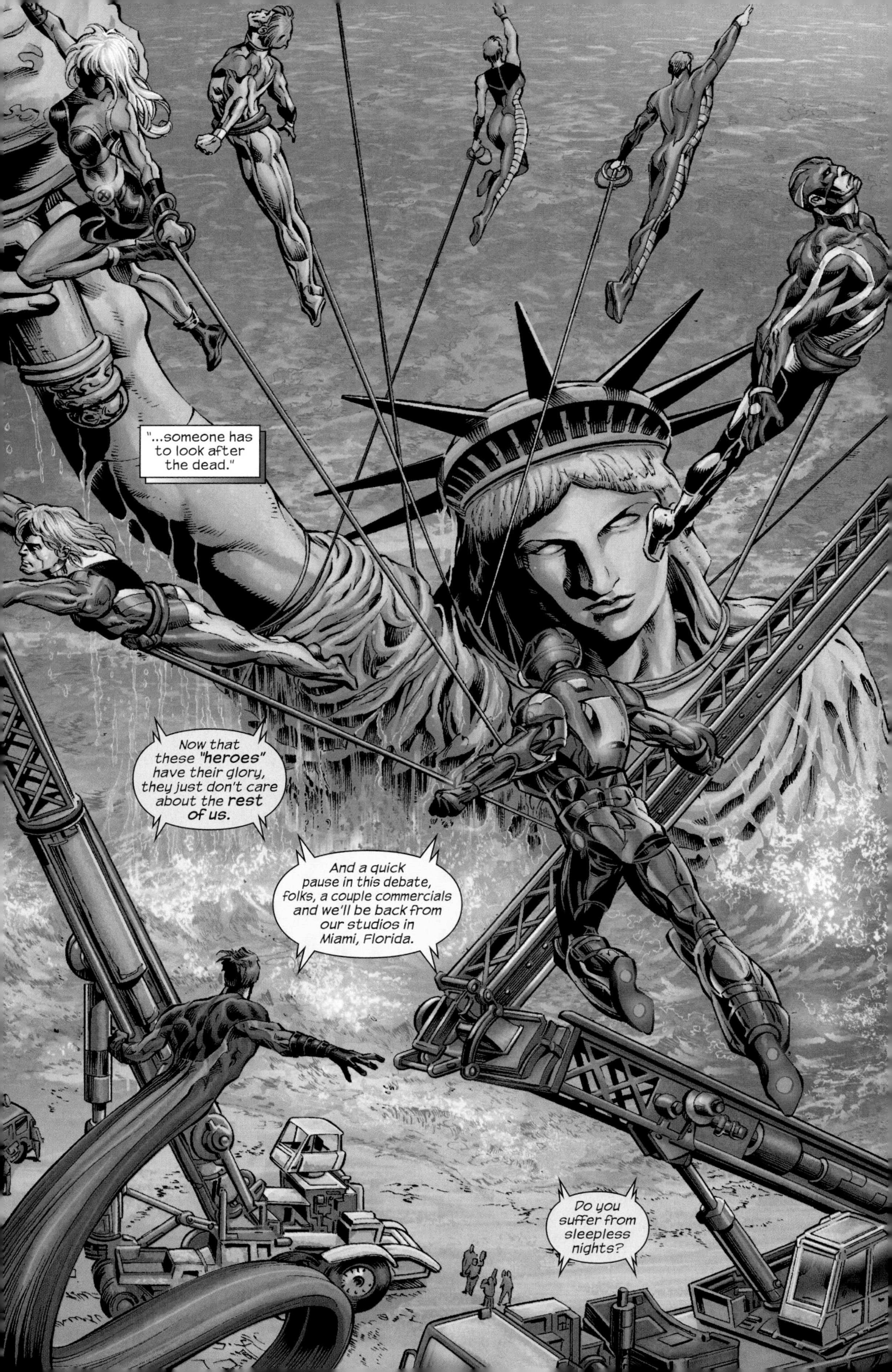
"...someone has to look after the dead."
Now that these "heroes" have their glory, they just don't care about the rest of us.
And a quick pause in this debate, folks, a couple commercials and we'll be back from our studios in Miami, Florida.
Do you suffer from sleepless nights?

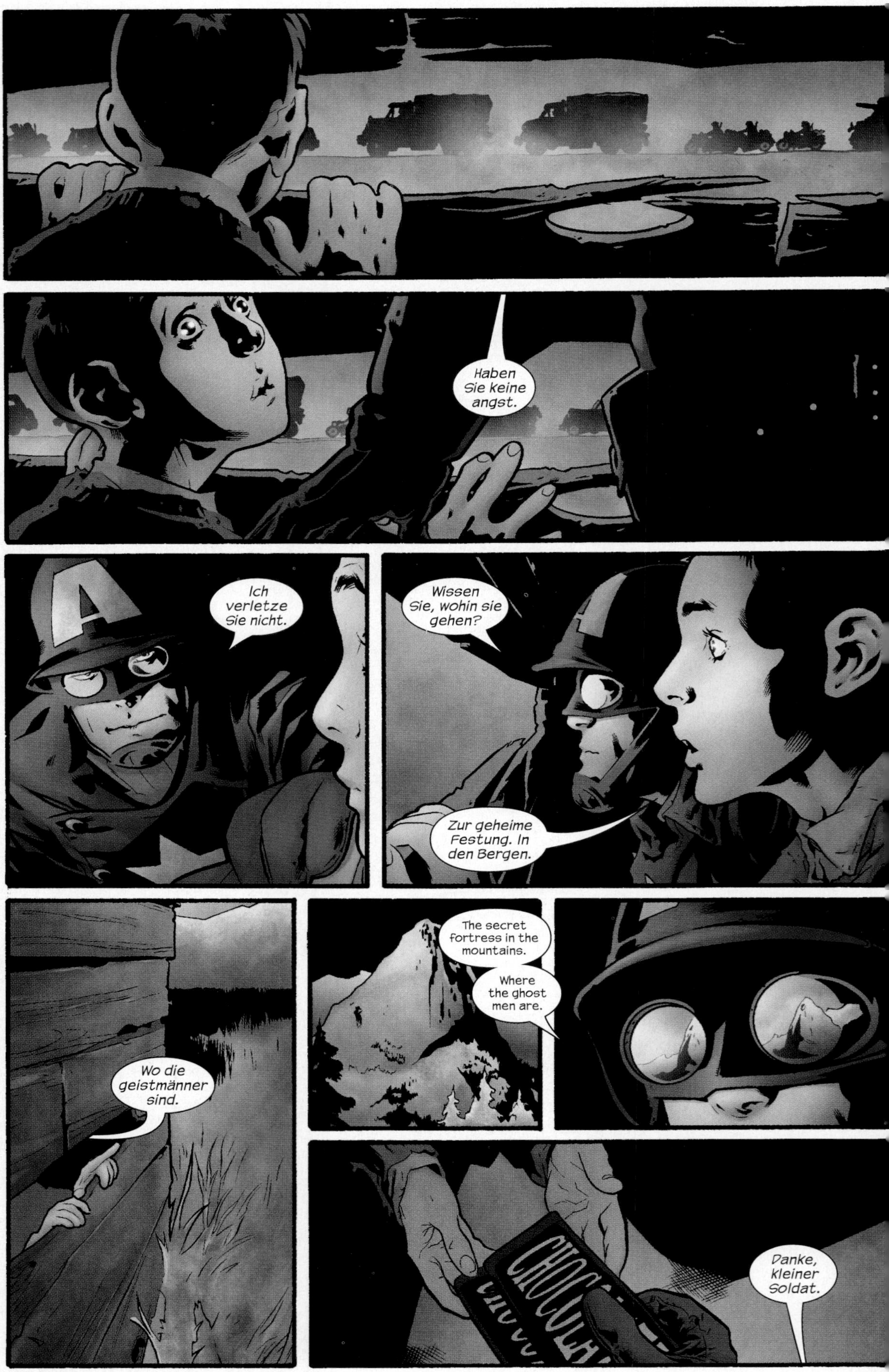
Haben Sie keine angst.
Ich verletze Sie nicht.
Wissen Sie, wohin sie gehen?
Zur geheime Festung. In den Bergen.
Wo die geistmänner sind.
The secret fortress in the mountains.
Where the ghost men are.
Danke, kleiner Soldat.

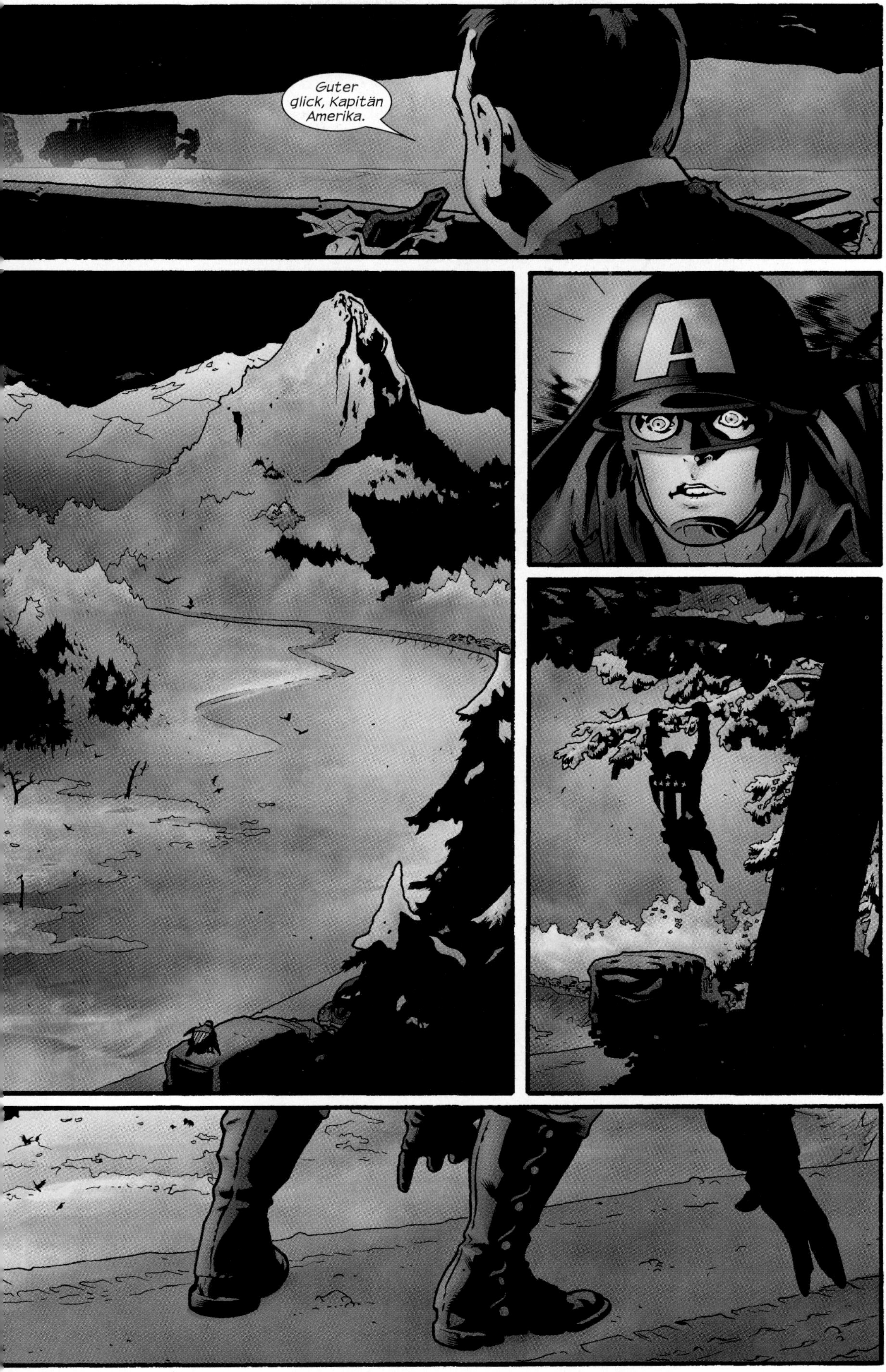
Guter glick, Kapitän Amerika.

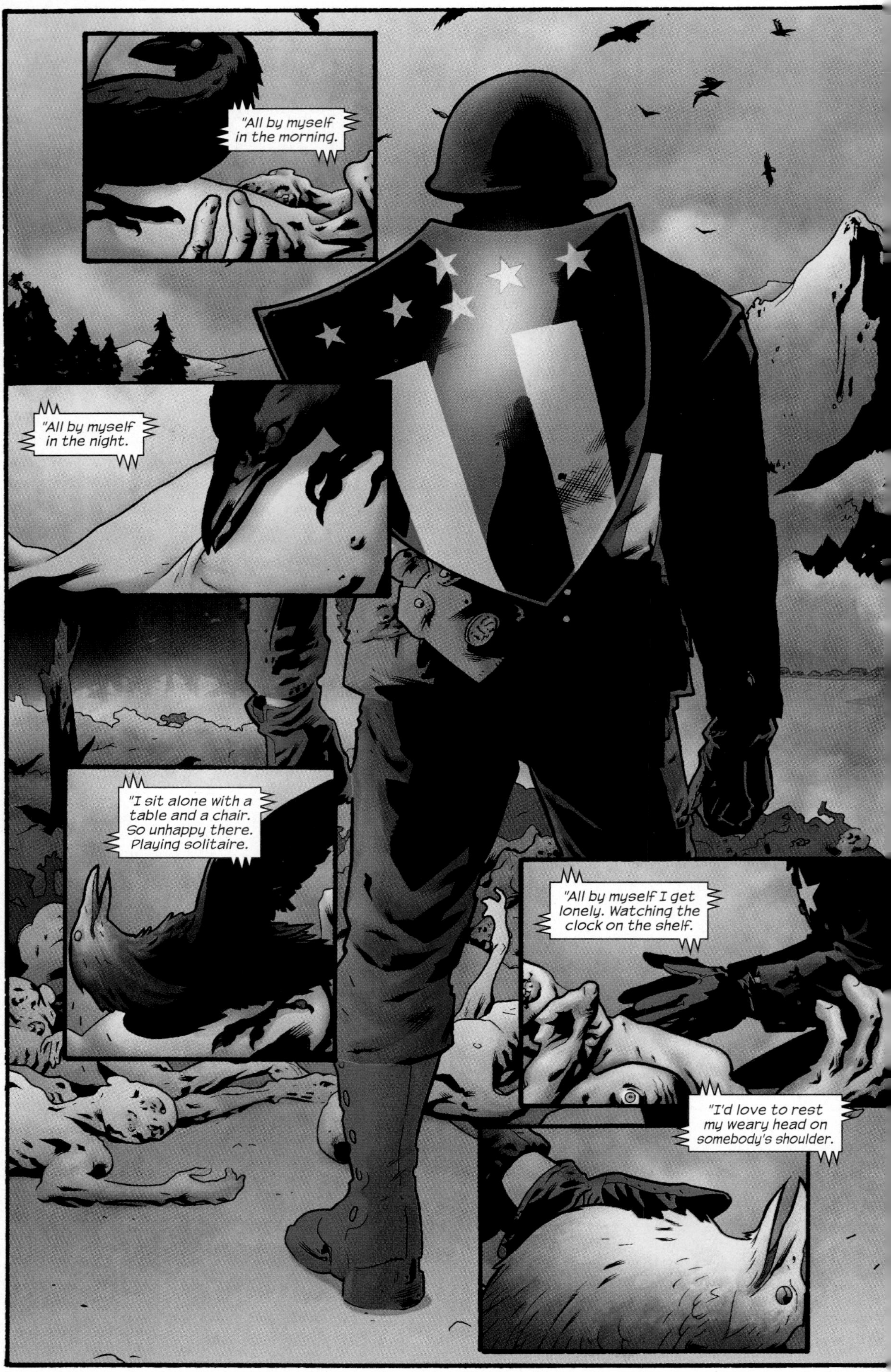
"All by myself in the morning.
"All by myself in the night.
"I sit alone with a table and a chair. So unhappy there. Playing solitaire.
"All by myself I get lonely. Watching the clock on the shelf.
"I'd love to rest my weary head on somebody's shoulder.

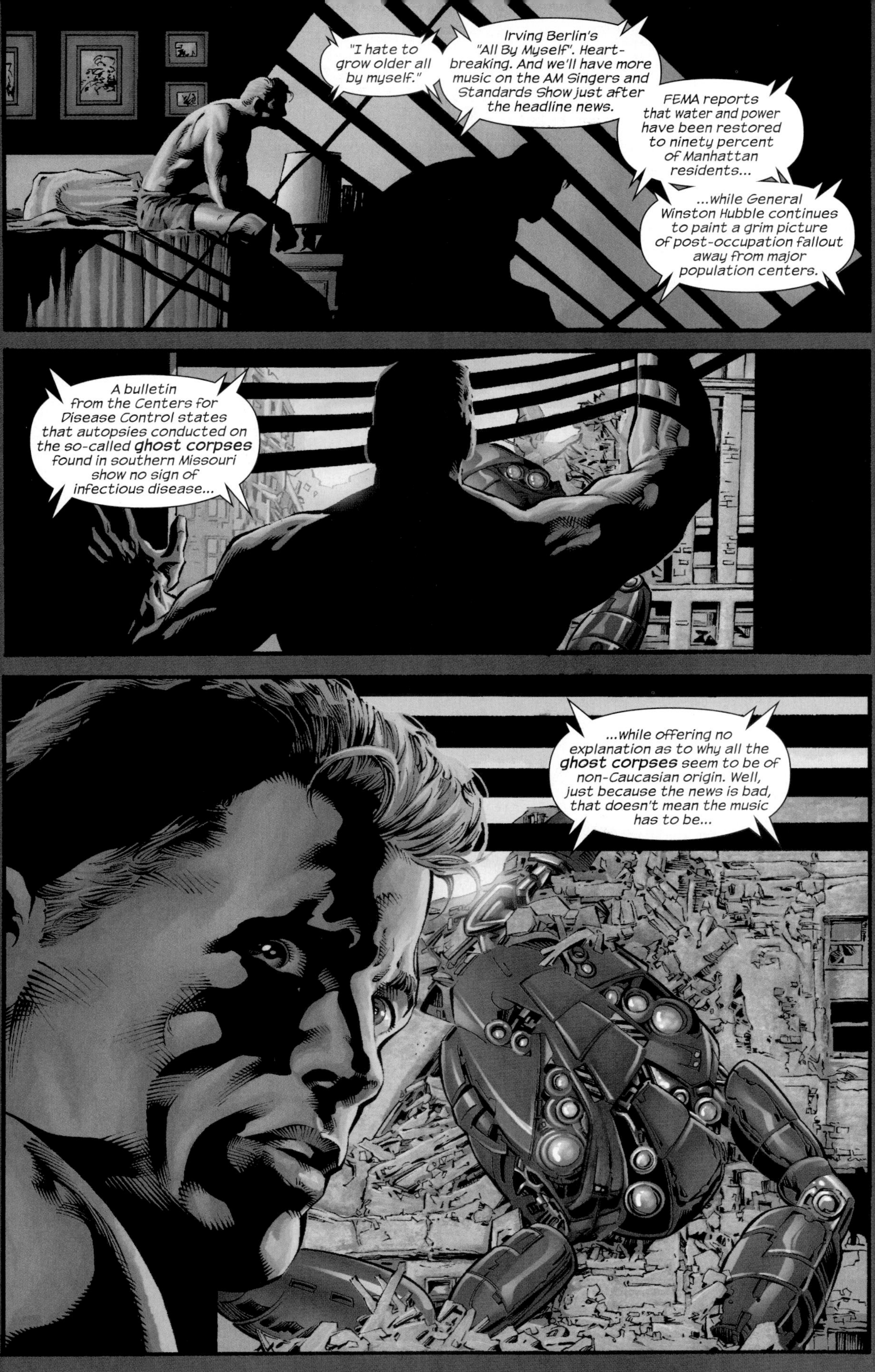
"I hate to grow older all by myself."
Irving Berlin's "All By Myself". Heart-breaking. And we'll have more music on the AM Singers and Standards Show just after the headline news.
FEMA reports that water and power have been restored to ninety percent of Manhattan residents...
...while General Winston Hubble continues to paint a grim picture of post-occupation fallout away from major population centers.
A bulletin from the Centers for Disease Control states that autopsies conducted on the so-called **ghost corpses** found in southern Missouri show no sign of infectious disease...
...while offering no explanation as to why all the **ghost corpses** seem to be of non-Caucasian origin. Well, just because the news is bad, that doesn't mean the music has to be...

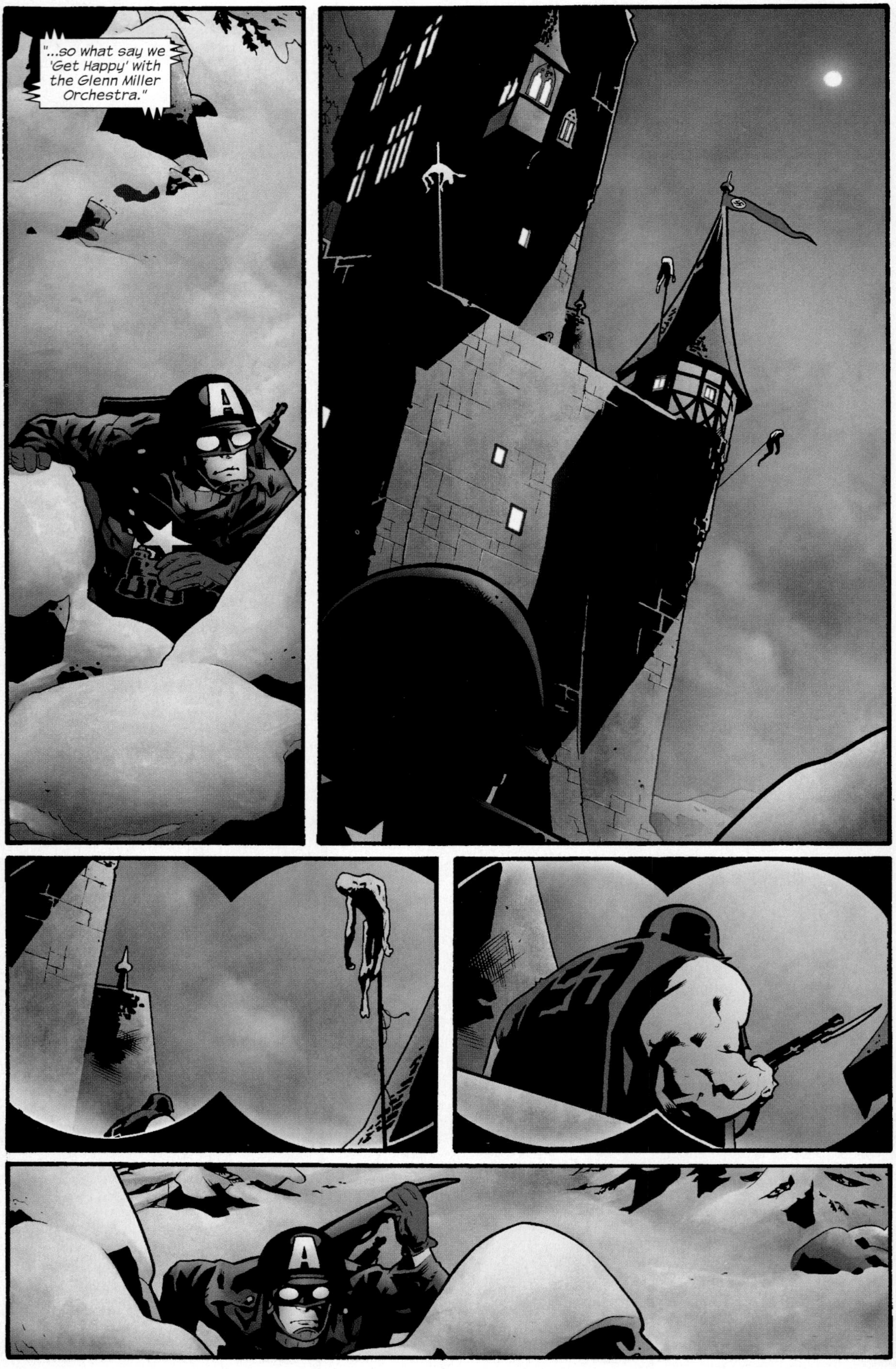
"...so what say we 'Get Happy' with the Glenn Miller Orchestra."

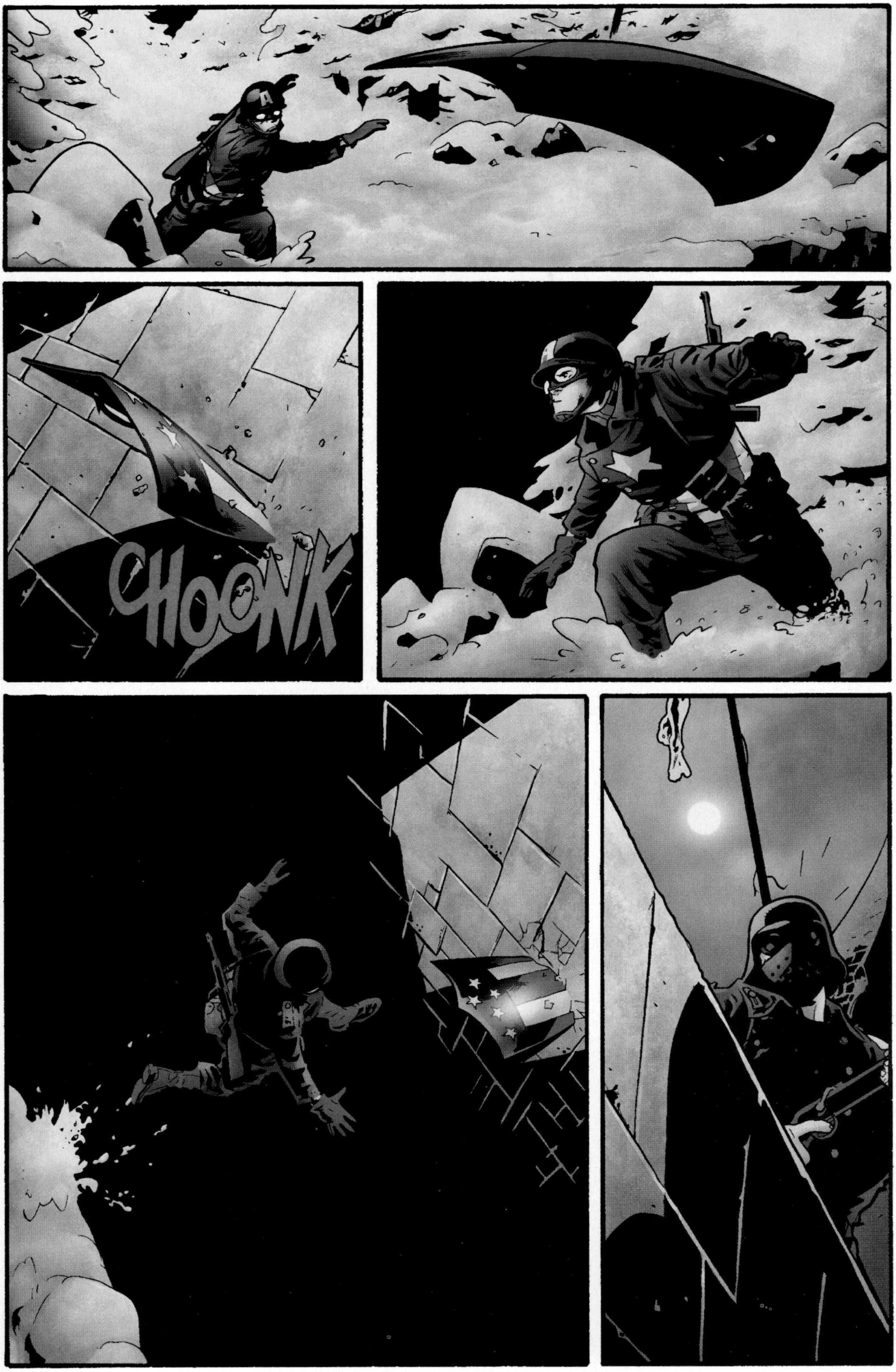
CHOONK

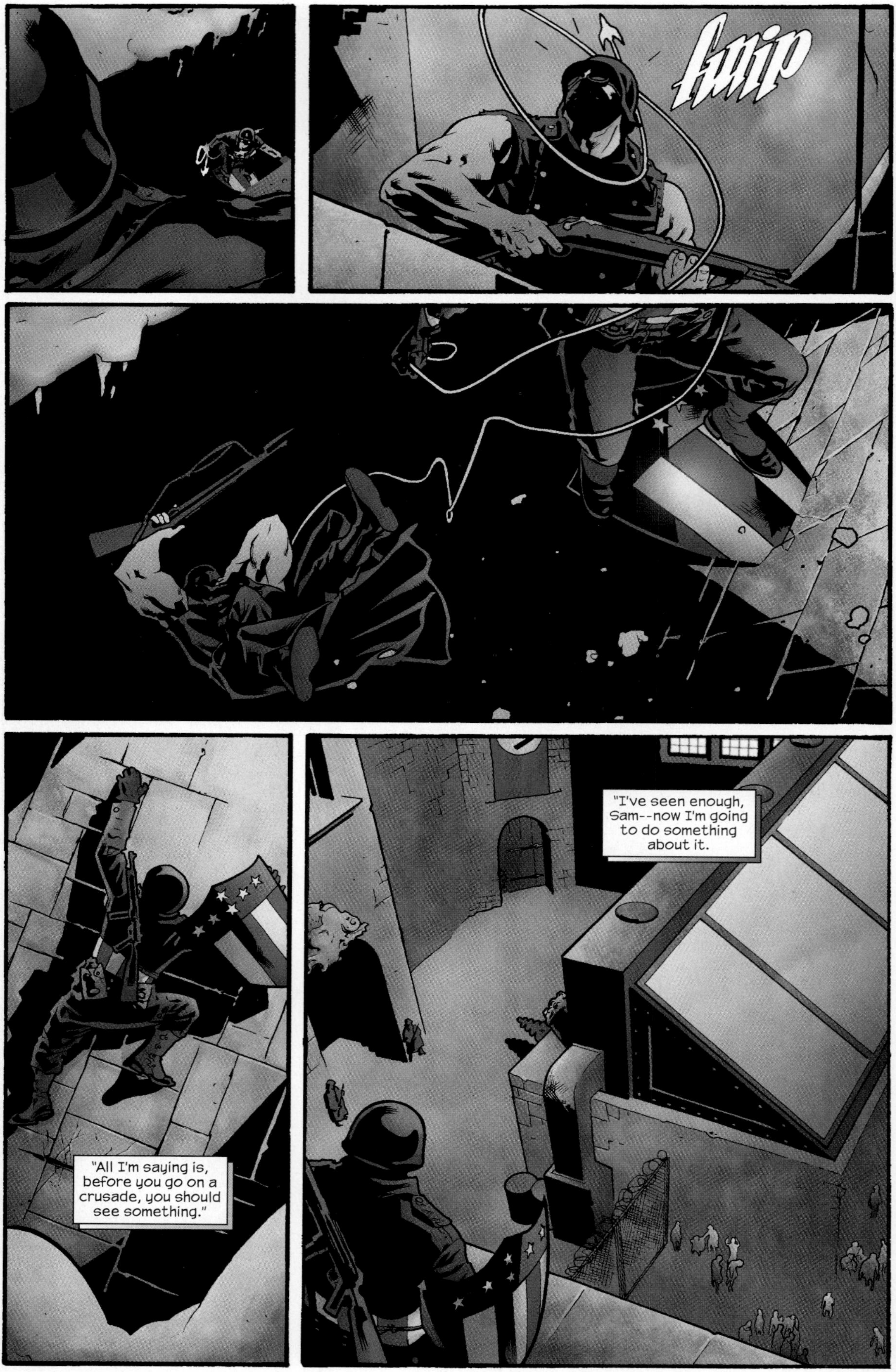

fwip
"All I'm saying is, before you go on a crusade, you should see something."
"I've seen enough, Sam--now I'm going to do something about it.

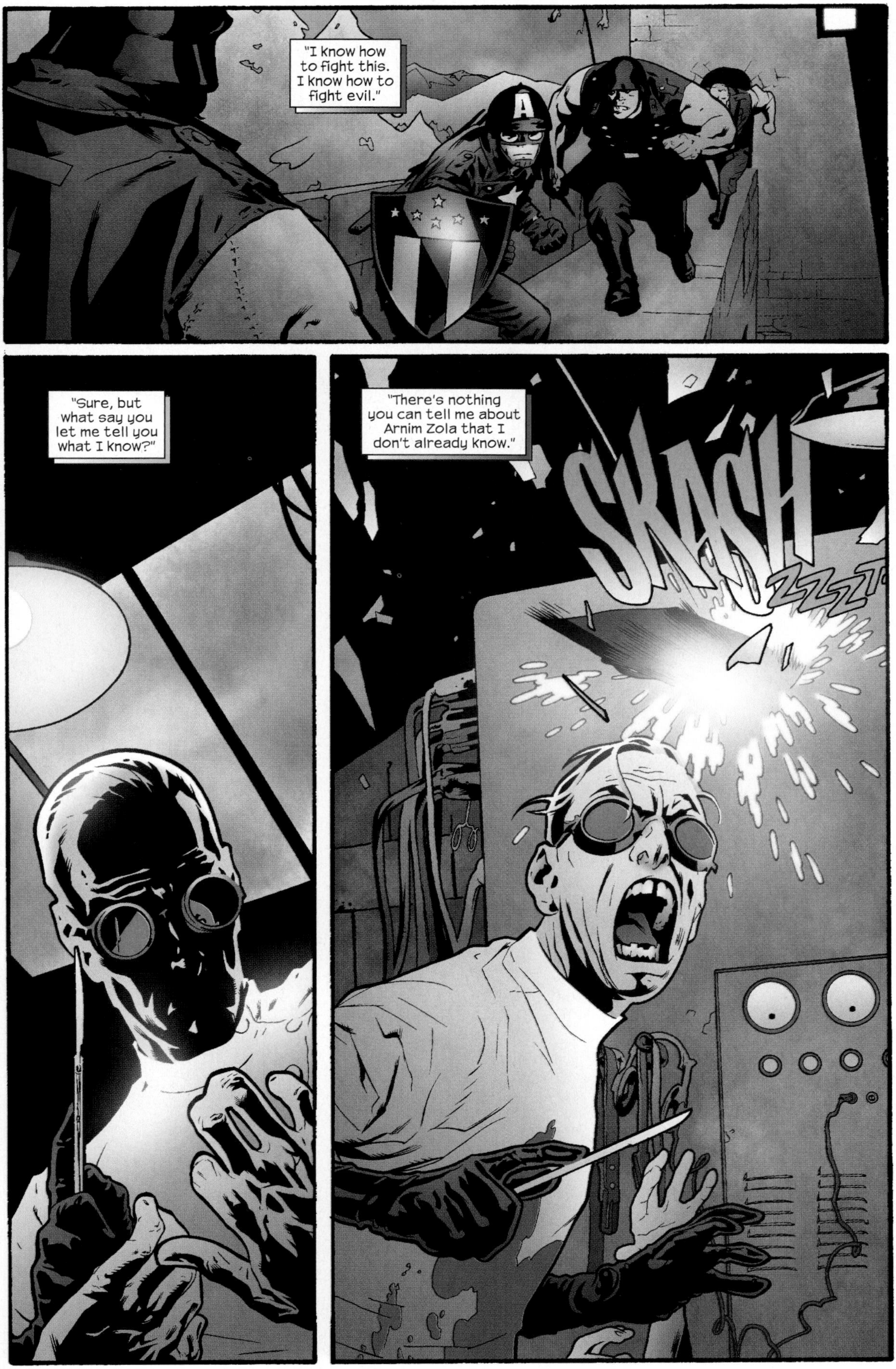
"I know how to fight this. I know how to fight evil."
"Sure, but what say you let me tell you what I know?"
"There's nothing you can tell me about Arnim Zola that I don't already know."
SKASH
ZZZZT

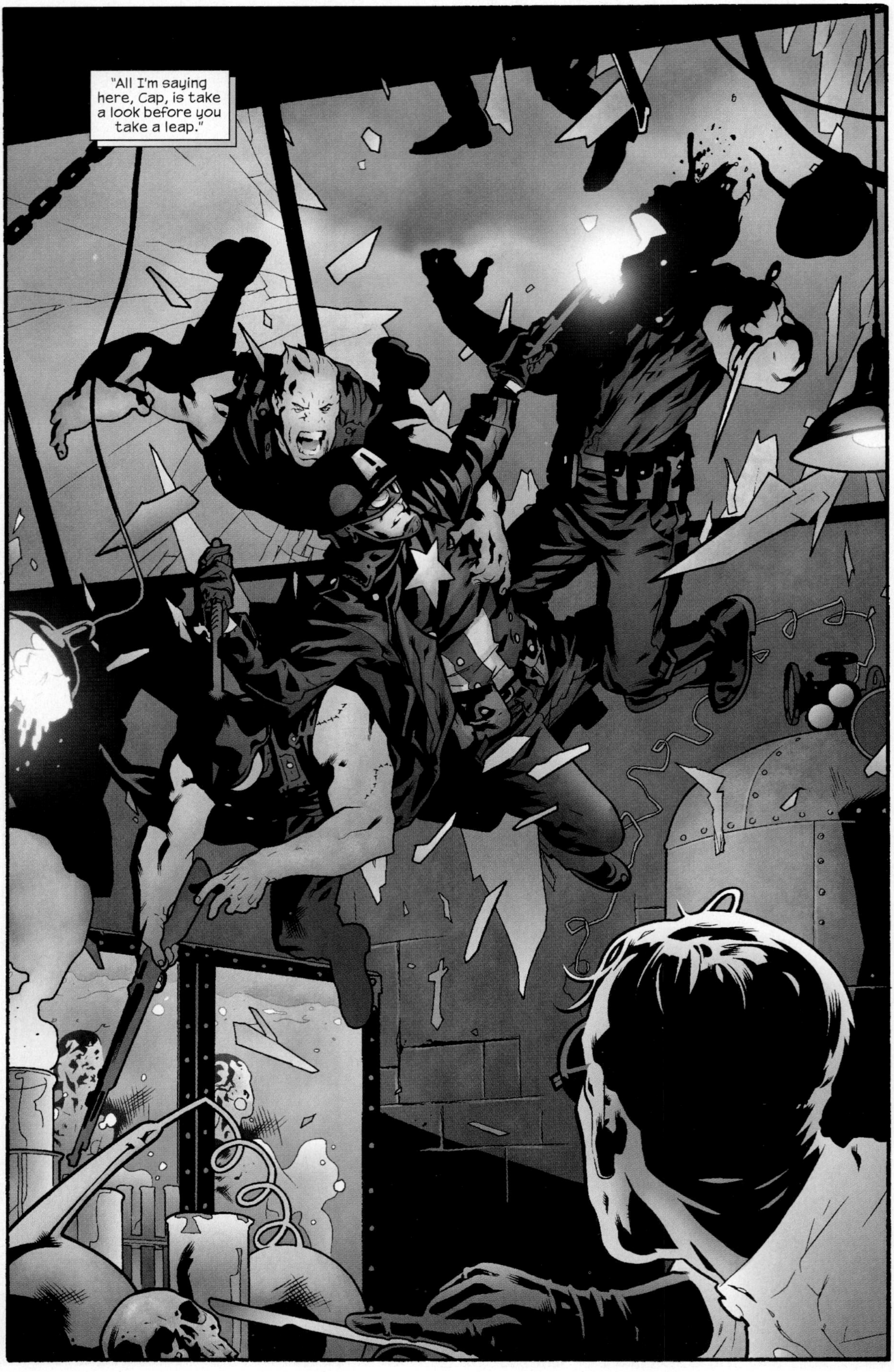
"All I'm saying here, Cap, is take a look before you take a leap."

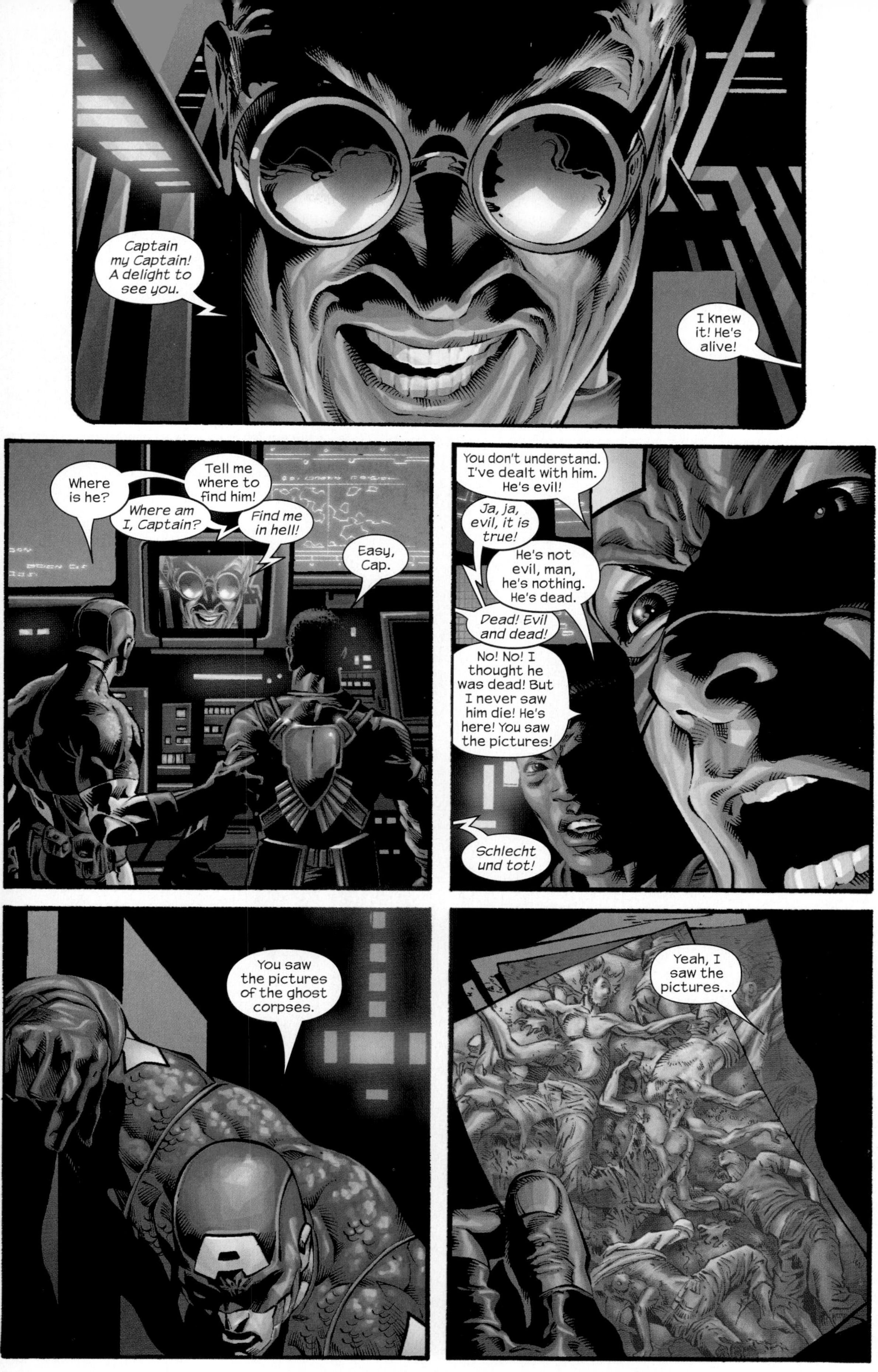

Captain my Captain! A delight to see you.
I knew it! He's alive!
Where is he?
Tell me where to find him!
Where am I, Captain?
Find me in hell!
Easy, Cap.
You don't understand. I've dealt with him. He's evil!
Ja, ja, evil, it is true!
He's not evil, man, he's nothing. He's dead.
Dead! Evil and dead!
No! No! I thought he was dead! But I never saw him die! He's here! You saw the pictures!
Schlecht und tot!
You saw the pictures of the ghost corpses.
Yeah, I saw the pictures...

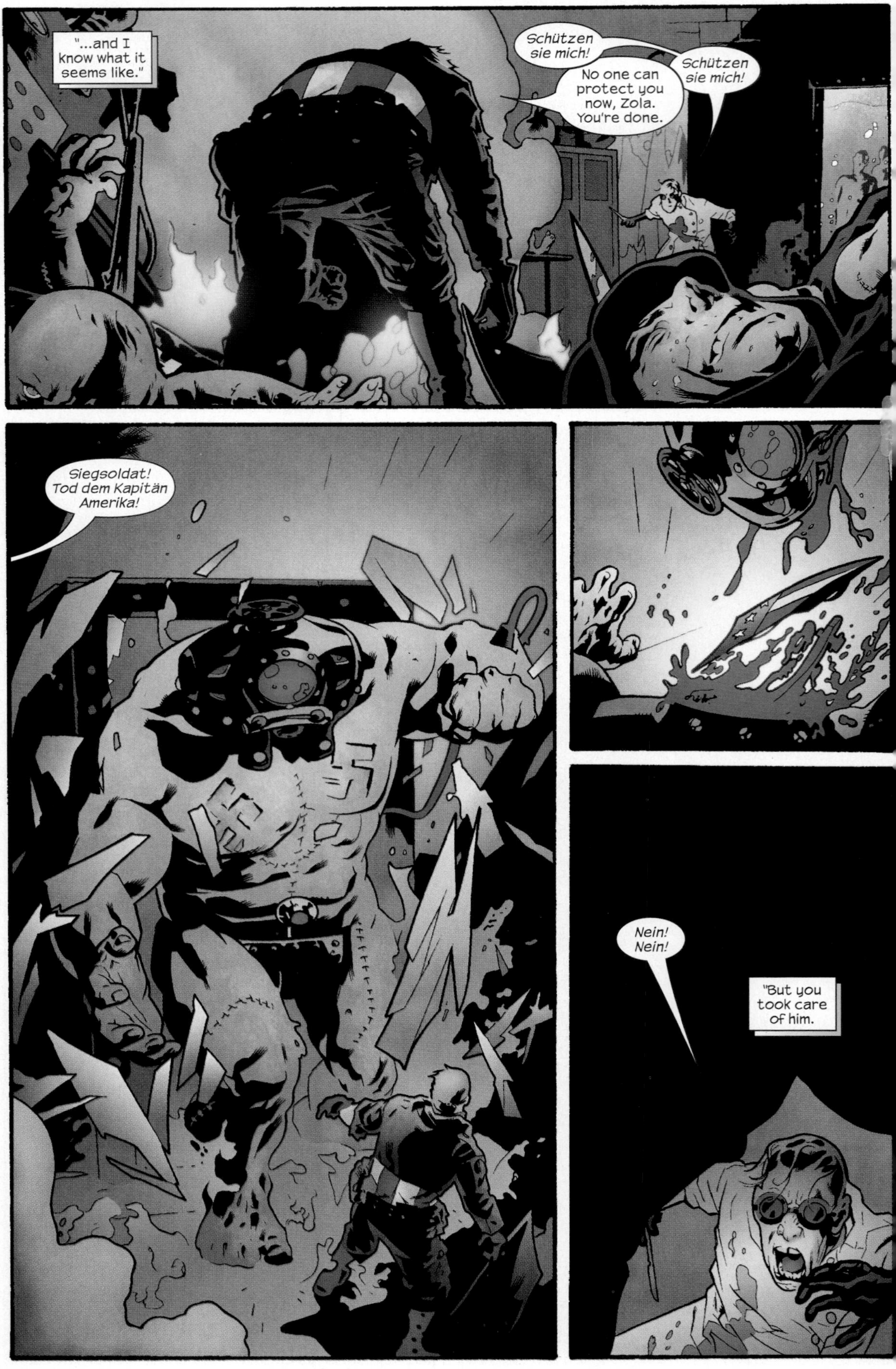
"...and I know what it seems like."
Schützen sie mich!
No one can protect you now, Zola. You're done.
Schützen sie mich!
Siegsoldat! Tod dem Kapitän Amerika!
Nein! Nein!
"But you took care of him.

"Crushing evil, man."

"It's what you do."

"Just, that wasn't the end of it."

"Ja. Sadly, *Kapitän*, that was not the end. Your Secret Service, they kept me alive."

"That's a lie."

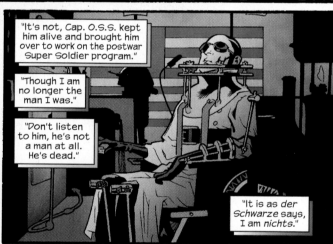

"It's not, Cap. O.S.S. kept him alive and brought him over to work on the postwar Super Soldier program."

"Though I am no longer the man I was."

"Don't listen to him, he's not a man at all. He's dead."

"It is as *der Schwarze* says, I am *nichts*."

"They mapped his brain before the tumors could eat it. Created an Artificial Intelligence. Didn't want to lose all that crazy intellect."

"*Ja*, to develop weapons! And it appears one of my weapons is loose, *ja*? The *Weiber Staub*. My White Dust. So beautiful."

"So good to know some part of me is still in the world. *Ich bin nur der Geist in dieser maschine*."

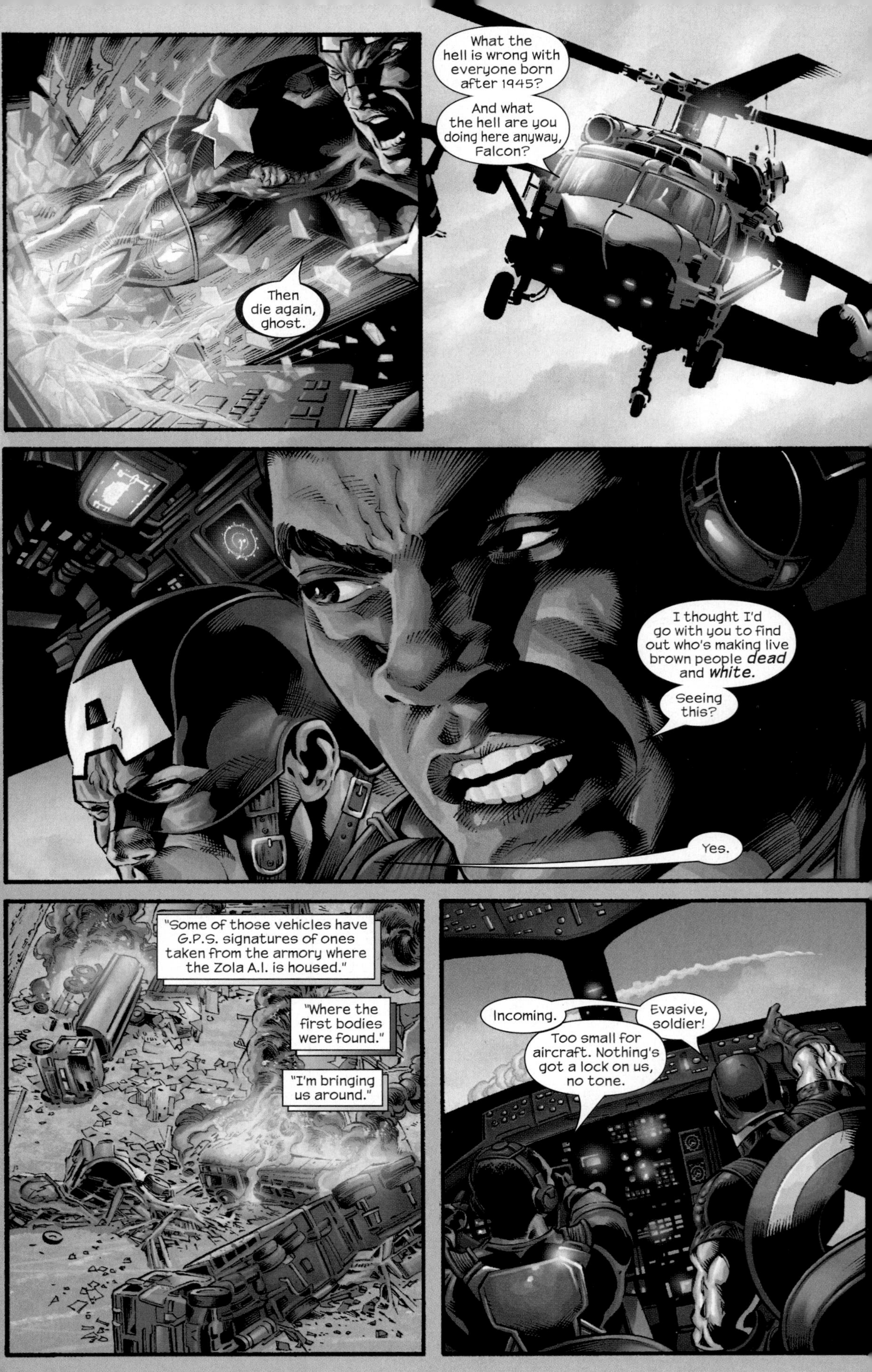
What the hell is wrong with everyone born after 1945?
And what the hell are you doing here anyway, Falcon?
Then die again, ghost.
I thought I'd go with you to find out who's making live brown people *dead* and *white.*
Seeing this?
Yes.
"Some of those vehicles have G.P.S. signatures of ones taken from the armory where the Zola A.I. is housed."
"Where the first bodies were found."
"I'm bringing us around."
Incoming.
Evasive, soldier!
Too small for aircraft. Nothing's got a lock on us, no tone.

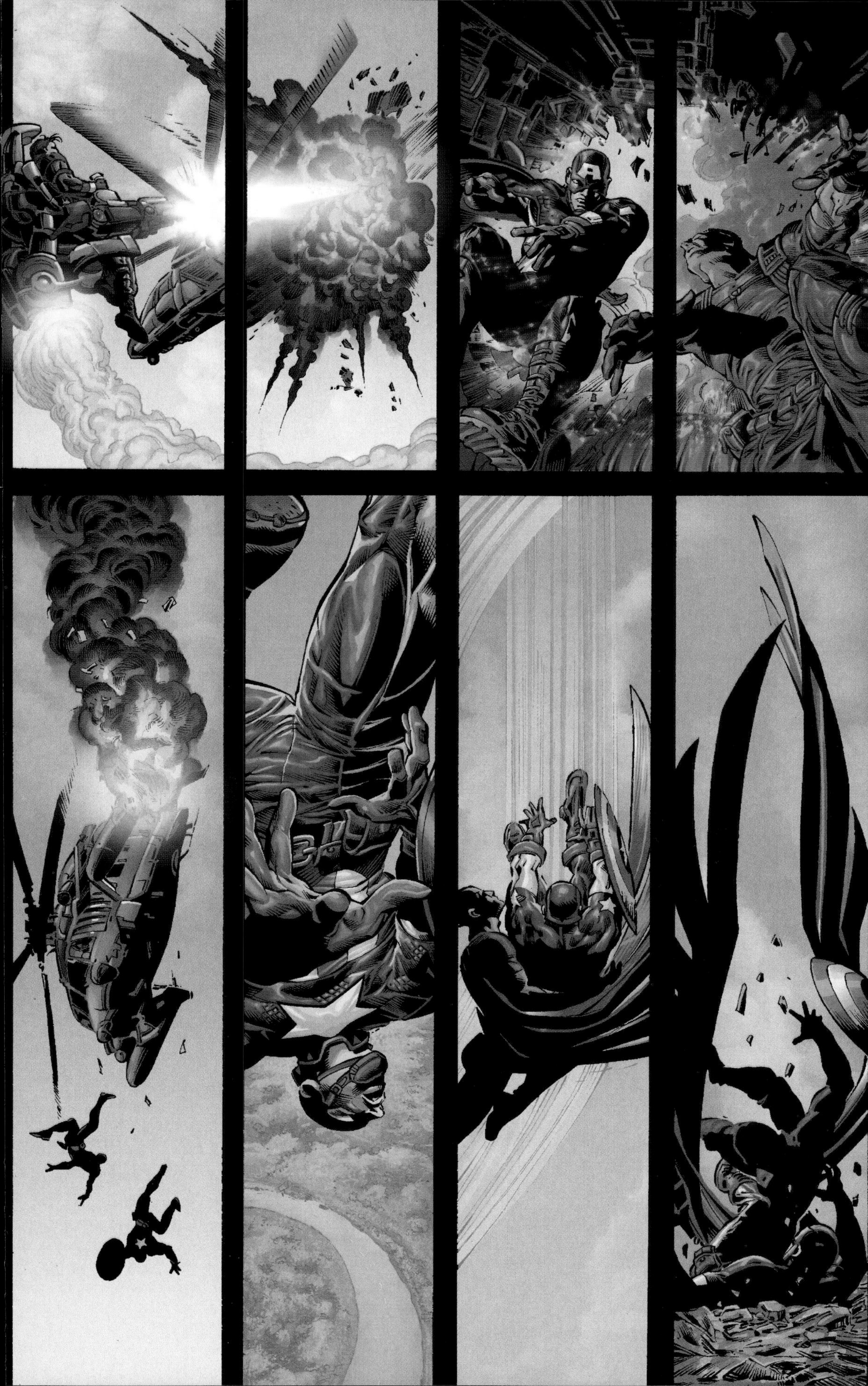

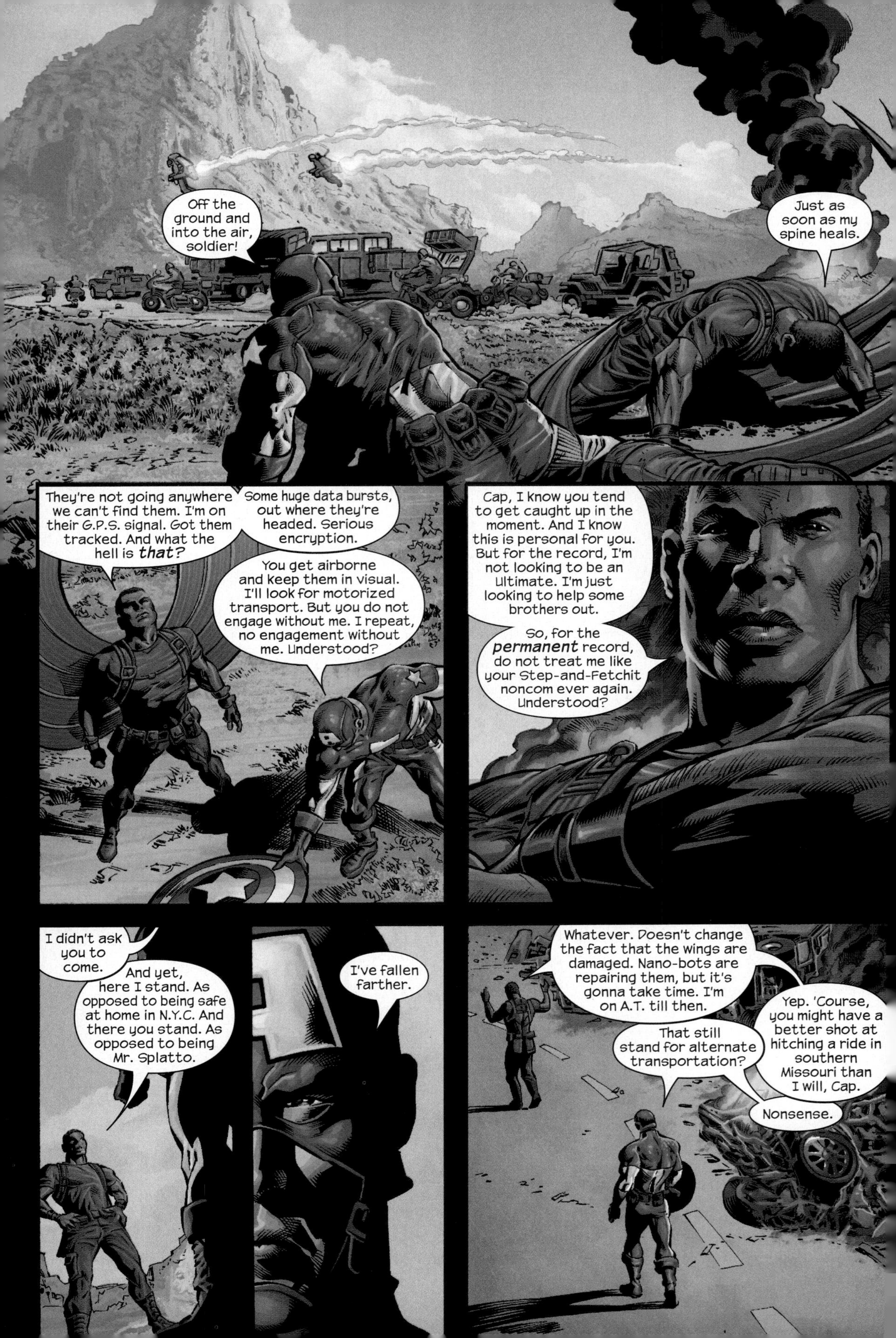
Off the ground and into the air, soldier!
Just as soon as my spine heals.
They're not going anywhere we can't find them. I'm on their G.P.S. signal. Got them tracked. And what the hell is *that?*
Some huge data bursts, out where they're headed. Serious encryption.
You get airborne and keep them in visual. I'll look for motorized transport. But you do not engage without me. I repeat, no engagement without me. Understood?
Cap, I know you tend to get caught up in the moment. And I know this is personal for you. But for the record, I'm not looking to be an Ultimate. I'm just looking to help some brothers out.
So, for the **permanent** record, do not treat me like your Step-and-Fetchit noncom ever again. Understood?
I didn't ask you to come.
And yet, here I stand. As opposed to being safe at home in N.Y.C. And there you stand. As opposed to being Mr. Splatto.
I've fallen farther.
Whatever. Doesn't change the fact that the wings are damaged. Nano-bots are repairing them, but it's gonna take time. I'm on A.T. till then.
That still stand for alternate transportation?
Yep. 'Course, you might have a better shot at hitching a ride in southern Missouri than I will, Cap.
Nonsense.

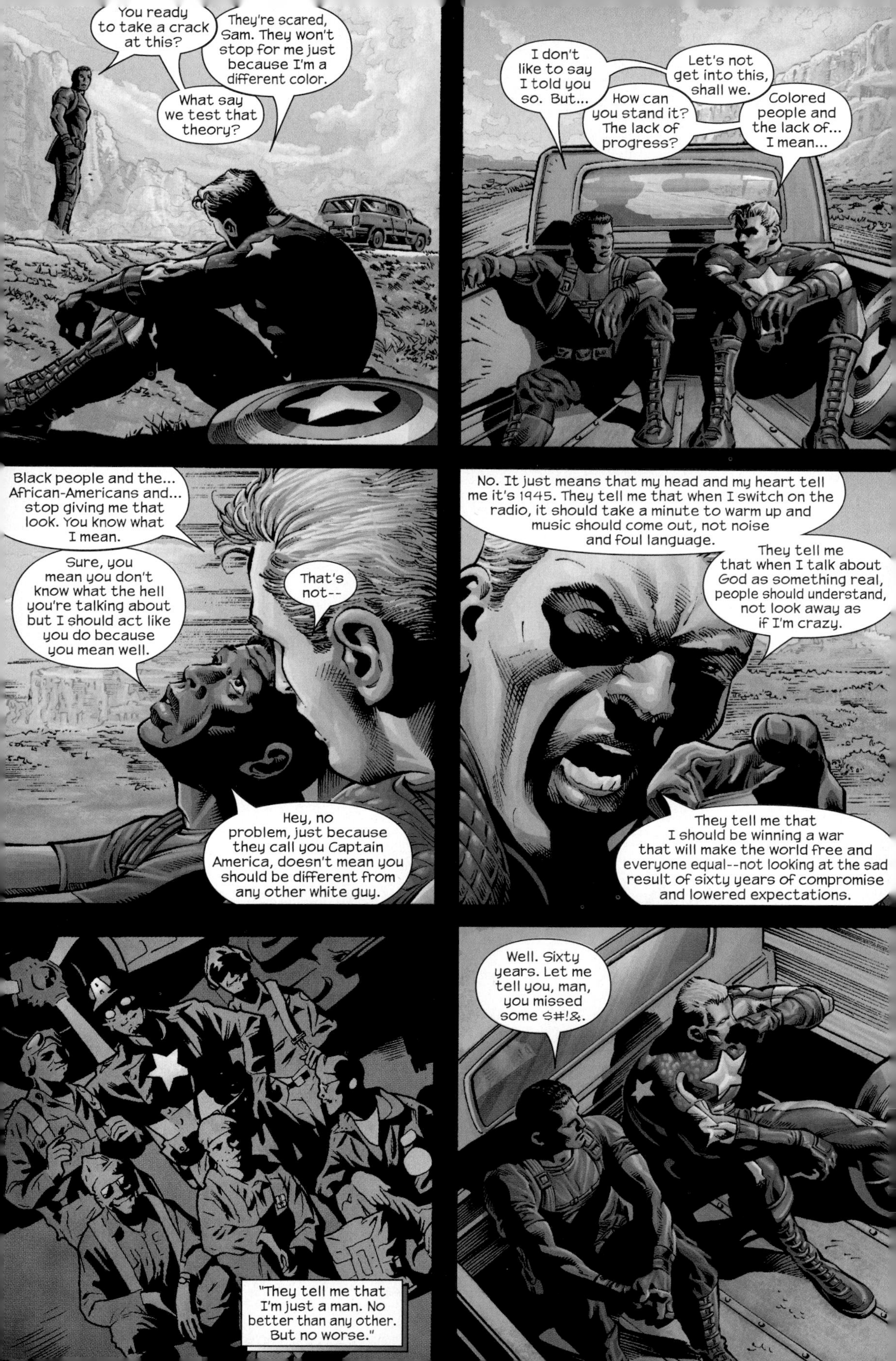
You ready to take a crack at this?
They're scared, Sam. They won't stop for me just because I'm a different color.
What say we test that theory?
I don't like to say I told you so. But...
Let's not get into this, shall we.
How can you stand it? The lack of progress?
Colored people and the lack of... I mean...
Black people and the... African-Americans and... stop giving me that look. You know what I mean.
Sure, you mean you don't know what the hell you're talking about but I should act like you do because you mean well.
That's not--
Hey, no problem, just because they call you Captain America, doesn't mean you should be different from any other white guy.
No. It just means that my head and my heart tell me it's 1945. They tell me that when I switch on the radio, it should take a minute to warm up and music should come out, not noise and foul language.
They tell me that when I talk about God as something real, people should understand, not look away as if I'm crazy.
They tell me that I should be winning a war that will make the world free and everyone equal--not looking at the sad result of sixty years of compromise and lowered expectations.
"They tell me that I'm just a man. No better than any other. But no worse."
Well. Sixty years. Let me tell you, man, you missed some $#!&.

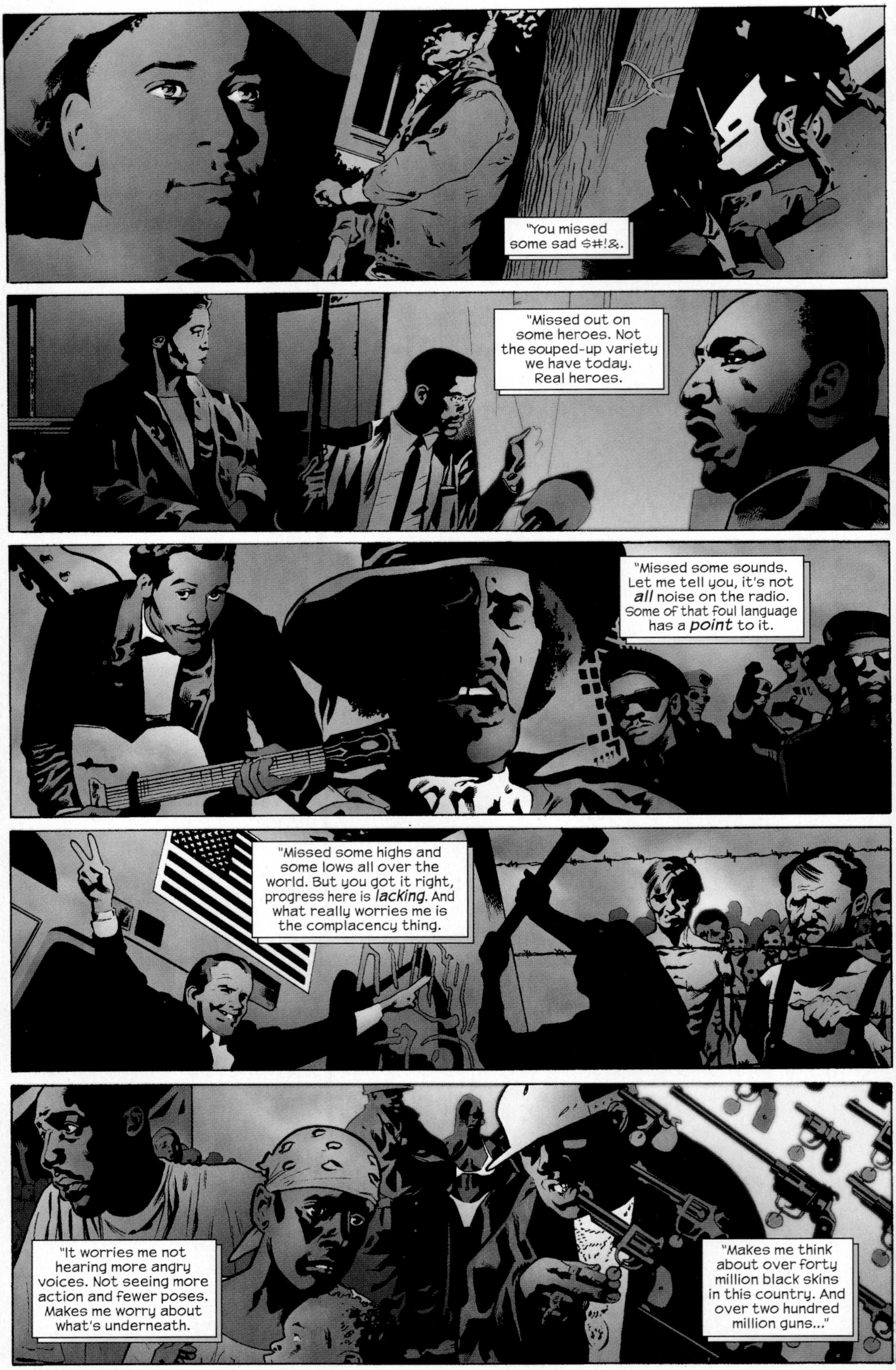
"You missed some sad $#!&.
"Missed out on some heroes. Not the souped-up variety we have today. Real heroes.
"Missed some sounds. Let me tell you, it's not *all* noise on the radio. Some of that foul language has a *point* to it.
"Missed some highs and some lows all over the world. But you got it right, progress here is *lacking.* And what really worries me is the complacency thing.
"It worries me not hearing more angry voices. Not seeing more action and fewer poses. Makes me worry about what's underneath.
"Makes me think about over forty million black skins in this country. And over two hundred million guns..."

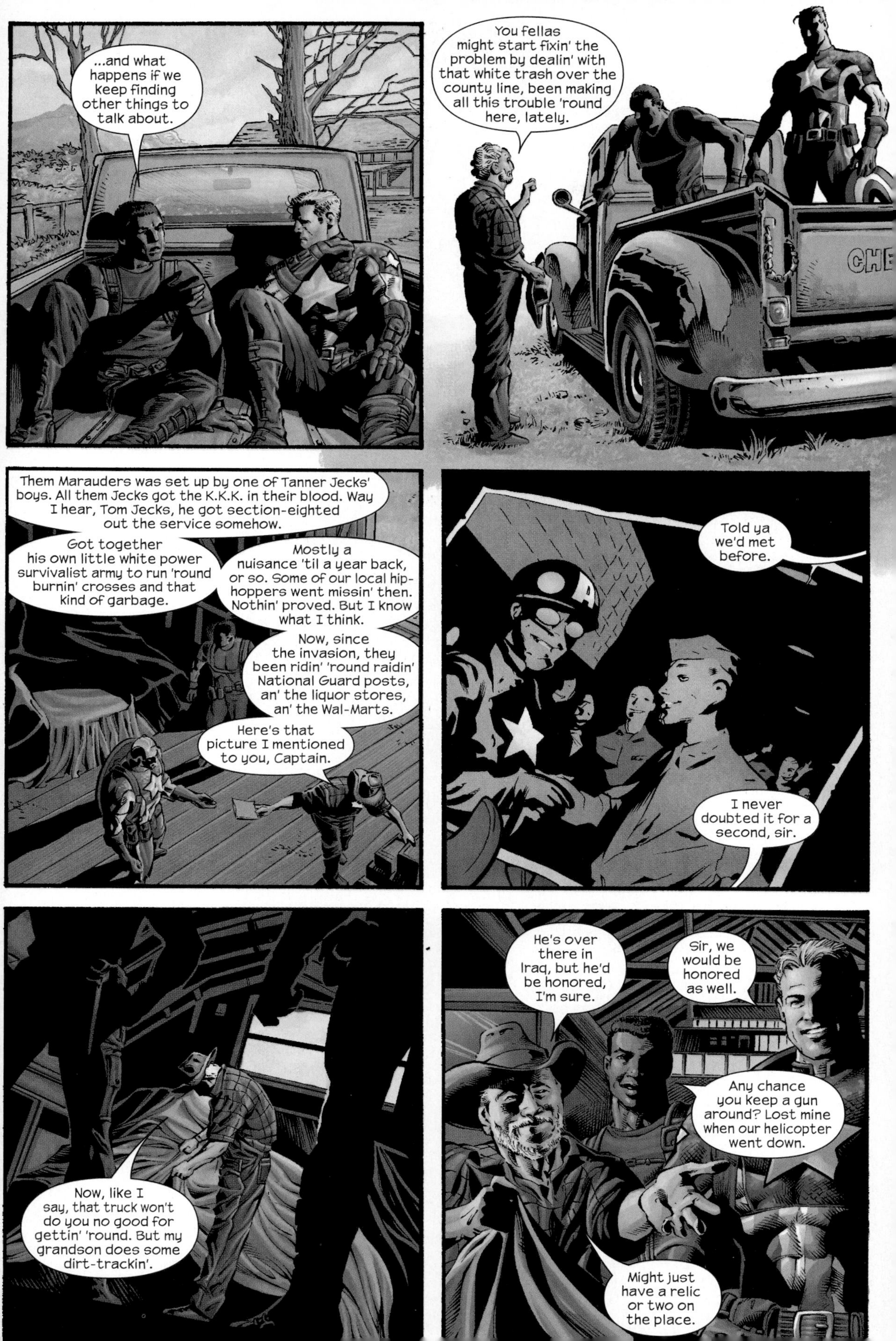

...and what happens if we keep finding other things to talk about.
You fellas might start fixin' the problem by dealin' with that white trash over the county line, been making all this trouble 'round here, lately.
CHE
Them Marauders was set up by one of Tanner Jecks' boys. All them Jecks got the K.K.K. in their blood. Way I hear, Tom Jecks, he got section-eighted out the service somehow.
Got together his own little white power survivalist army to run 'round burnin' crosses and that kind of garbage.
Mostly a nuisance 'til a year back, or so. Some of our local hip-hoppers went missin' then. Nothin' proved. But I know what I think.
Now, since the invasion, they been ridin' 'round raidin' National Guard posts, an' the liquor stores, an' the Wal-Marts.
Here's that picture I mentioned to you, Captain.
Told ya we'd met before.
I never doubted it for a second, sir.
Now, like I say, that truck won't do you no good for gettin' 'round. But my grandson does some dirt-trackin'.
He's over there in Iraq, but he'd be honored, I'm sure.
Sir, we would be honored as well.
Any chance you keep a gun around? Lost mine when our helicopter went down.
Might just have a relic or two on the place.

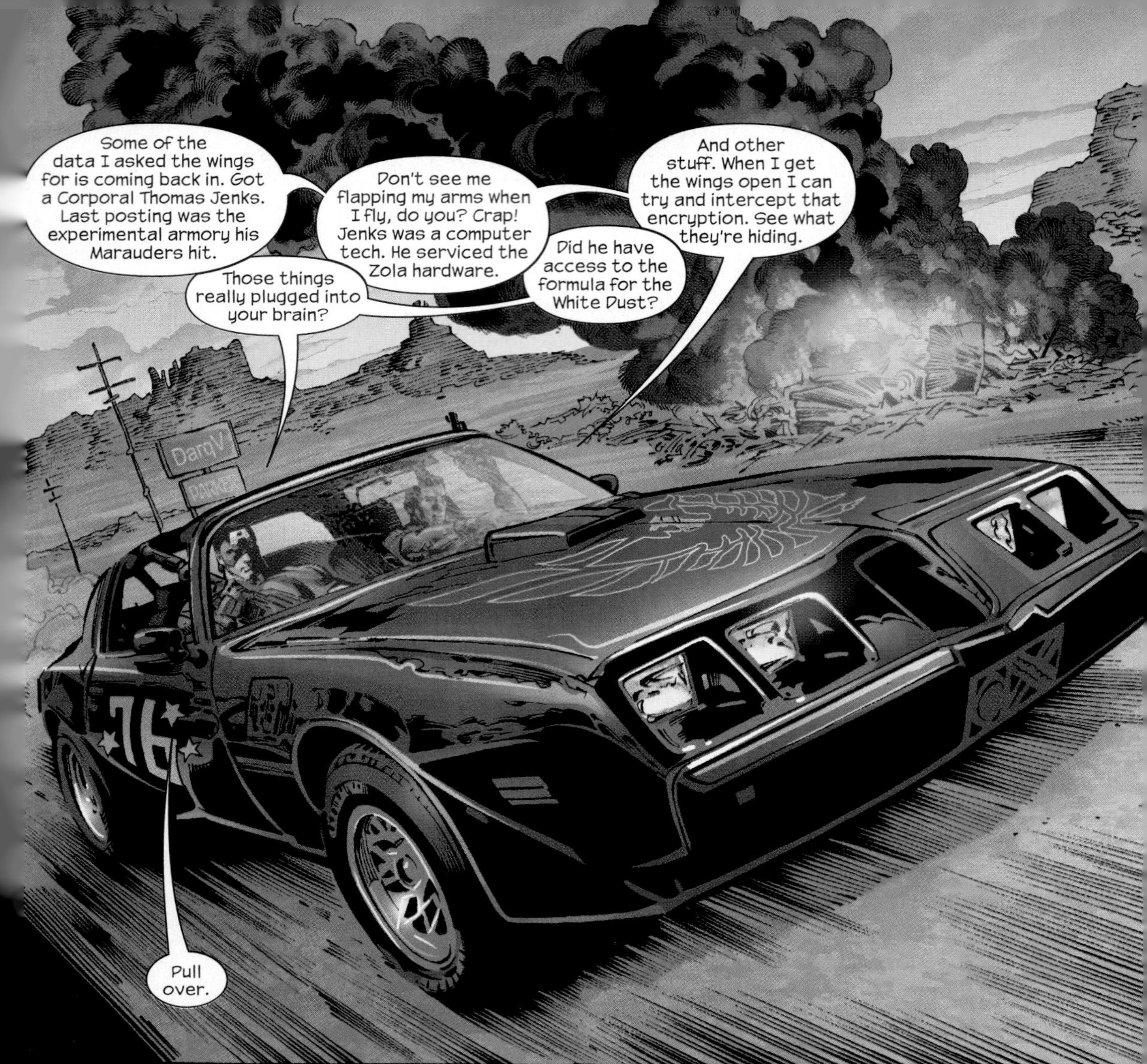
Some of the data I asked the wings for is coming back in. Got a Corporal Thomas Jenks. Last posting was the experimental armory his Marauders hit.
Those things really plugged into your brain?
Don't see me flapping my arms when I fly, do you? Crap! Jenks was a computer tech. He serviced the Zola hardware.
Did he have access to the formula for the White Dust?
And other stuff. When I get the wings open I can try and intercept that encryption. See what they're hiding.
Pull over.
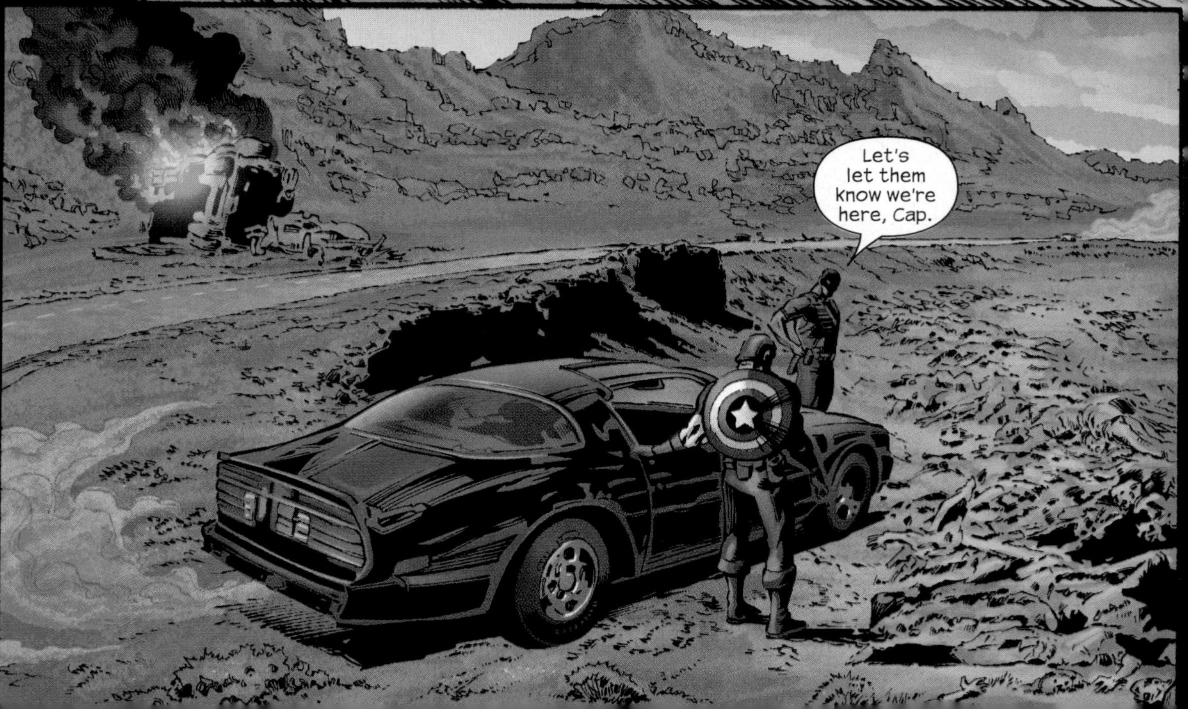
Let's let them know we're here, Cap.

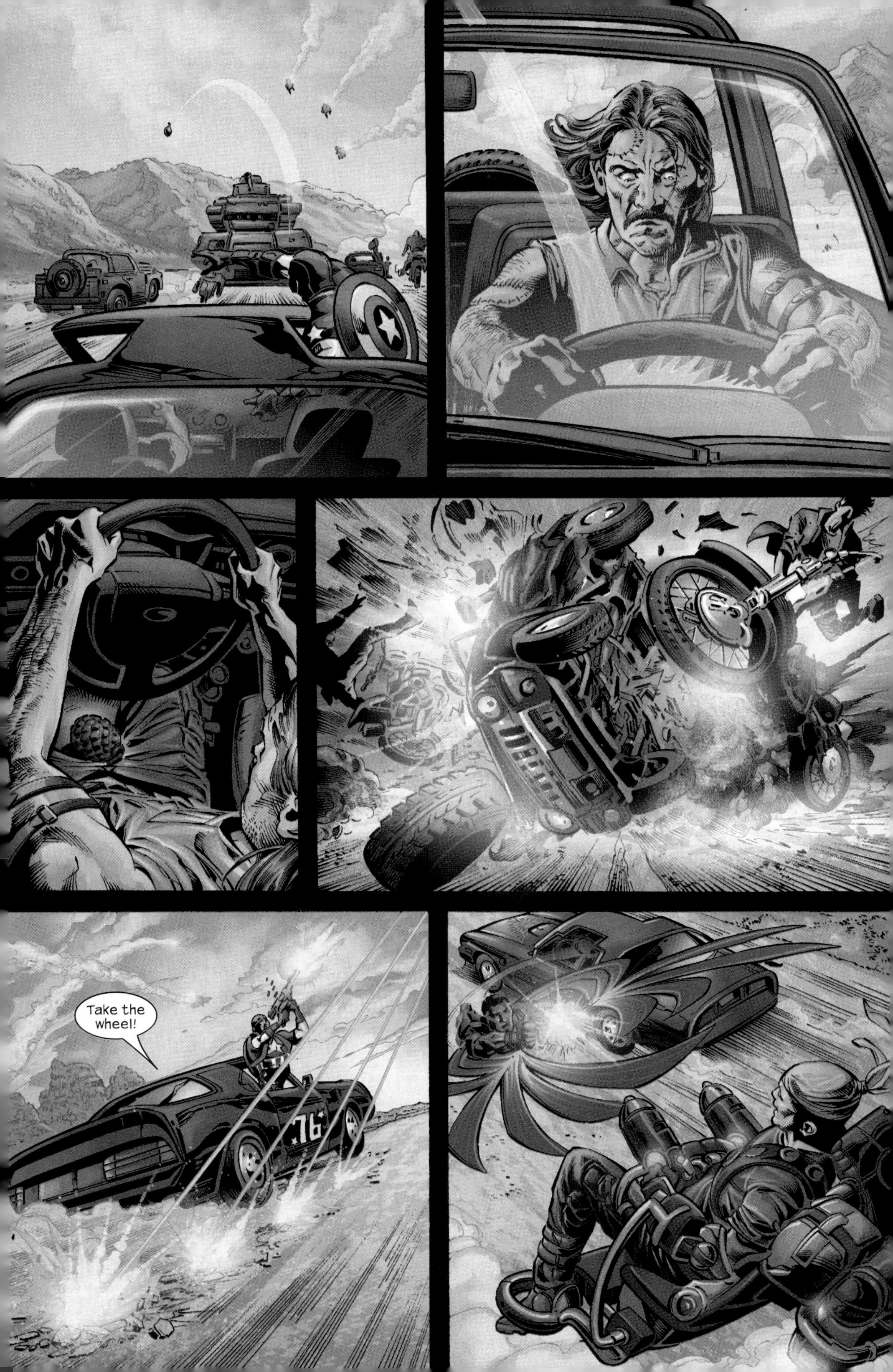
Take the wheel!
76

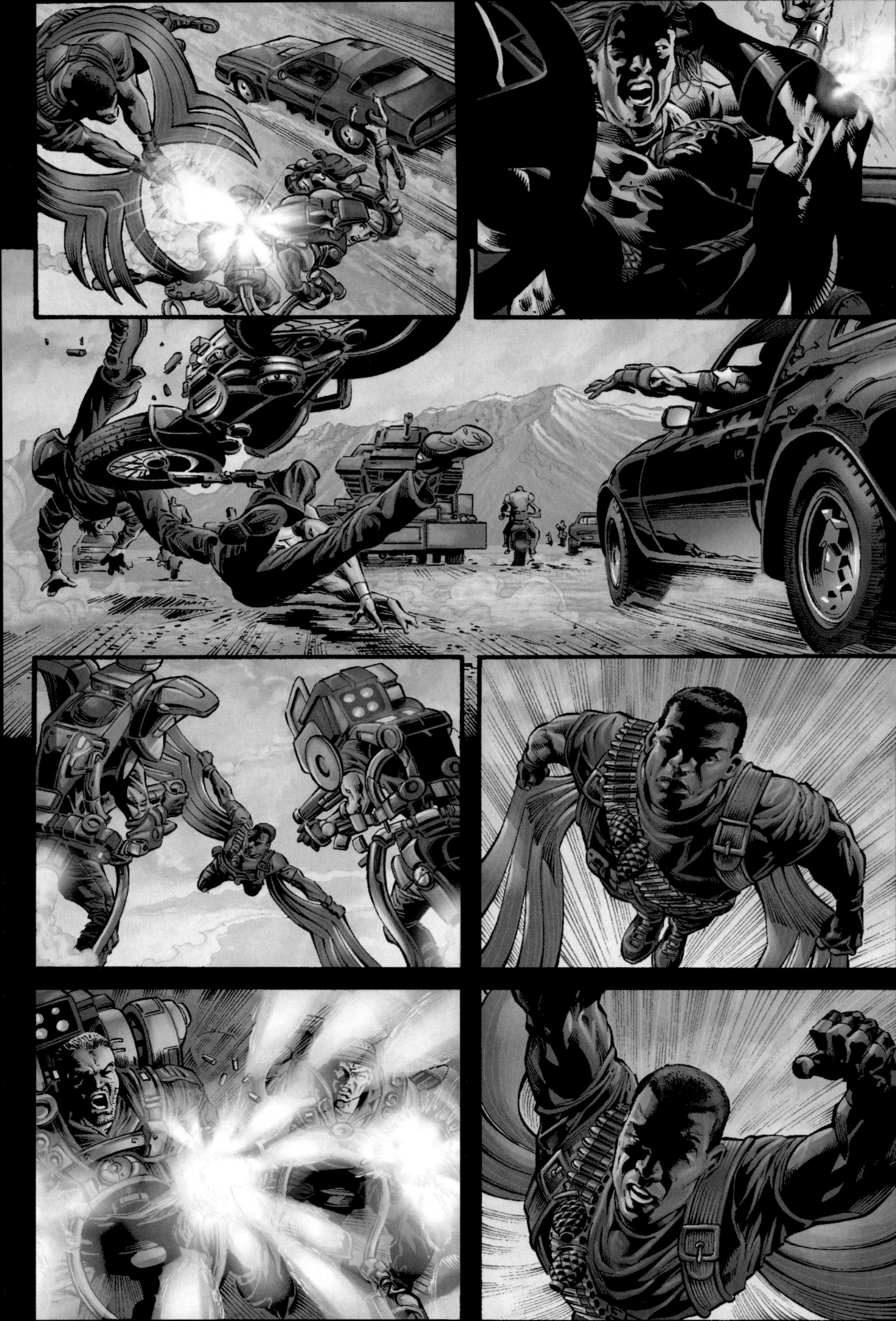

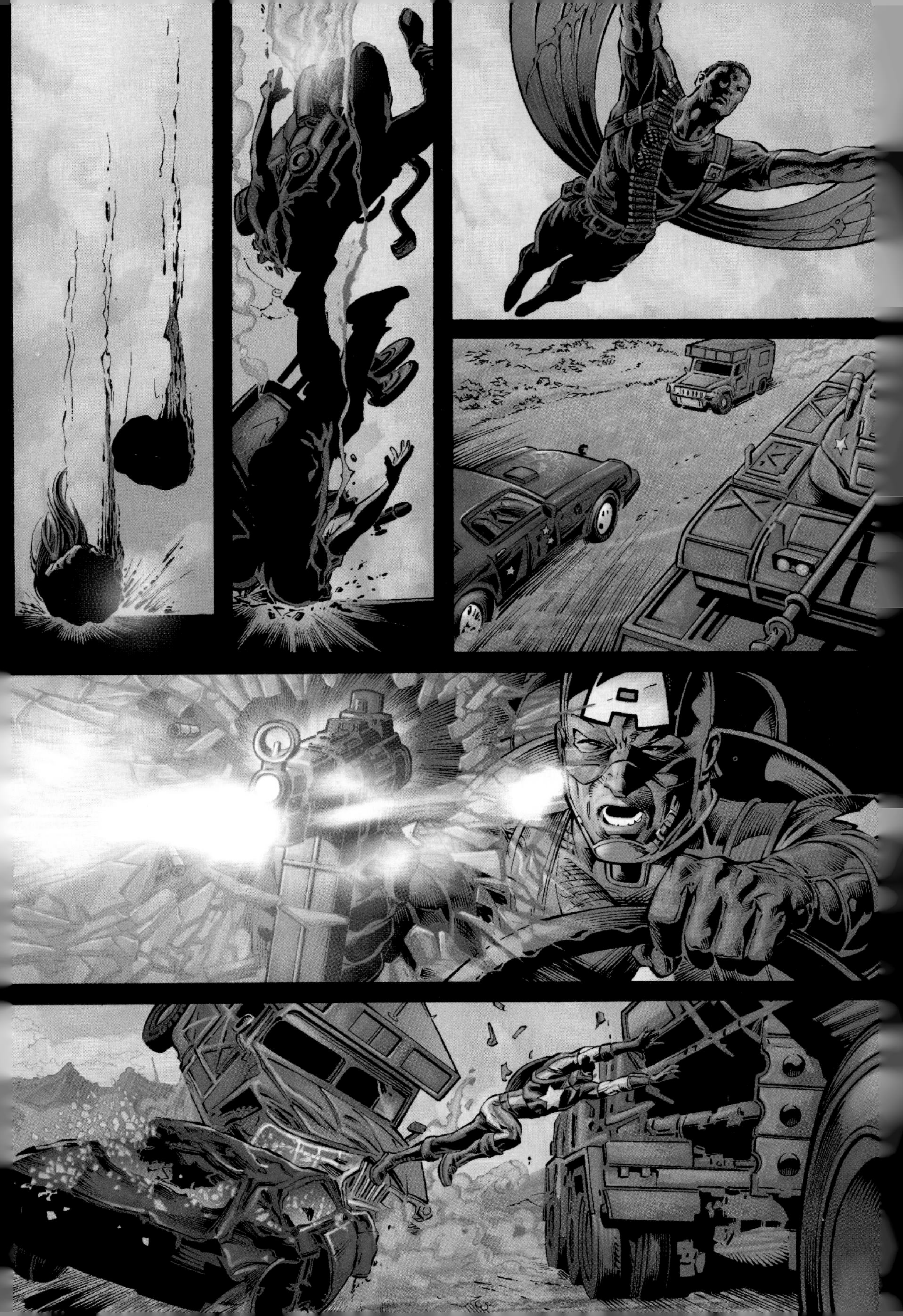

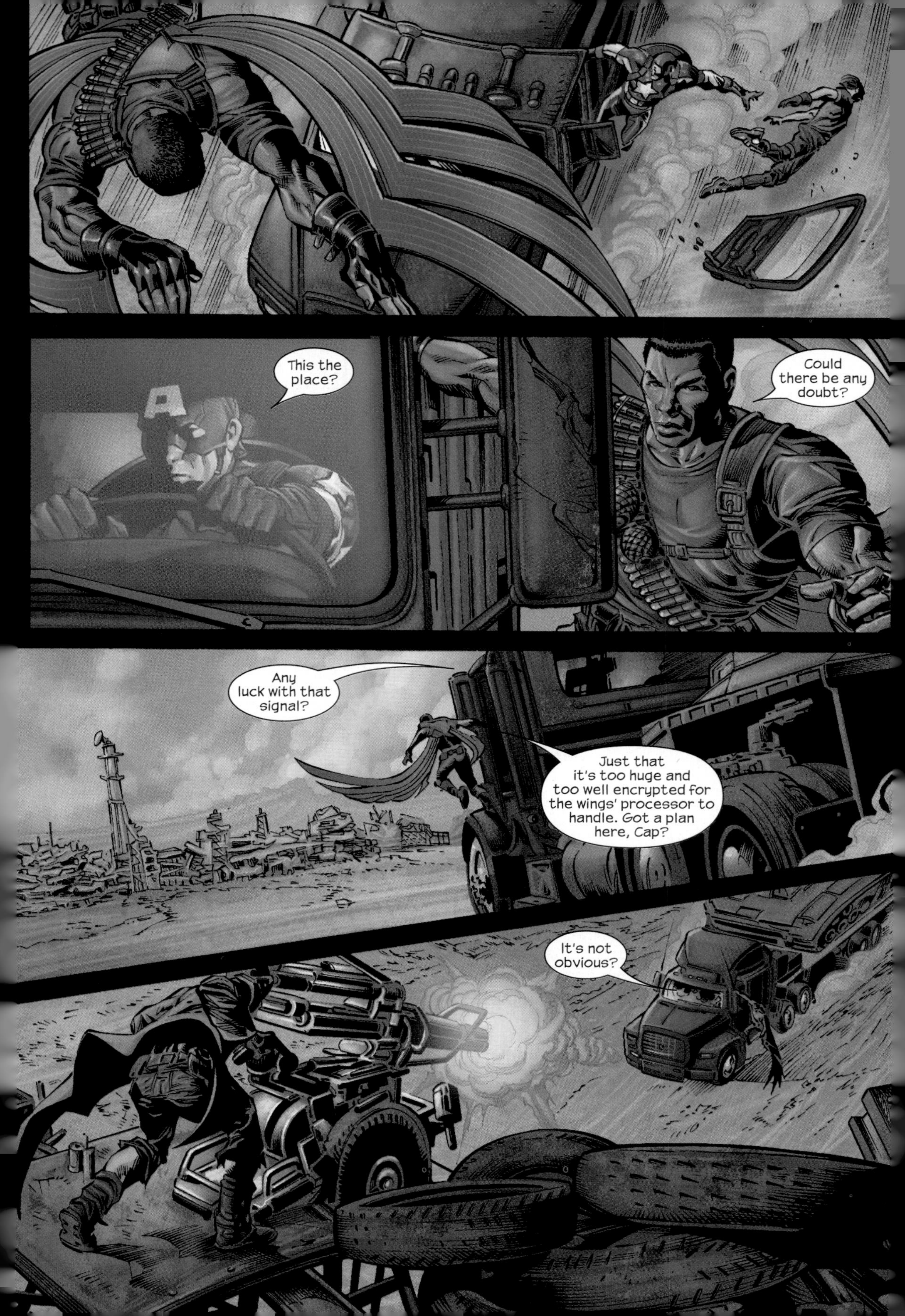
This the place?
Could there be any doubt?
Any luck with that signal?
Just that it's too huge and too well encrypted for the wings' processor to handle. Got a plan here, Cap?
It's not obvious?

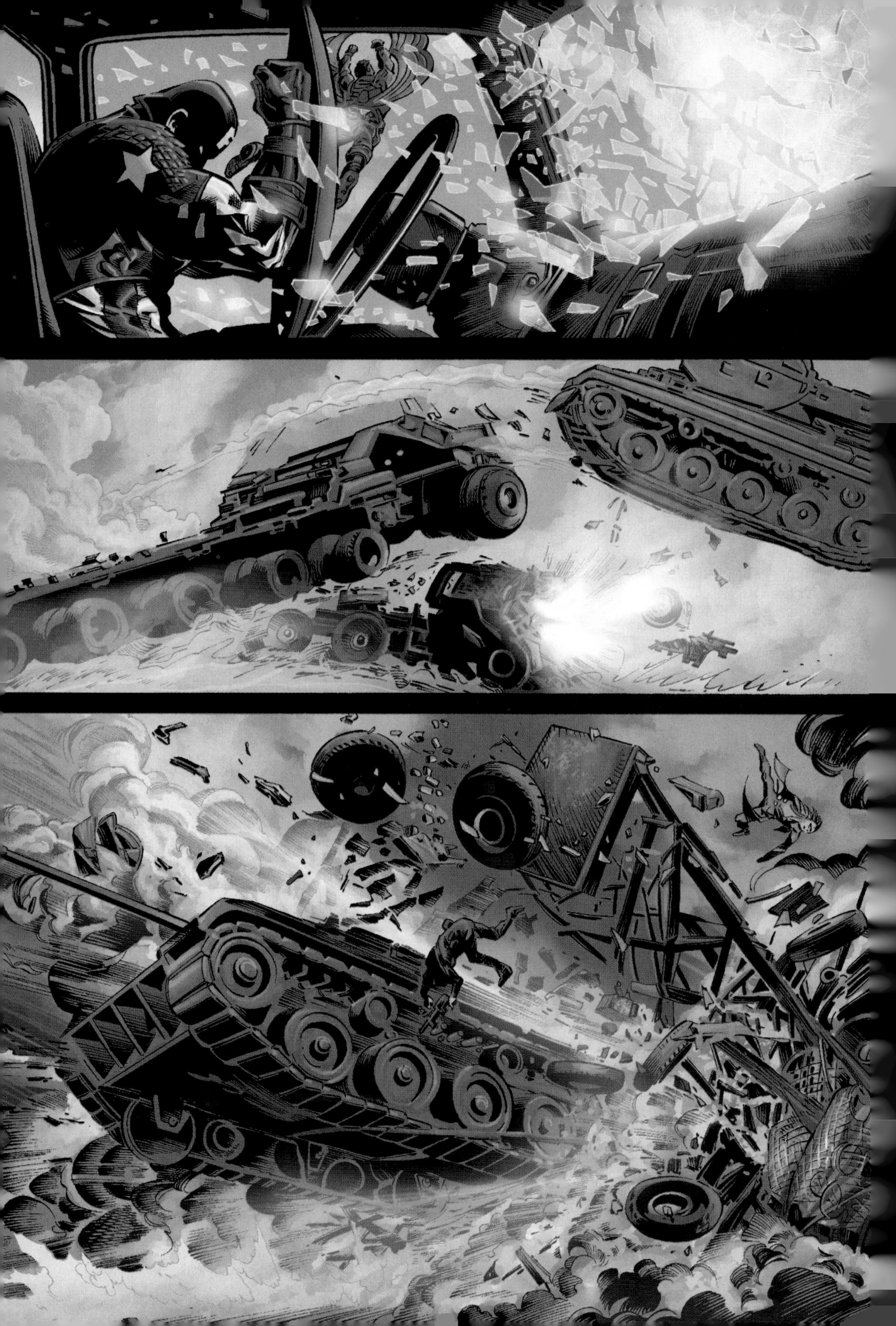

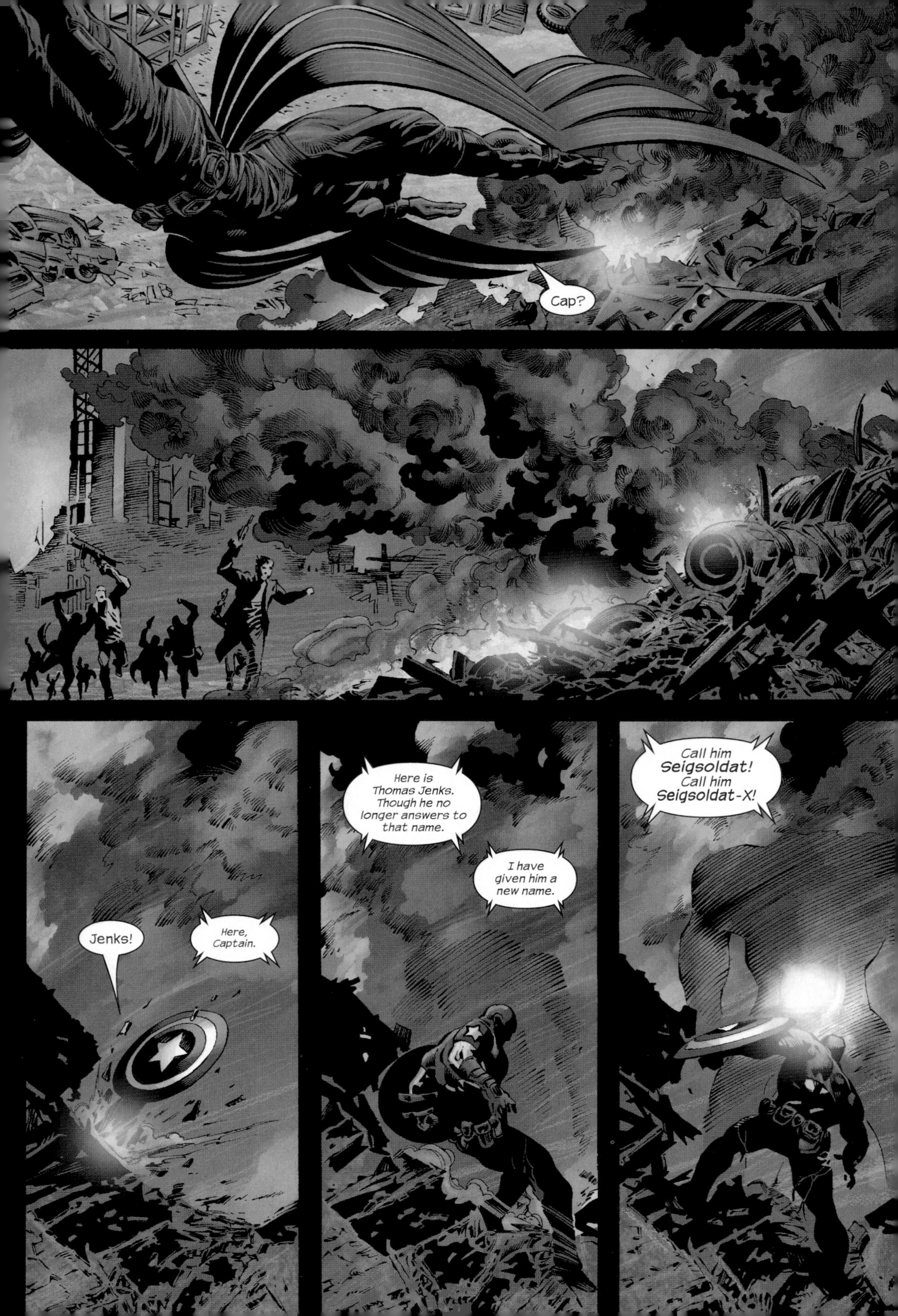
Cap?
Jenks!
Here, Captain.
Here is Thomas Jenks. Though he no longer answers to that name.
I have given him a new name.
Call him Seigsoldat! Call him Seigsoldat-X!

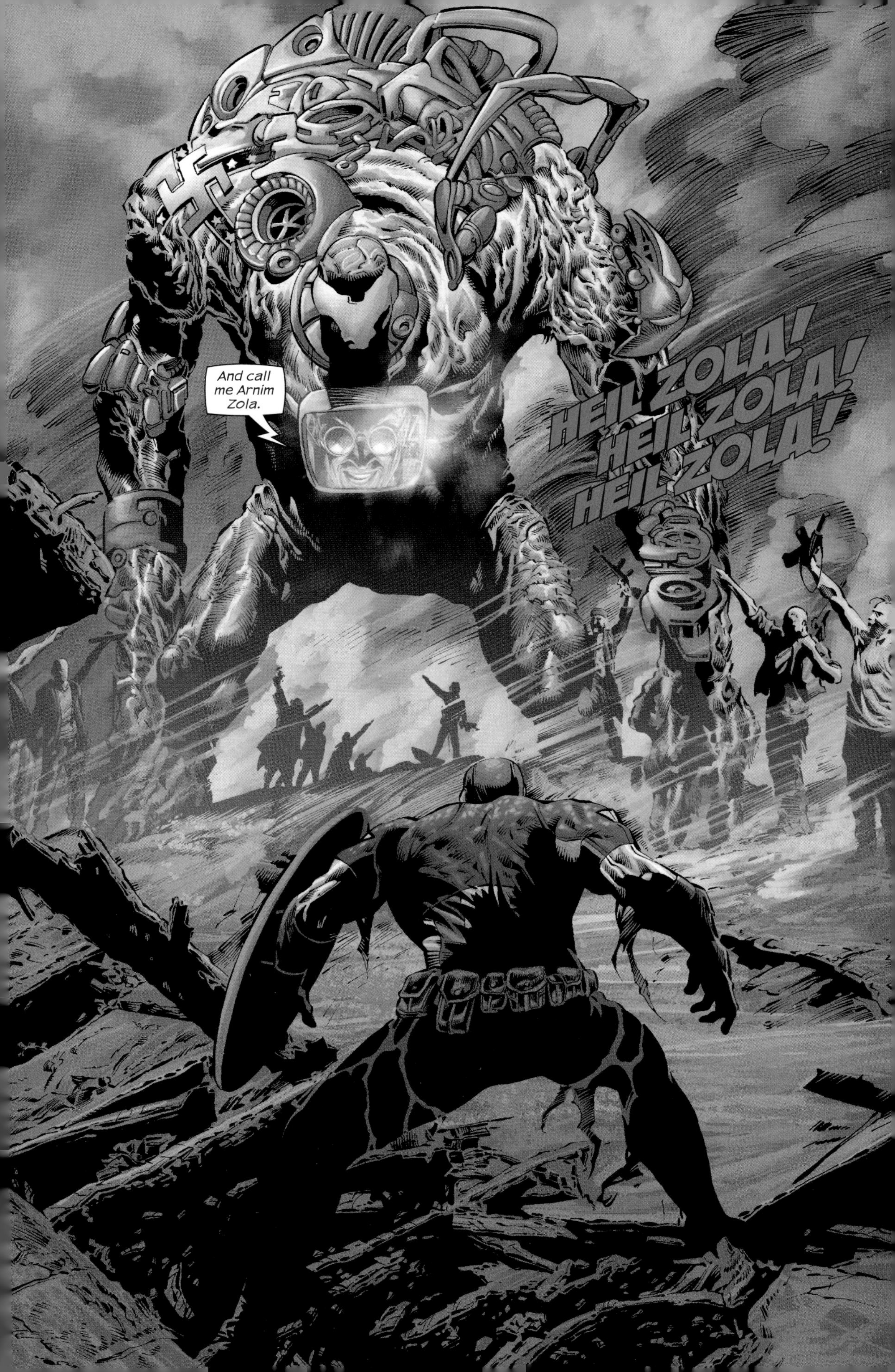
And call me Arnim Zola.
HEIL ZOLA! HEIL ZOLA! HEIL ZOLA!

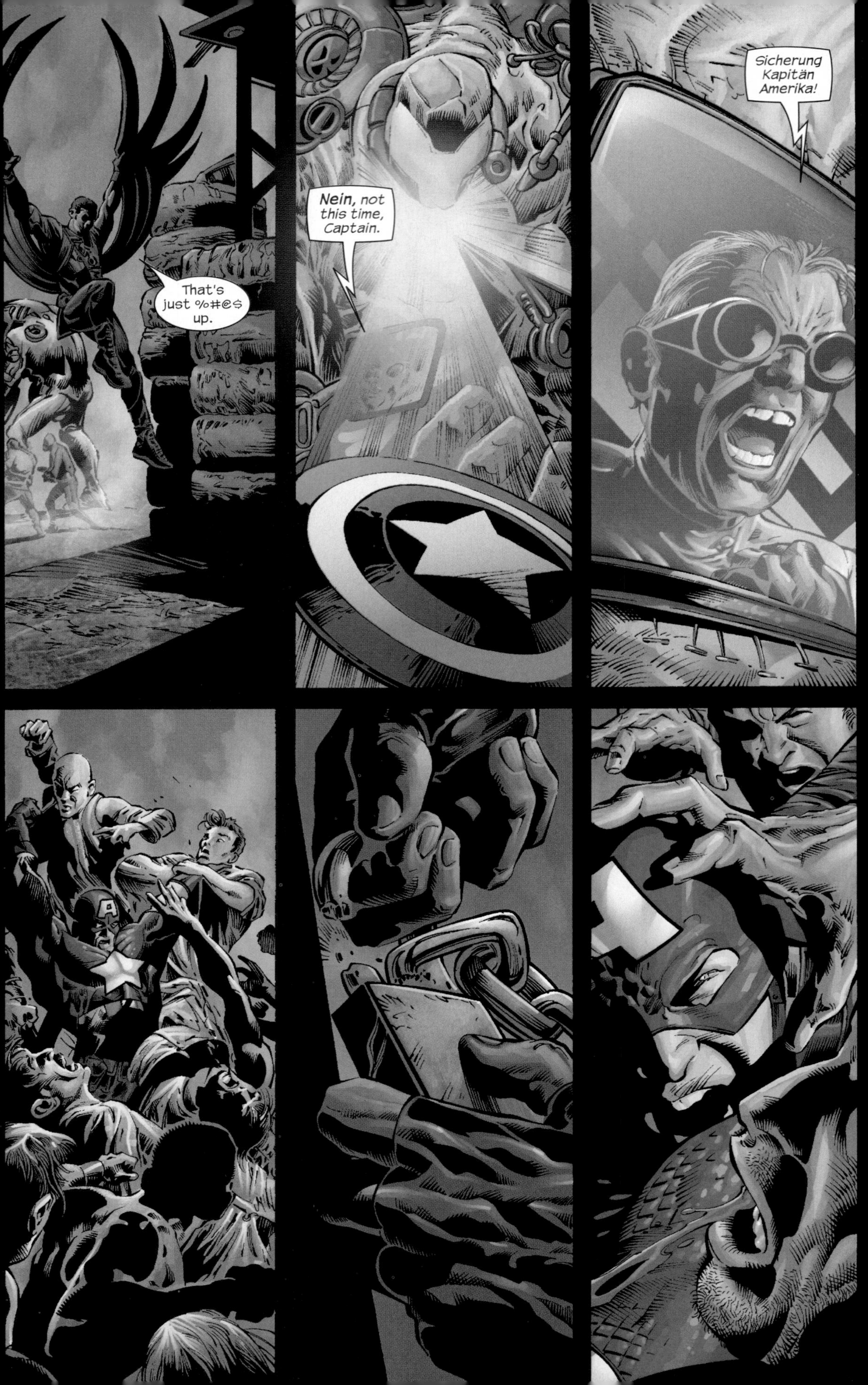
That's just %#@$ up.
Nein, not this time, Captain.
Sicherung Kapitän Amerika!

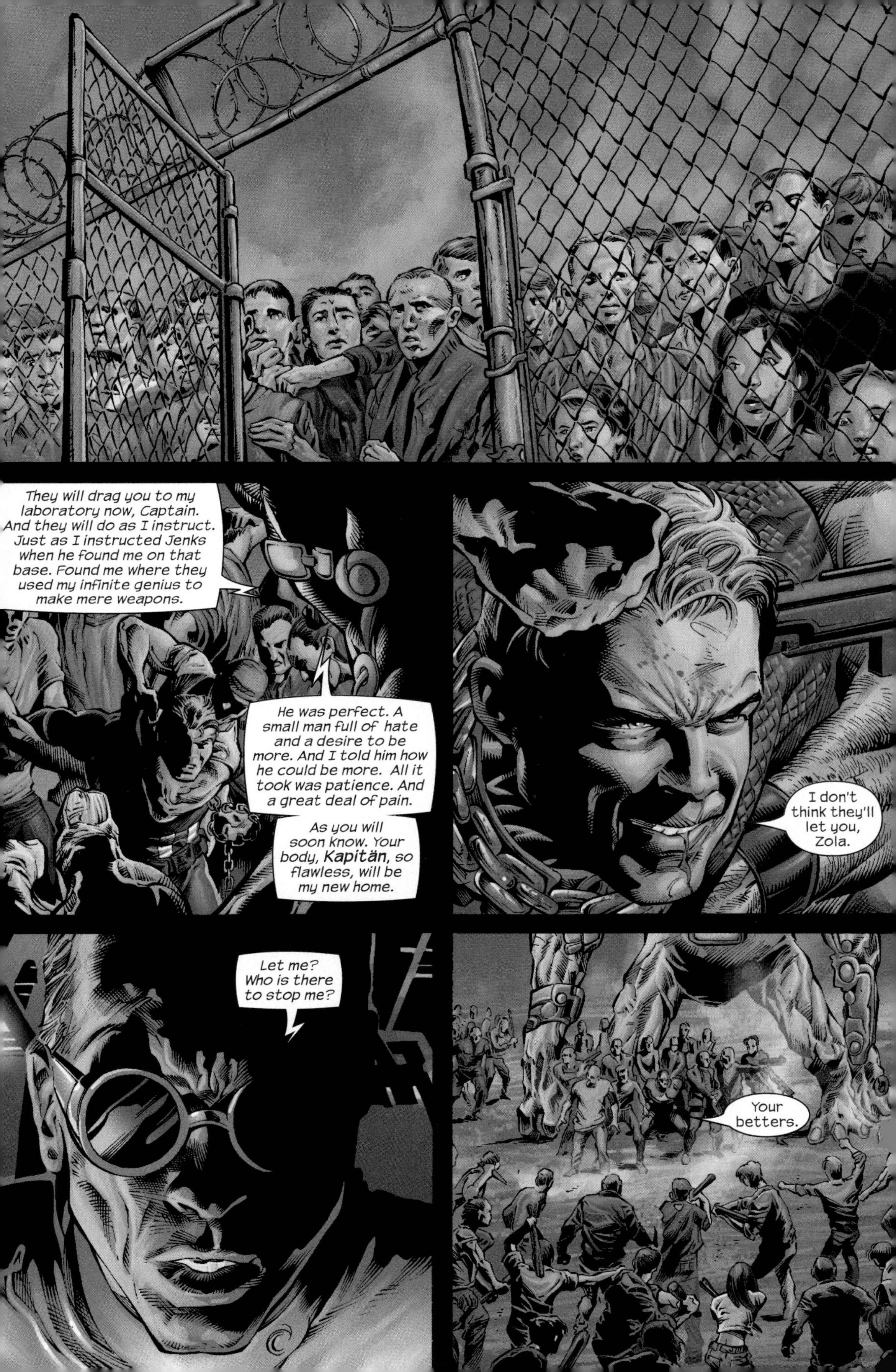

They will drag you to my laboratory now, Captain. And they will do as I instruct. Just as I instructed Jenks when he found me on that base. Found me where they used my infinite genius to make mere weapons.
He was perfect. A small man full of hate and a desire to be more. And I told him how he could be more. All it took was patience. And a great deal of pain.
As you will soon know. Your body, Kapitän, so flawless, will be my new home.
I don't think they'll let you, Zola.
Let me? Who is there to stop me?
Your betters.

Nein! Nein!

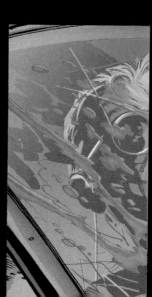

"Sorry to bother you on your down-time, Cap."

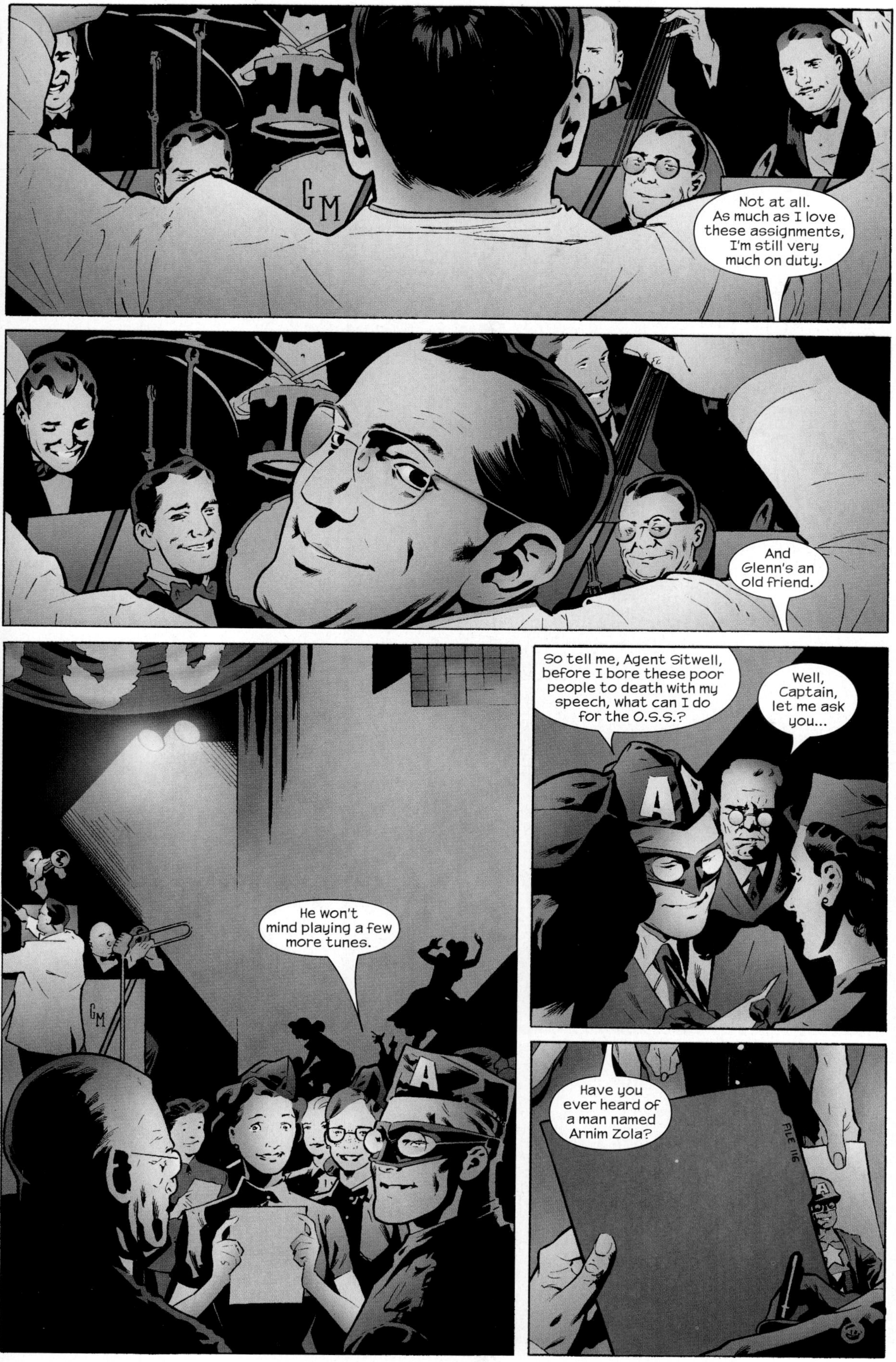

Not at all. As much as I love these assignments, I'm still very much on duty.
And Glenn's an old friend.
He won't mind playing a few more tunes.
So tell me, Agent Sitwell, before I bore these poor people to death with my speech, what can I do for the O.S.S.?
Well, Captain, let me ask you...
Have you ever heard of a man named Arnim Zola?
FILE 116

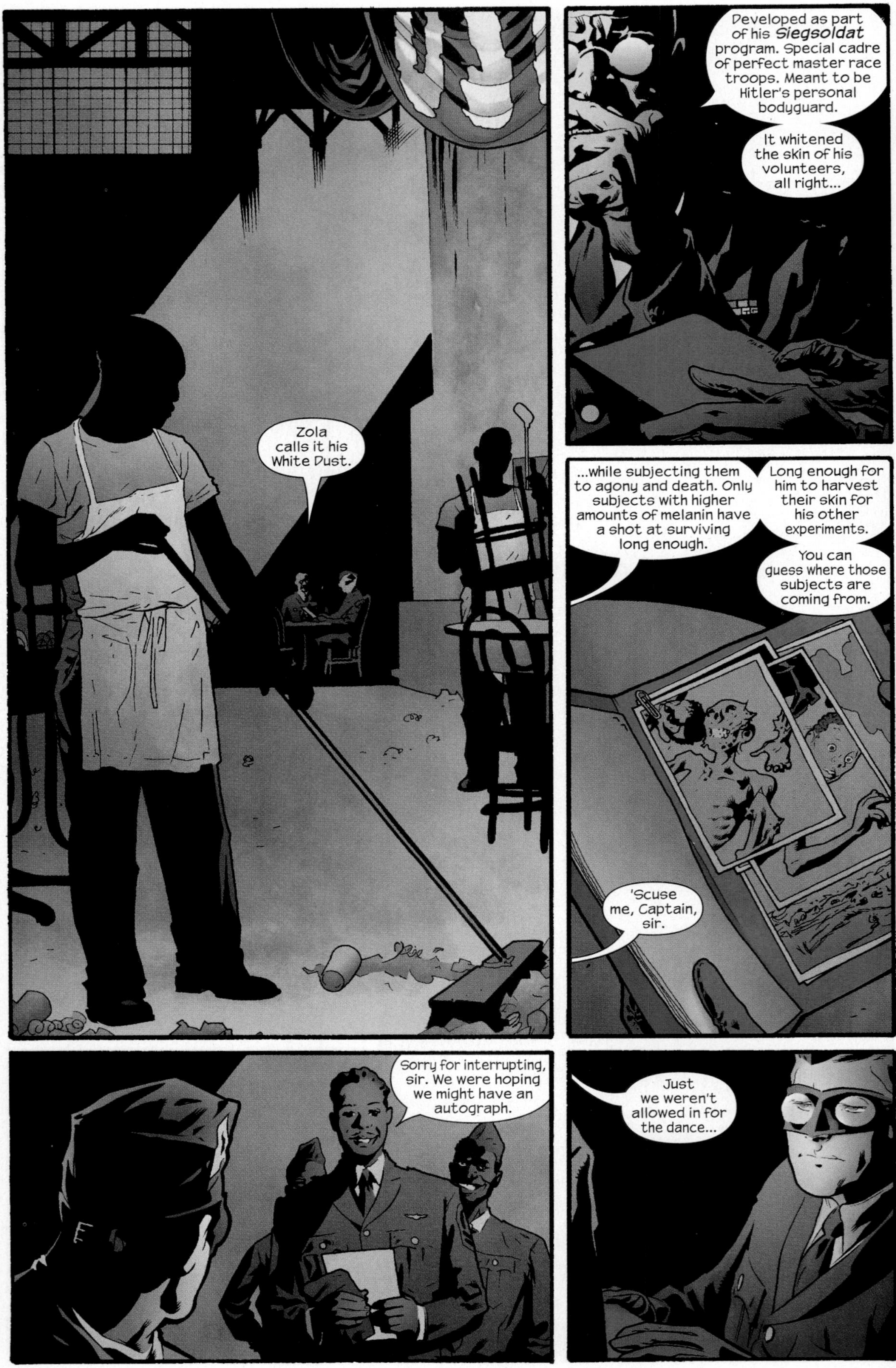
Zola calls it his White Dust.
Developed as part of his *Siegsoldat* program. Special cadre of perfect master race troops. Meant to be Hitler's personal bodyguard.
It whitened the skin of his volunteers, all right...
...while subjecting them to agony and death. Only subjects with higher amounts of melanin have a shot at surviving long enough.
Long enough for him to harvest their skin for his other experiments.
You can guess where those subjects are coming from.
'Scuse me, Captain, sir.
Sorry for interrupting, sir. We were hoping we might have an autograph.
Just we weren't allowed in for the dance...

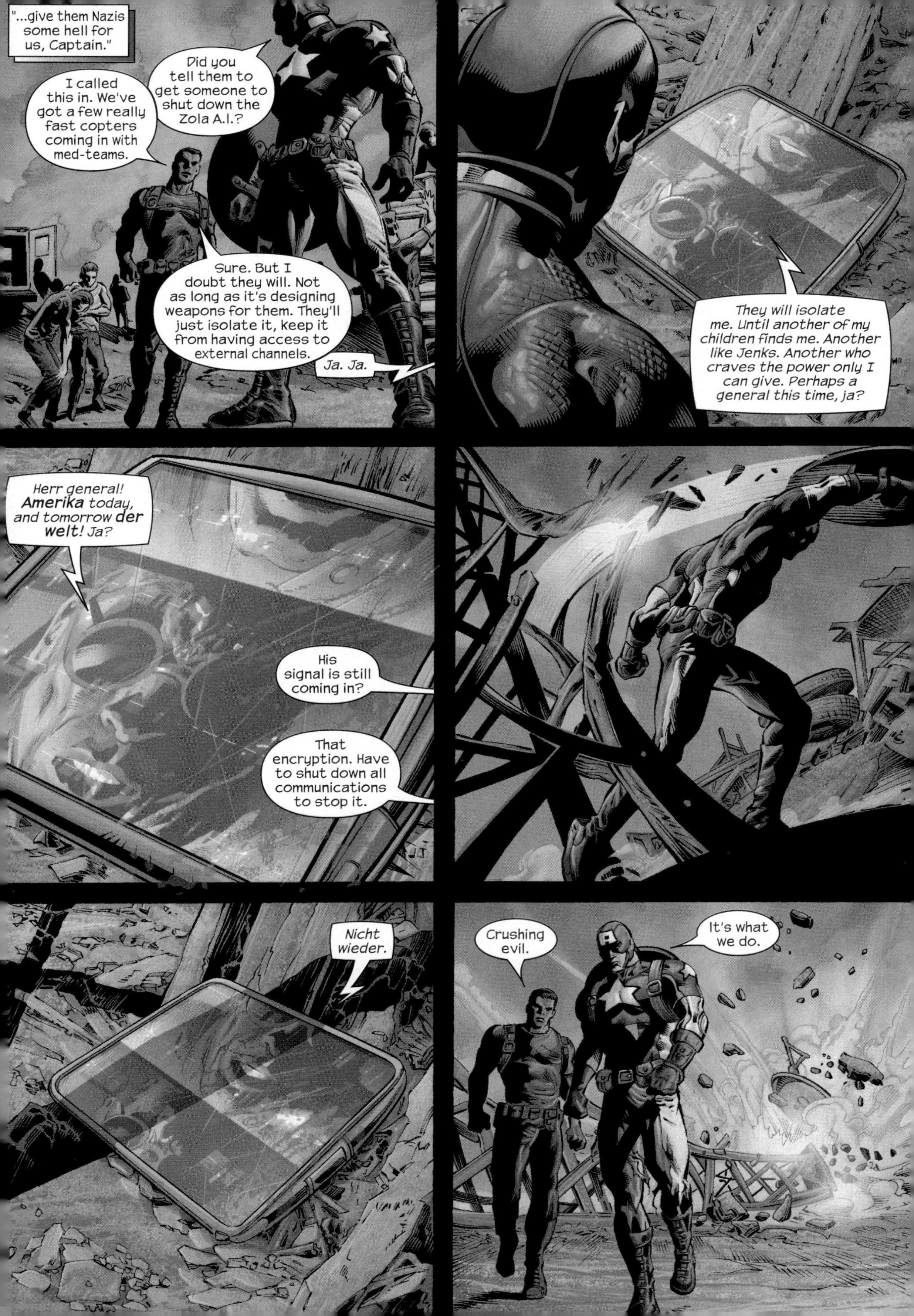
"...give them Nazis some hell for us, Captain."
I called this in. We've got a few really fast copters coming in with med-teams.
Did you tell them to get someone to shut down the Zola A.I.?
Sure. But I doubt they will. Not as long as it's designing weapons for them. They'll just isolate it, keep it from having access to external channels.
Ja. Ja.
They will isolate me. Until another of my children finds me. Another like Jenks. Another who craves the power only I can give. Perhaps a general this time, ja?
Herr general! Amerika today, and tomorrow der welt! Ja?
His signal is still coming in?
That encryption. Have to shut down all communications to stop it.
Nicht wieder.
Crushing evil.
It's what we do.

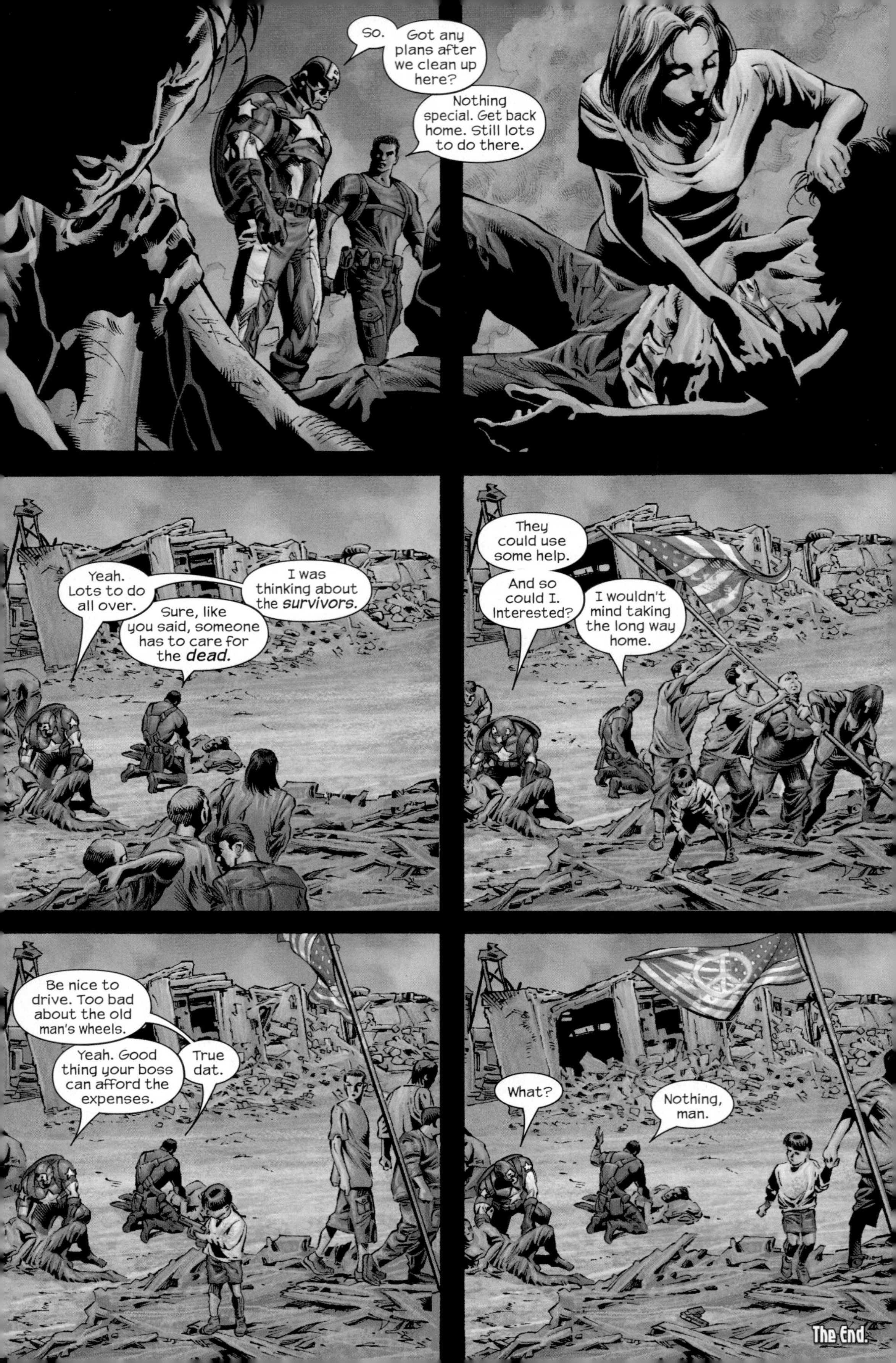
So.
Got any plans after we clean up here?
Nothing special. Get back home. Still lots to do there.
Yeah. Lots to do all over.
I was thinking about the *survivors.*
Sure, like you said, someone has to care for the *dead.*
They could use some help.
And so could I. Interested?
I wouldn't mind taking the long way home.
Be nice to drive. Too bad about the old man's wheels.
True dat.
Yeah. Good thing your boss can afford the expenses.
What?
Nothing, man.
The End.

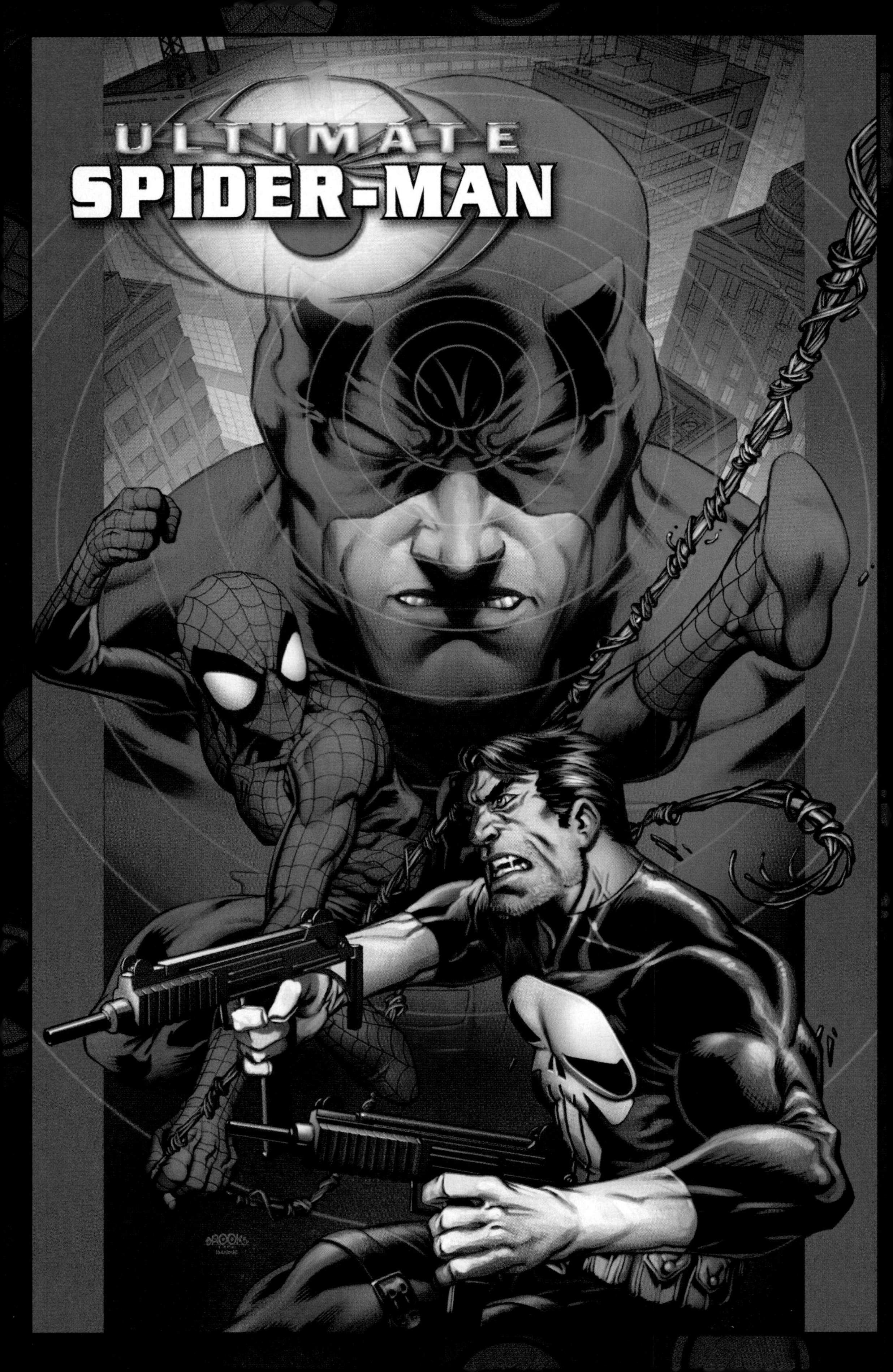
ULTIMATE
SPIDER-MAN

ULTIMATE SPIDER-MAN

PREVIOUSLY IN ULTIMATE SPIDER-MAN

The bite of a genetically-altered spider granted high school student Peter Parker incredible, arachnid-like powers! When a burglar killed his beloved Uncle Ben, a grief-stricken Peter vowed to use his amazing abilities to protect his fellow man. He learned the invaluable lesson that with great power must also come great responsibility...

Now the fledgling super hero tries to balance a full High School curriculum, a night job as a web designer for the *Daily Bugle* tabloid, a friendship with the beautiful Mary Jane Watson, and swing time as the misunderstood, web-slinging Spider-Man.

Spider-Man has had several confrontations with New York crime boss Wilson Fisk, a.k.a. the Kingpin of Crime. After his last run-in with Fisk, Spidey befriended NYPD Captain Jeanne De Wolfe...not knowing that she is actually under the Kingpin's influence — she's a rotten cop.

Spider-Man has also had a couple of run-ins with the guardian of Hell's Kitchen, Manhattan — the mystery known as Daredevil. They haven't been the friendliest of run-ins, and Spidey has no idea that Daredevil is secretly Matt Murdock, who, along with Franklin "Foggy" Nelson, runs a law firm.

Ex-cop Frank Castle is the only one in his family that survived a gangland-style assassination by his fellow cops, after Frank refused to take a bribe. He now fights crime as the brutal, unflinching Punisher — and was last seen being carted away by the NYPD after a battle with Spidey.

Moon Knight is just one of four personalities of a mystery crime fighter who barely survived his last encounter with Spider-Man — a battle with Kingpin's assassin Elektra. Moon Knight has been in a coma ever since...

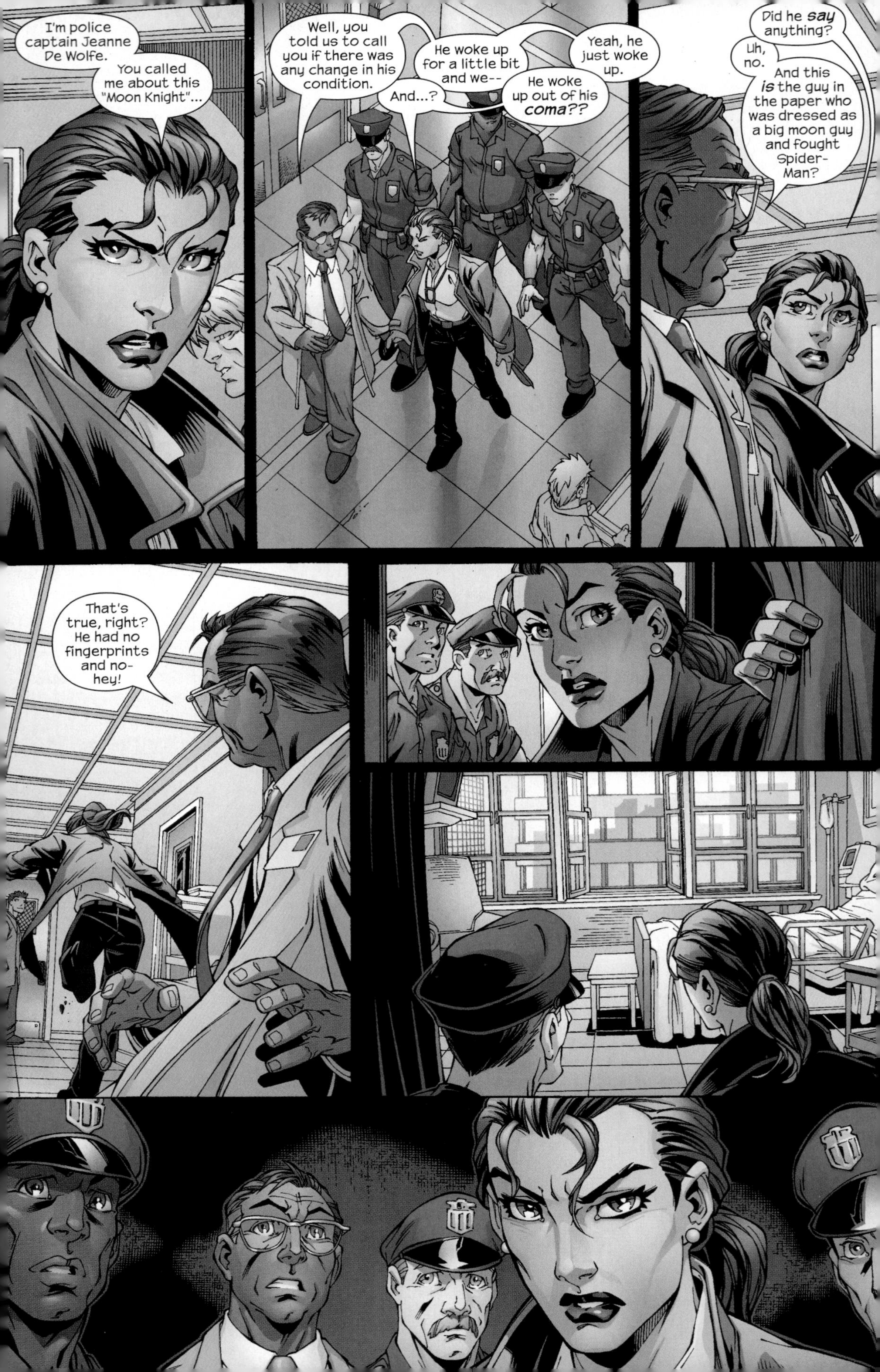
I'm police captain Jeanne De Wolfe.
You called me about this "Moon Knight"...
Well, you told us to call you if there was any change in his condition.
He woke up for a little bit and we--
Yeah, he just woke up.
And...?
He woke up out of his *coma??*
Did he *say* anything?
Uh, no.
And this *is* the guy in the paper who was dressed as a big moon guy and fought Spider-Man?
That's true, right? He had no fingerprints and no-- hey!

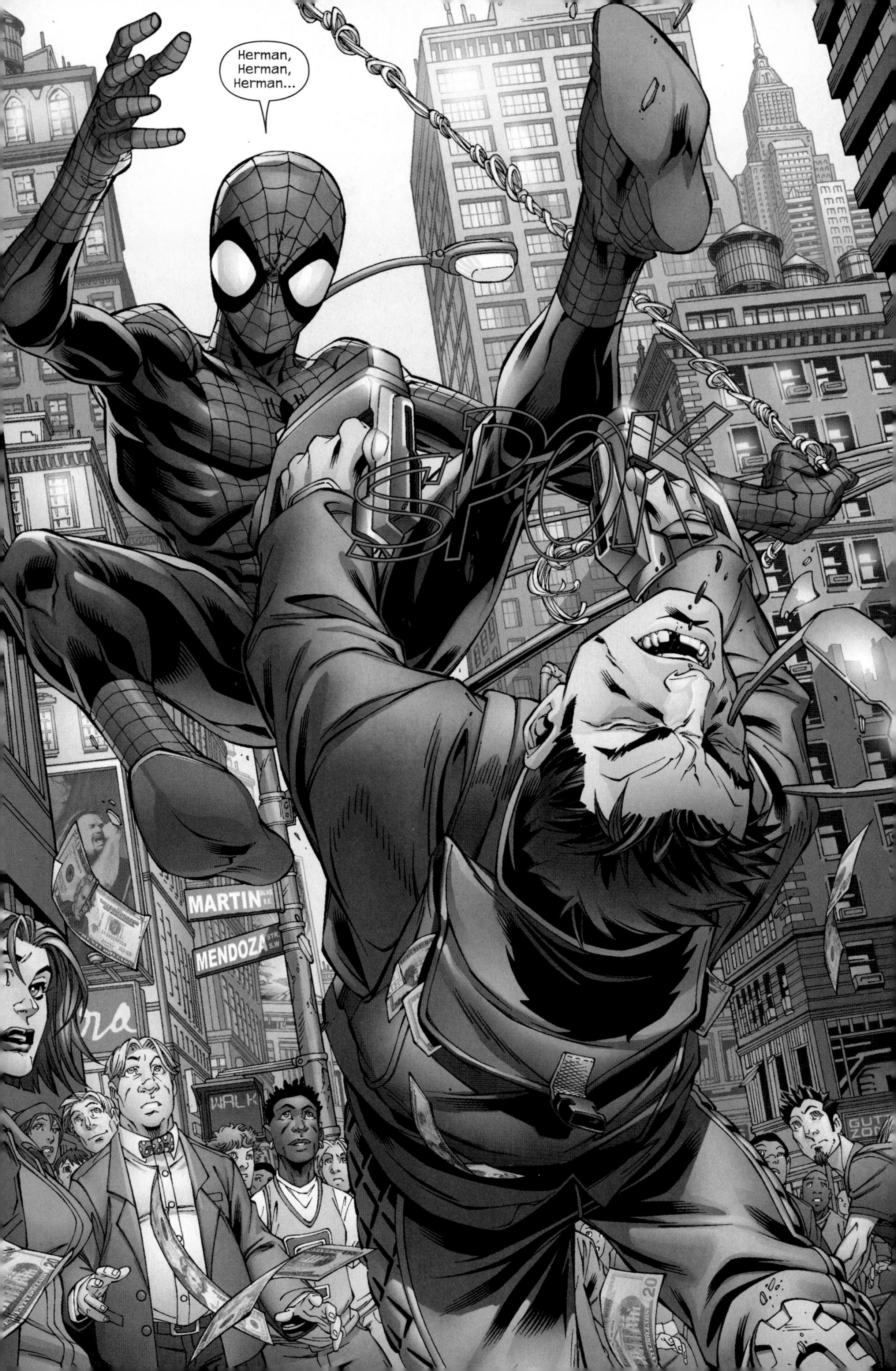
Herman, Herman, Herman...
SPOK
MARTIN
MENDOZA
WALK

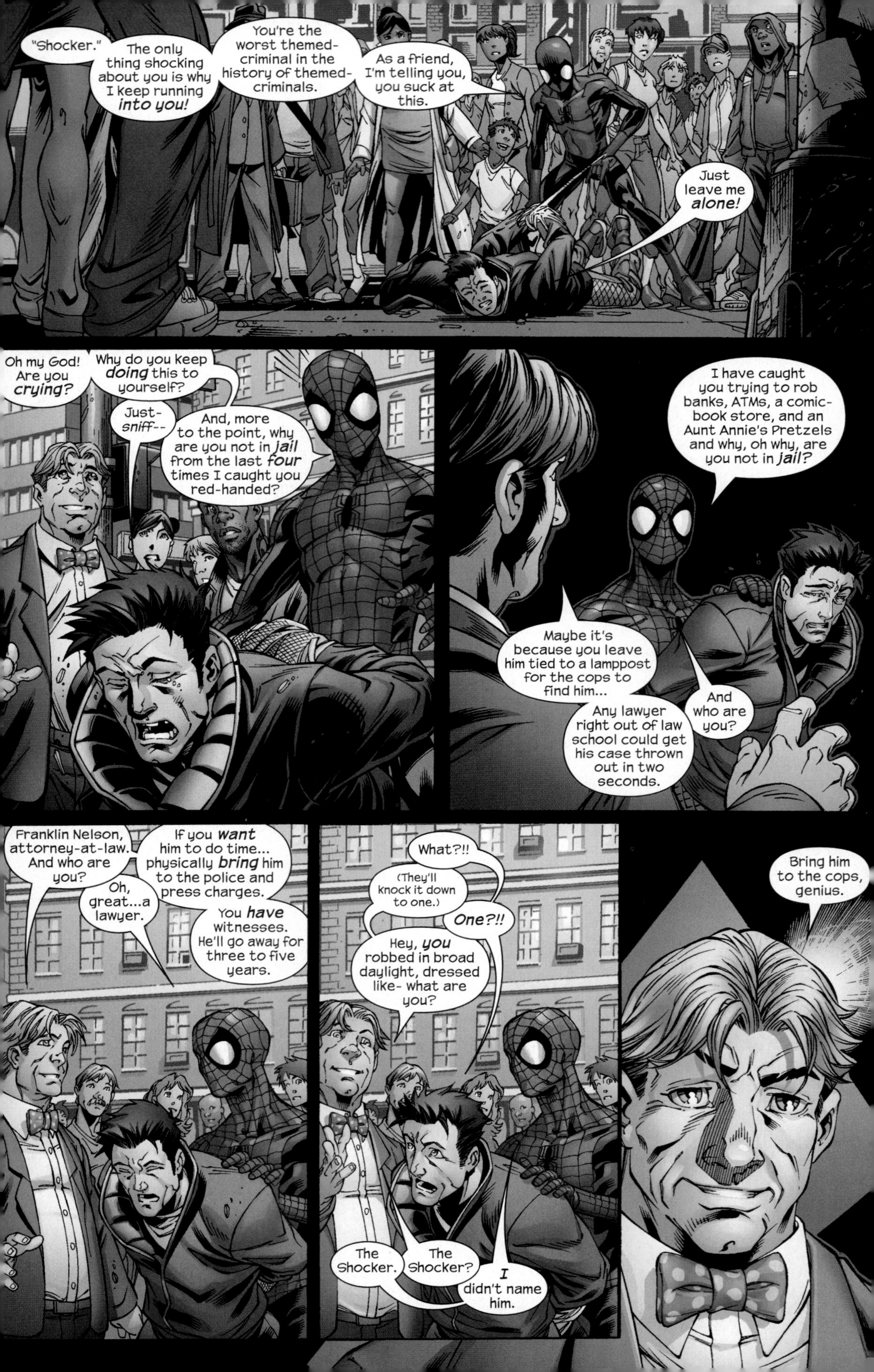
"Shocker."
The only thing shocking about you is why I keep running *into you!*
You're the worst themed-criminal in the history of themed-criminals.
As a friend, I'm telling you, you suck at this.
Just leave me *alone!*
Oh my God! Are you *crying?*
Why do you keep *doing* this to yourself?
Just- *sniff*--
And, more to the point, why are you not in *jail* from the last *four* times I caught you red-handed?
I have caught you trying to rob banks, ATMs, a comic-book store, and an Aunt Annie's Pretzels and why, oh why, are you not in *jail?*
Maybe it's because you leave him tied to a lamppost for the cops to find him...
Any lawyer right out of law school could get his case thrown out in two seconds.
And who are you?
Franklin Nelson, attorney-at-law. And who are you?
Oh, great...a lawyer.
If you *want* him to do time... physically *bring* him to the police and press charges.
You *have* witnesses. He'll go away for three to five years.
What?!!
(They'll knock it down to one.)
One?!!
Hey, *you* robbed in broad daylight, dressed like- what are you?
The Shocker.
The Shocker?
I didn't name him.
Bring him to the cops, genius.

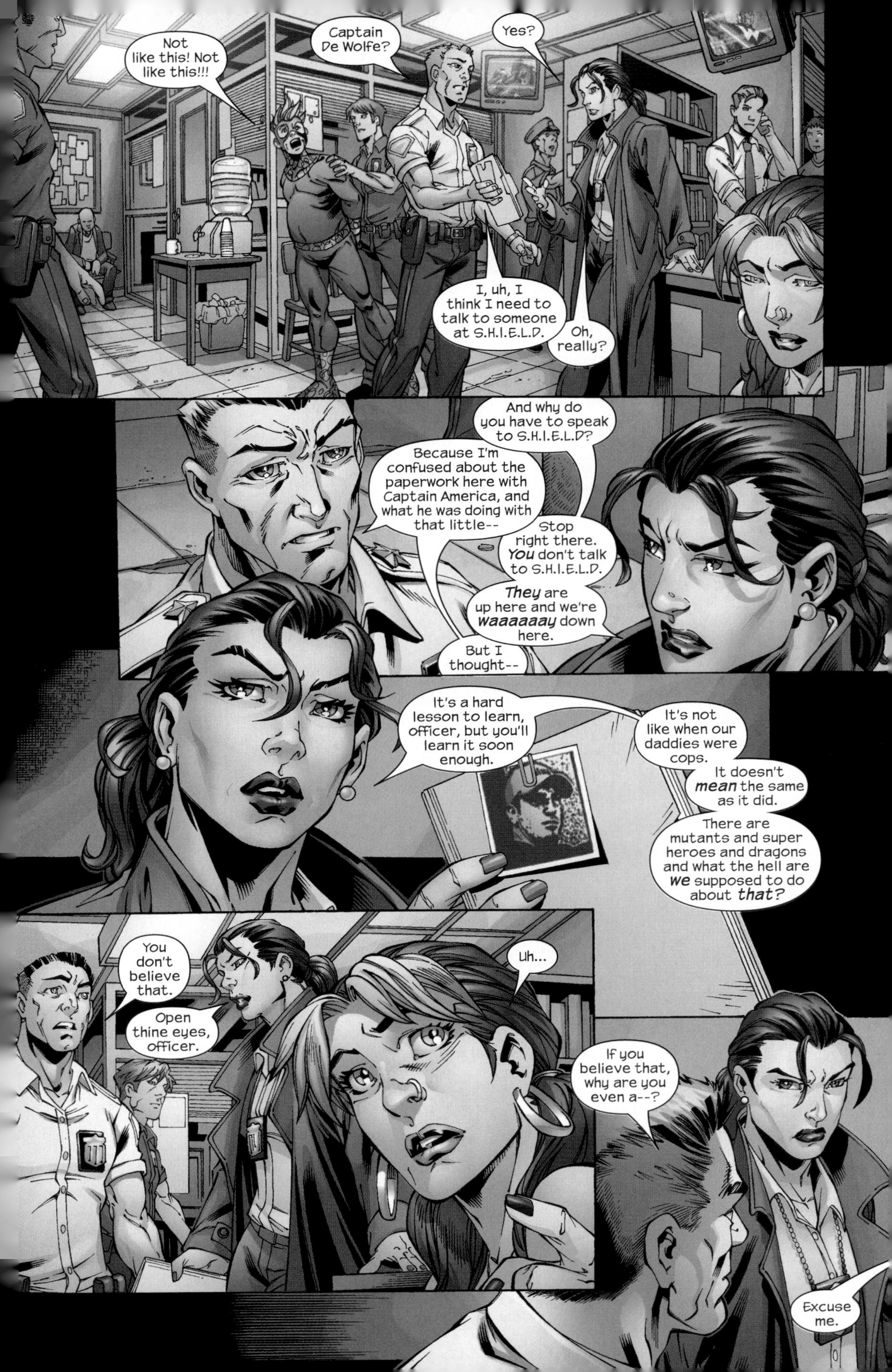

Not like this! Not like this!!!
Captain De Wolfe?
Yes?
I, uh, I think I need to talk to someone at S.H.I.E.L.D.
Oh, really?
And why do you have to speak to S.H.I.E.L.D?
Because I'm confused about the paperwork here with Captain America, and what he was doing with that little--
Stop right there. *You* don't talk to S.H.I.E.L.D.
They are up here and we're *waaaaaay* down here.
But I thought--
It's a hard lesson to learn, officer, but you'll learn it soon enough.
It's not like when our daddies were cops.
It doesn't *mean* the same as it did.
There are mutants and super heroes and dragons and what the hell are *we* supposed to do about *that?*
You don't believe that.
Open thine eyes, officer.
Uh...
If you believe that, why are you even a--?
Excuse me.

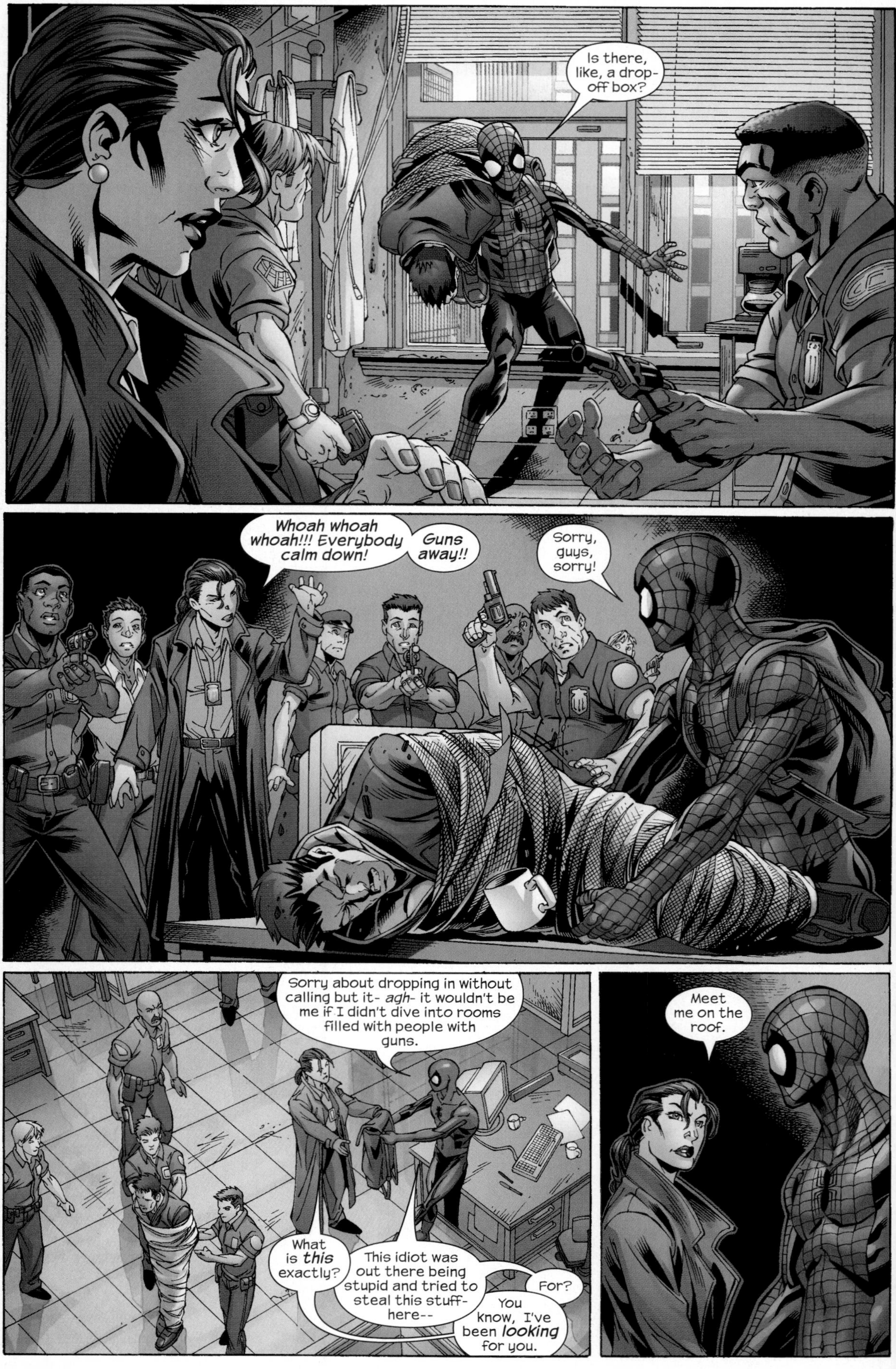

Is there, like, a drop-off box?
Whoah whoah whoah!!! Everybody calm down!
Guns away!!
Sorry, guys, sorry!
Sorry about dropping in without calling but it- *agh*- it wouldn't be me if I didn't dive into rooms filled with people with guns.
What is *this* exactly?
This idiot was out there being stupid and tried to steal this stuff- here--
For?
You know, I've been *looking* for you.
Meet me on the roof.

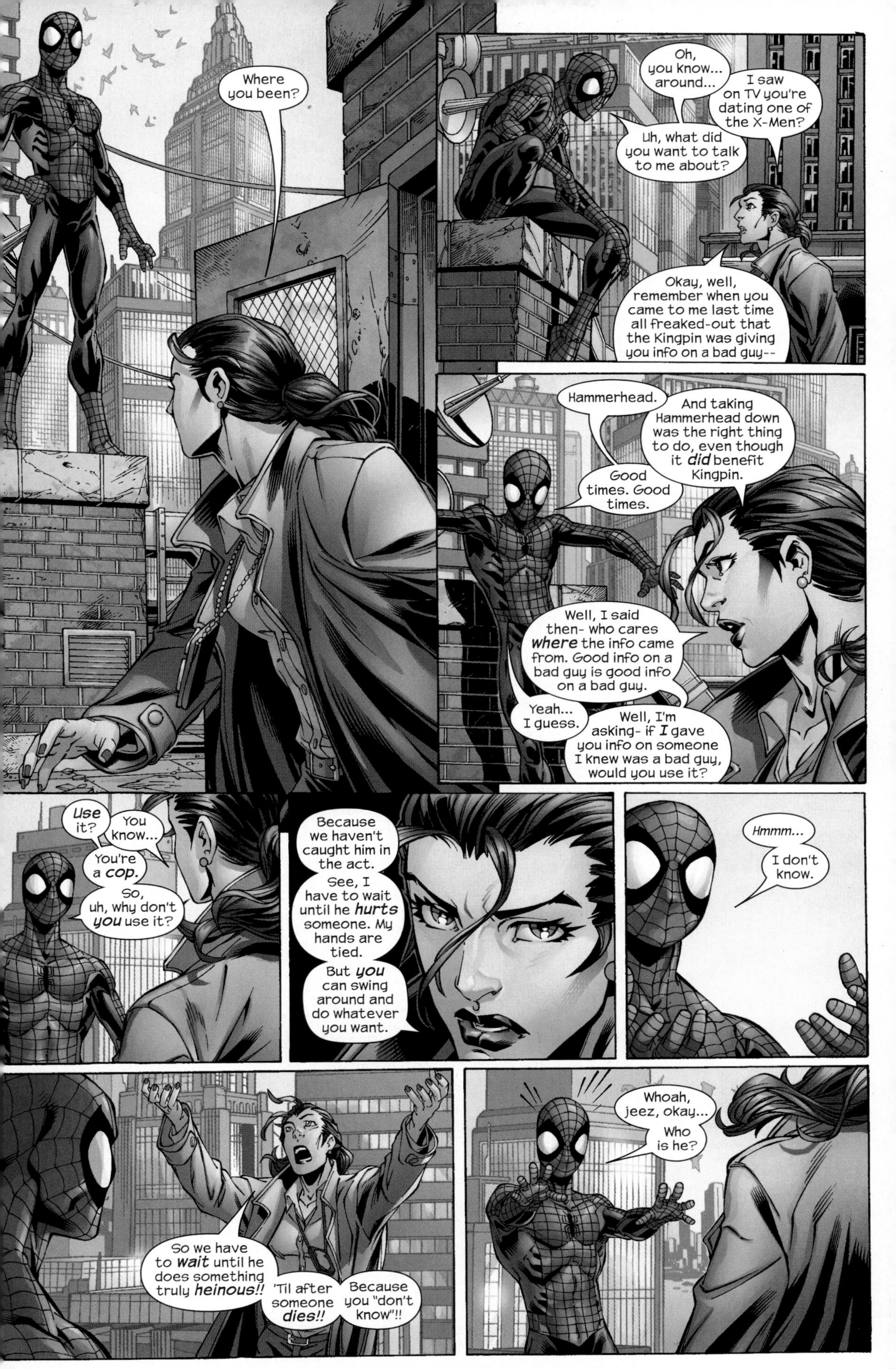
Where you been?
Oh, you know... around...
I saw on TV you're dating one of the X-Men?
Uh, what did you want to talk to me about?
Okay, well, remember when you came to me last time all freaked-out that the Kingpin was giving you info on a bad guy--
Hammerhead.
And taking Hammerhead down was the right thing to do, even though it did benefit Kingpin.
Good times. Good times.
Well, I said then- who cares where the info came from. Good info on a bad guy is good info on a bad guy.
Yeah... I guess.
Well, I'm asking- if I gave you info on someone I knew was a bad guy, would you use it?
Use it?
You know...
You're a cop.
So, uh, why don't you use it?
Because we haven't caught him in the act.
See, I have to wait until he hurts someone. My hands are tied.
But you can swing around and do whatever you want.
Hmmm...
I don't know.
So we have to wait until he does something truly heinous!!
'Til after someone dies!!
Because you "don't know"!!
Whoah, jeez, okay...
Who is he?

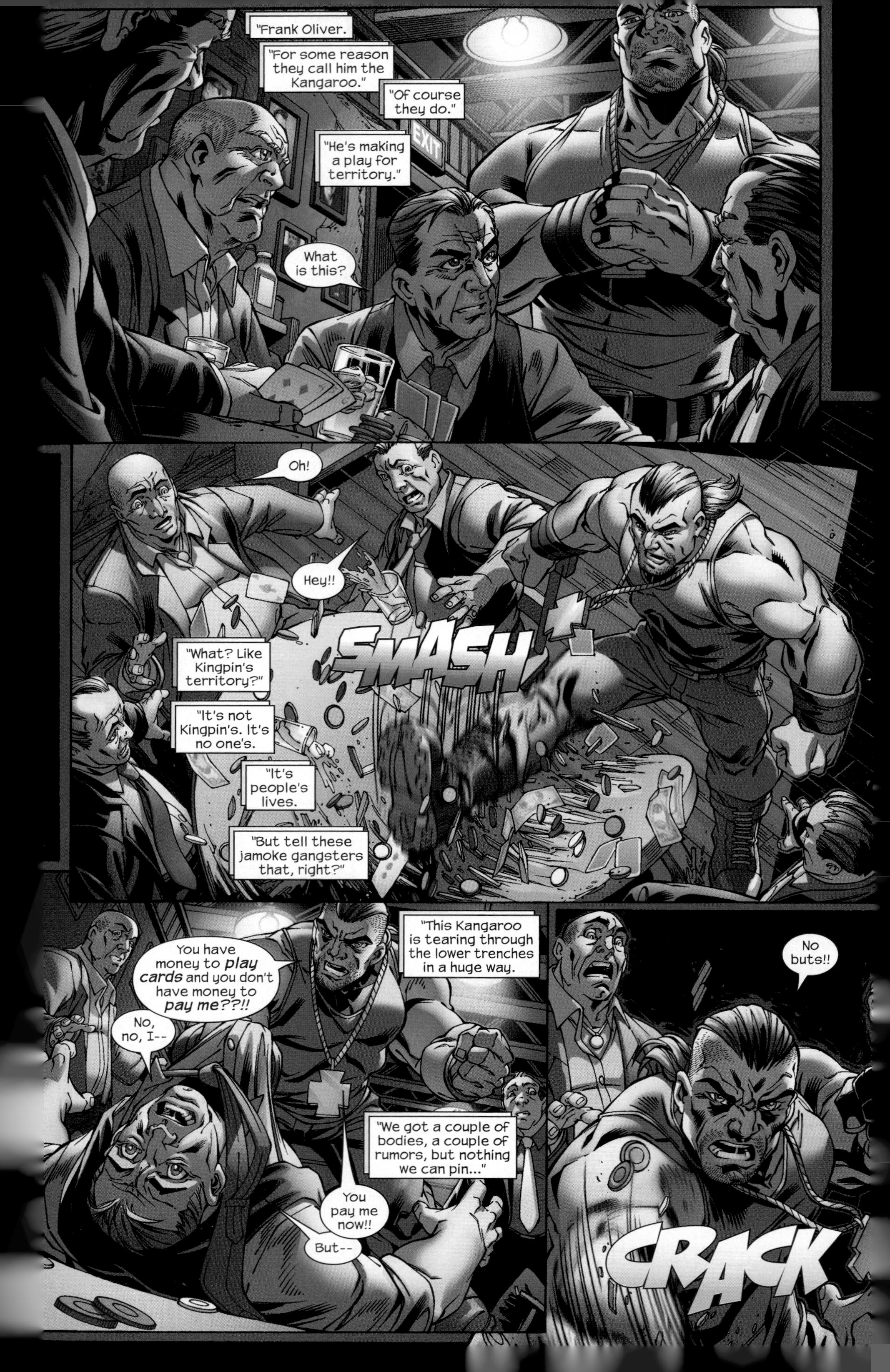
"Frank Oliver.
"For some reason they call him the Kangaroo."
"Of course they do."
"He's making a play for territory."
EXIT
What is this?
Oh!
Hey!!
SMASH
"What? Like Kingpin's territory?"
"It's not Kingpin's. It's no one's.
"It's people's lives.
"But tell these jamoke gangsters that, right?"
You have money to **play cards** and you don't have money to **pay me**??!!
"This Kangaroo is tearing through the lower trenches in a huge way.
No, no, I--
"We got a couple of bodies, a couple of rumors, but nothing we can pin..."
You pay me now!!
But--
No buts!!
CRACK

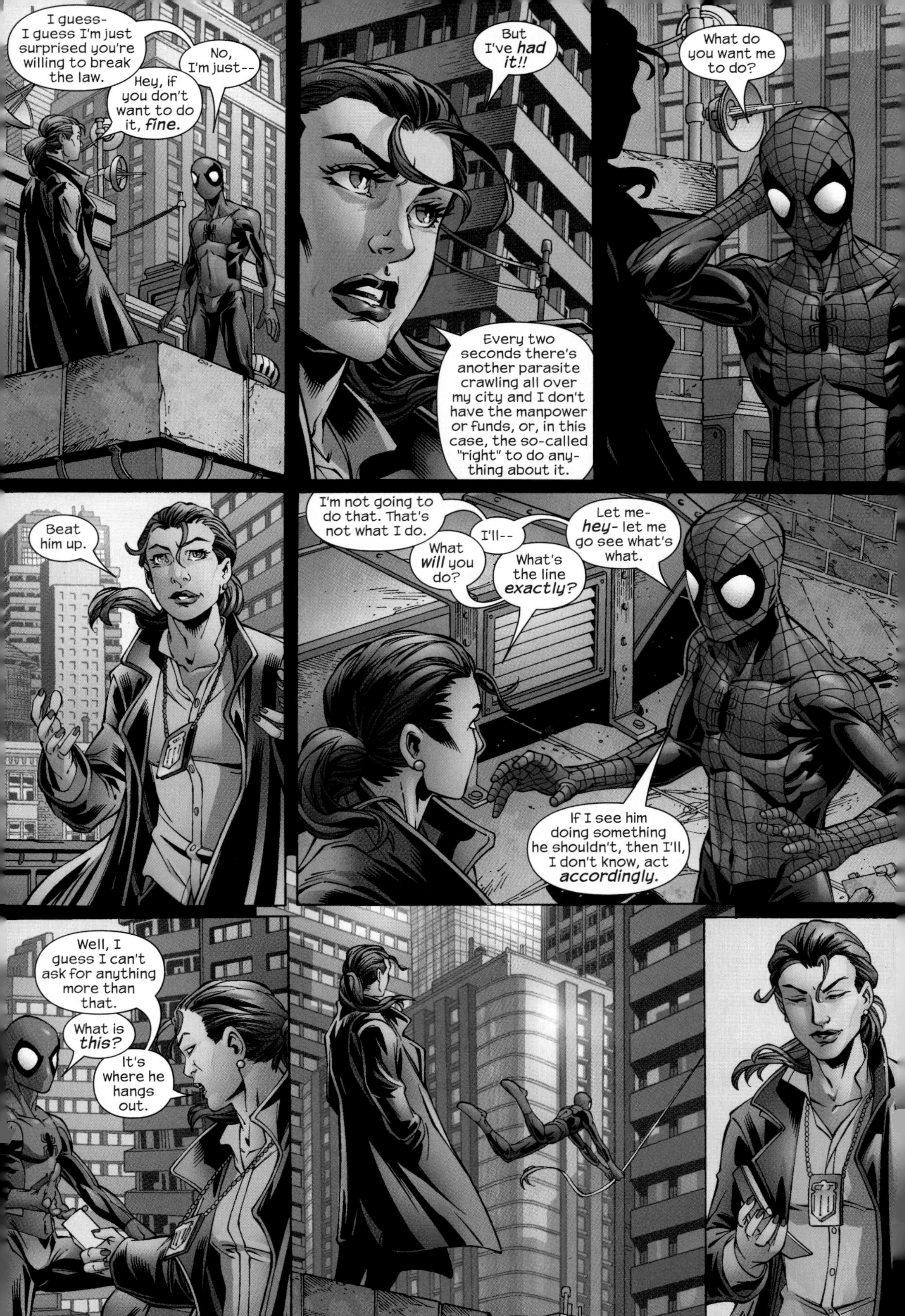
I guess- I guess I'm just surprised you're willing to break the law.
No, I'm just--
Hey, if you don't want to do it, *fine.*
But I've *had it!!*
Every two seconds there's another parasite crawling all over my city and I don't have the manpower or funds, or, in this case, the so-called "right" to do anything about it.
What do you want me to do?
Beat him up.
I'm not going to do that. That's not what I do.
What *will* you do?
I'll--
What's the line *exactly?*
Let me- *hey*- let me go see what's what.
If I see him doing something he shouldn't, then I'll, I don't know, act *accordingly.*
Well, I guess I can't ask for anything more than that.
What is *this?*
It's where he hangs out.

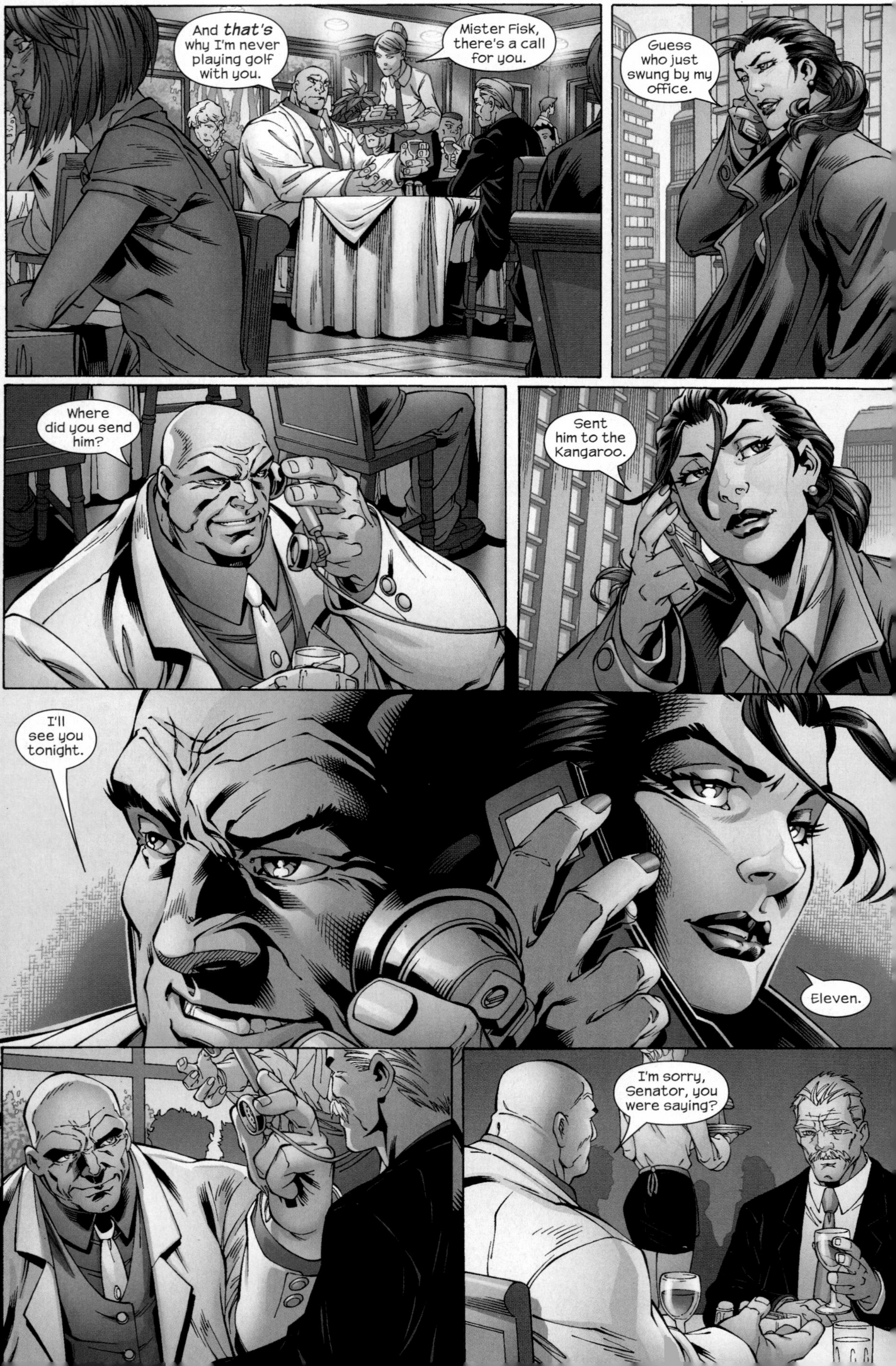
And *that's* why I'm never playing golf with you.
Mister Fisk, there's a call for you.
Guess who just swung by my office.
Where did you send him?
Sent him to the Kangaroo.
I'll see you tonight.
Eleven.
I'm sorry, Senator, you were saying?

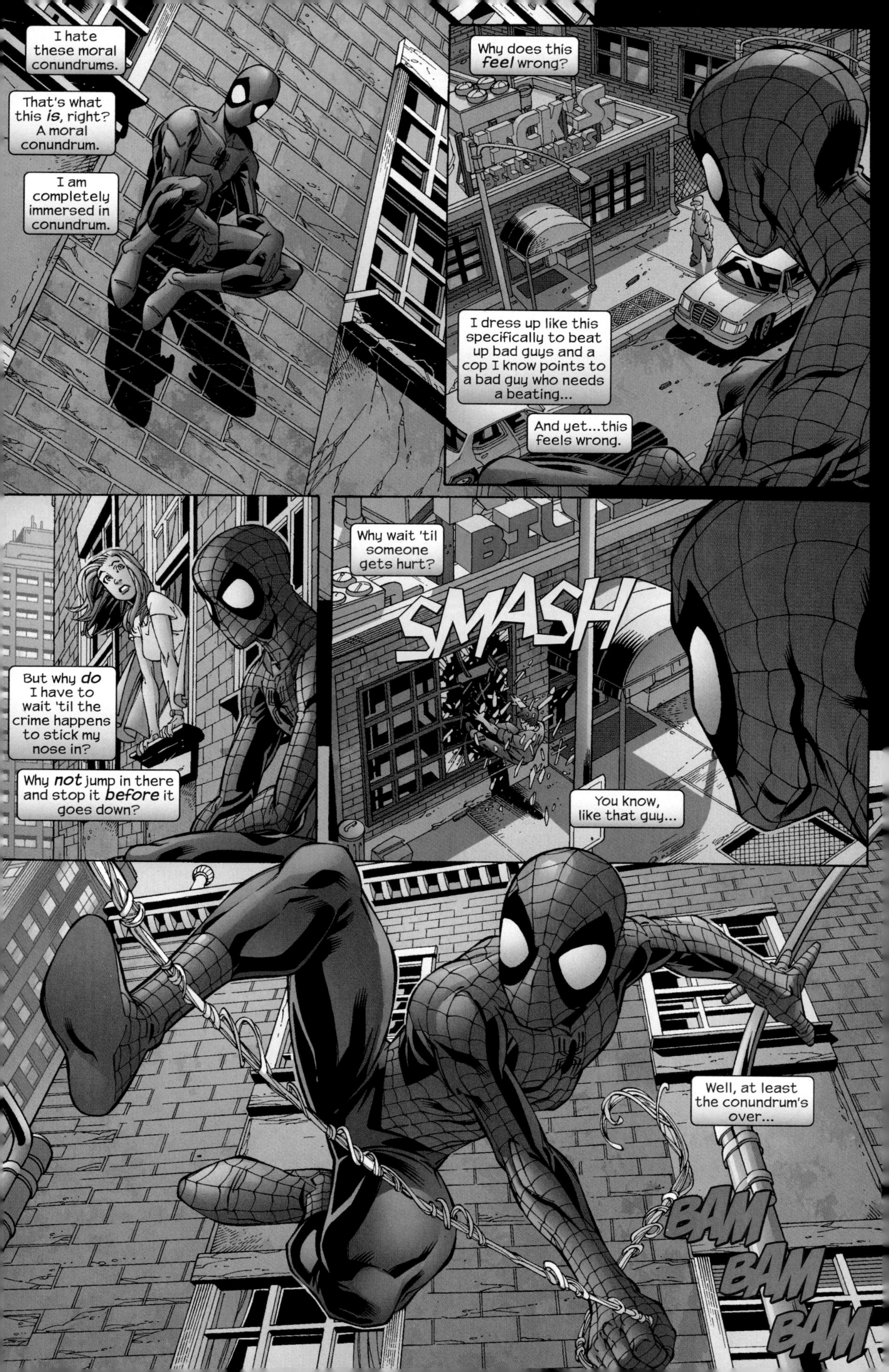

I hate these moral conundrums.
That's what this *is*, right? A moral conundrum.
I am completely immersed in conundrum.
Why does this *feel* wrong?
I dress up like this specifically to beat up bad guys and a cop I know points to a bad guy who needs a beating...
And yet...this feels wrong.
But why *do* I have to wait 'til the crime happens to stick my nose in?
Why *not* jump in there and stop it *before* it goes down?
Why wait 'til someone gets hurt?
SMASH
You know, like that guy...
Well, at least the conundrum's over...
BAM
BAM
BAM

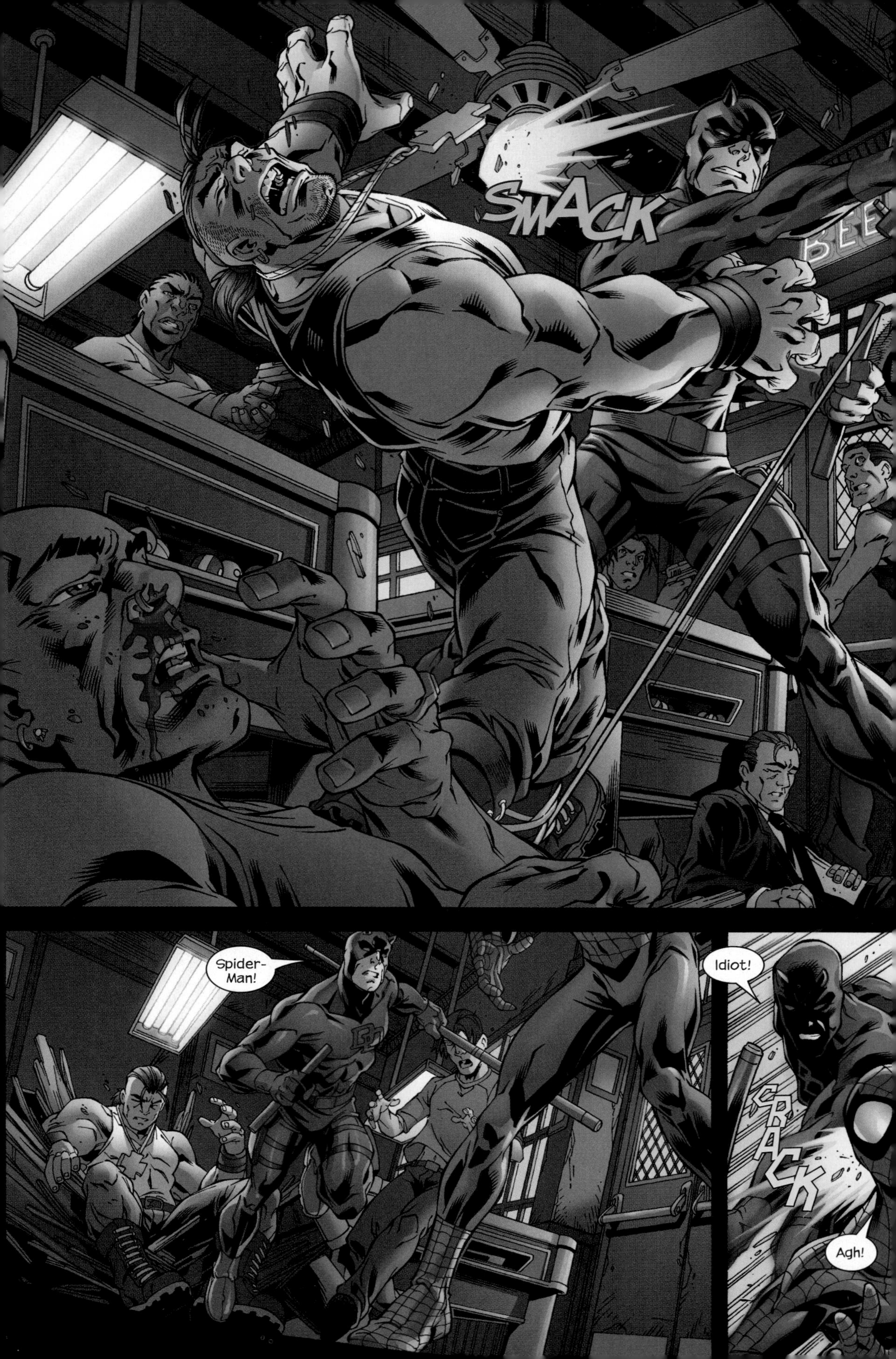
SMACK
Spider-Man!
Idiot!
CRACK
Agh!

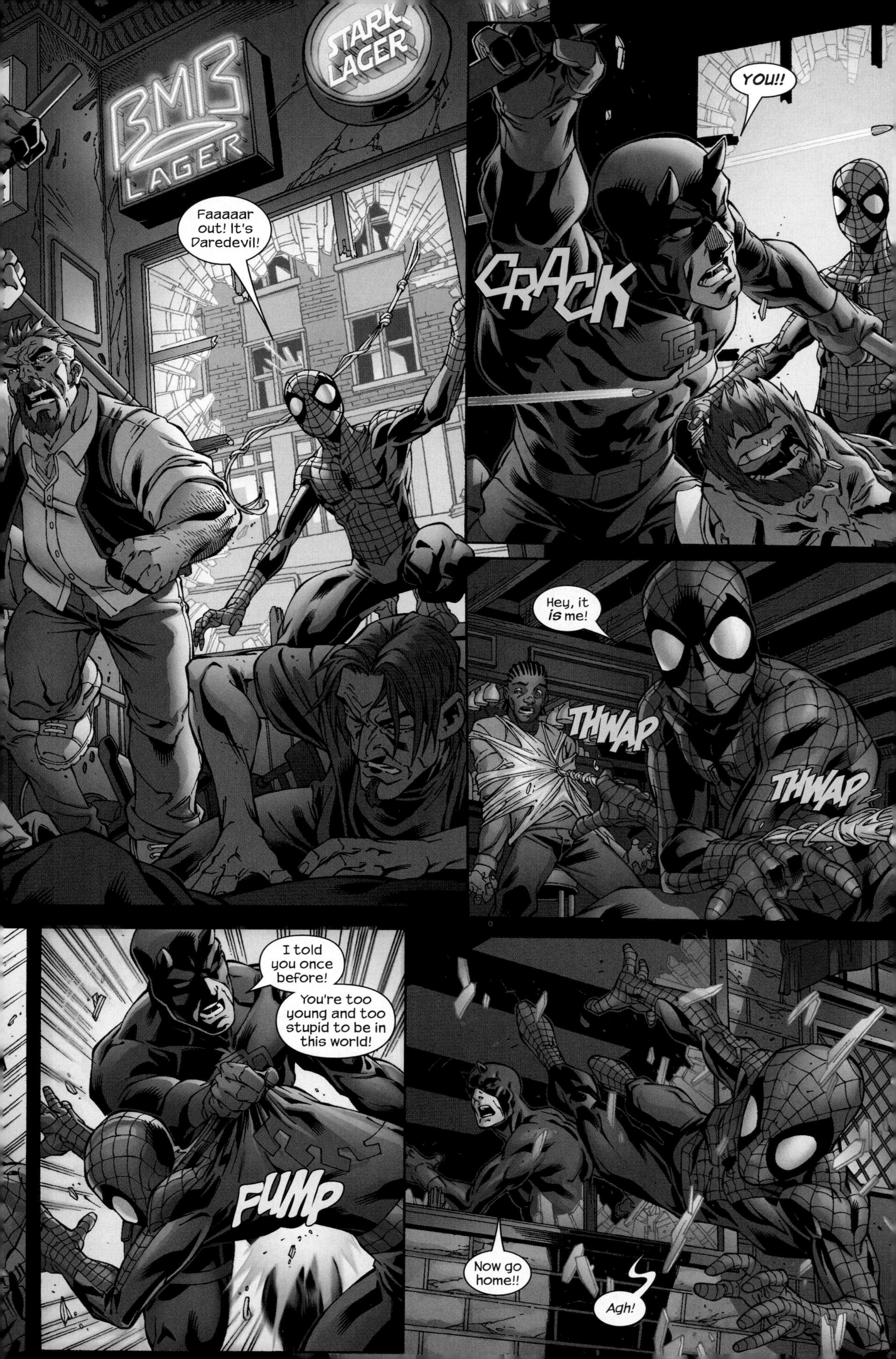
BMB LAGER
STARK LAGER
Faaaaar out! It's Daredevil!
CRACK
YOU!!
Hey, it *is* me!
THWAP
THWAP
I told you once before!
You're too young and too stupid to be in this world!
FUMP
Now go home!!
Agh!

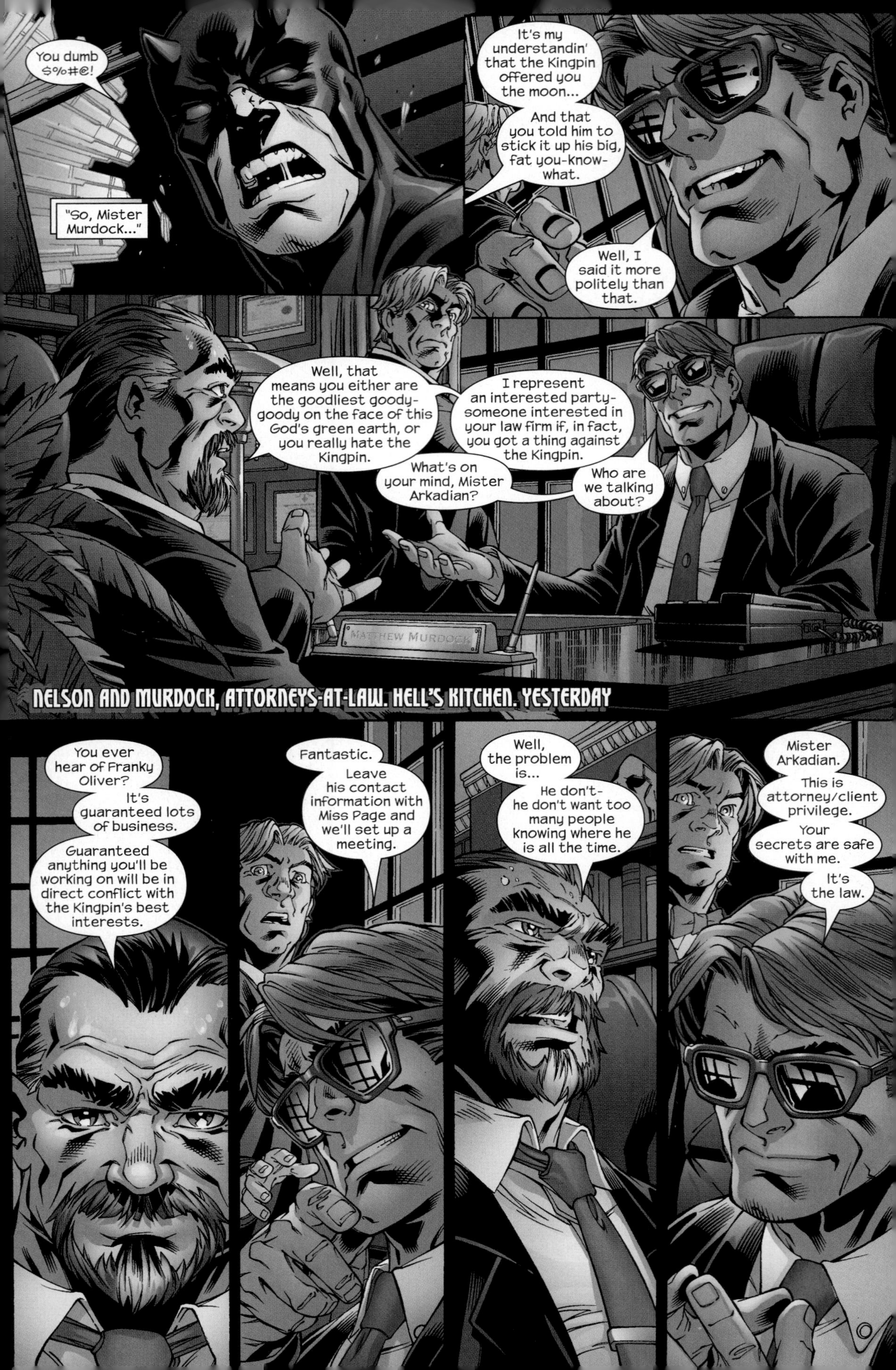

You dumb $%#@!
"So, Mister Murdock..."
It's my understandin' that the Kingpin offered you the moon...
And that you told him to stick it up his big, fat you-know-what.
Well, I said it more politely than that.
Well, that means you either are the goodliest goody-goody on the face of this God's green earth, or you really hate the Kingpin.
What's on your mind, Mister Arkadian?
I represent an interested party-someone interested in your law firm if, in fact, you got a thing against the Kingpin.
Who are we talking about?
MATTHEW MURDOCK
NELSON AND MURDOCK, ATTORNEYS-AT-LAW. HELL'S KITCHEN. YESTERDAY
You ever hear of Franky Oliver?
It's guaranteed lots of business.
Guaranteed anything you'll be working on will be in direct conflict with the Kingpin's best interests.
Fantastic.
Leave his contact information with Miss Page and we'll set up a meeting.
Well, the problem is...
He don't-he don't want too many people knowing where he is all the time.
Mister Arkadian.
This is attorney/client privilege.
Your secrets are safe with me.
It's the law.

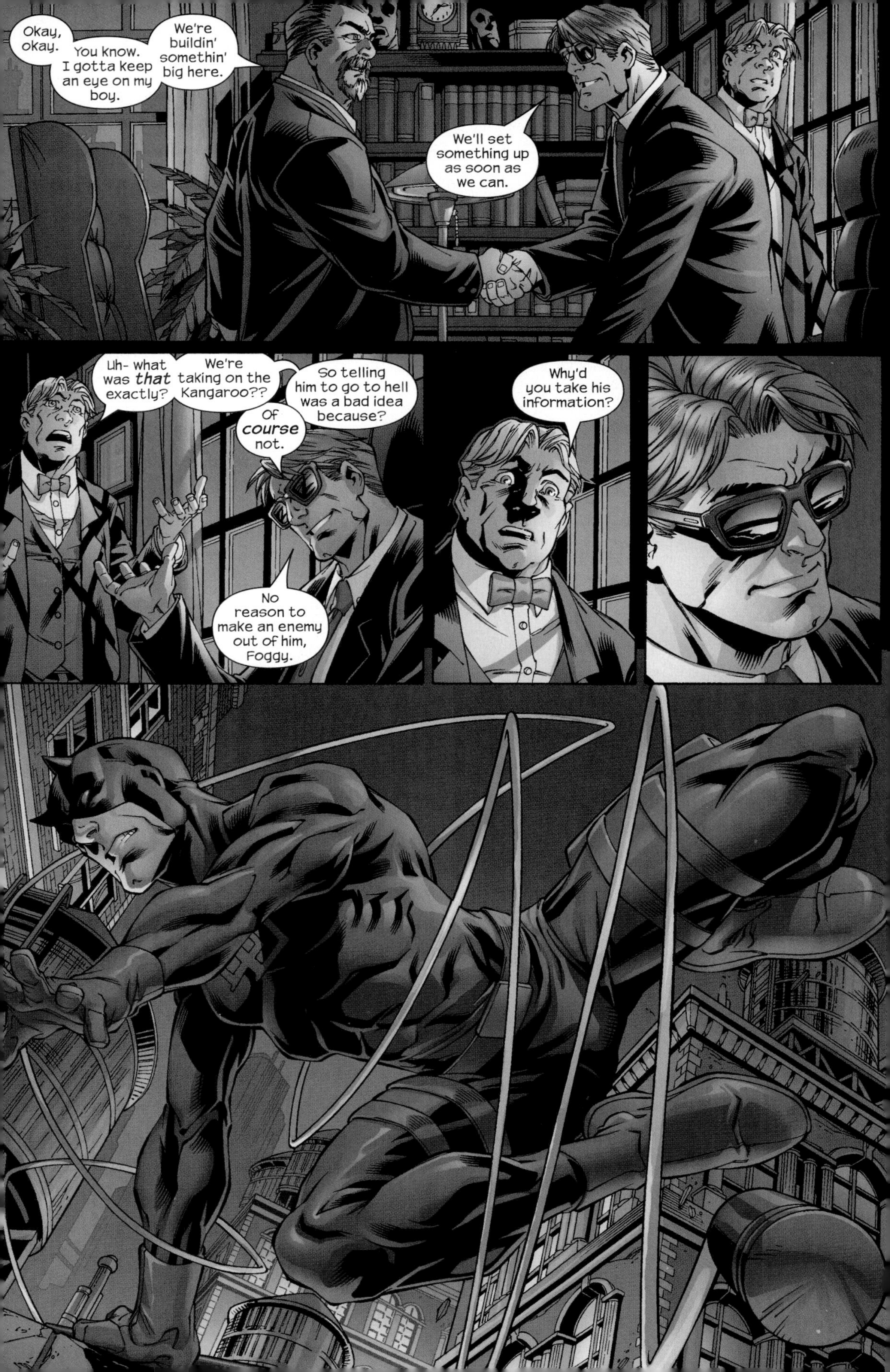

Okay, okay.
You know. I gotta keep an eye on my boy.
We're buildin' somethin' big here.
We'll set something up as soon as we can.
Uh- what was *that* exactly?
We're taking on the Kangaroo??
So telling him to go to hell was a bad idea because?
Of *course* not.
No reason to make an enemy out of him, Foggy.
Why'd you take his information?

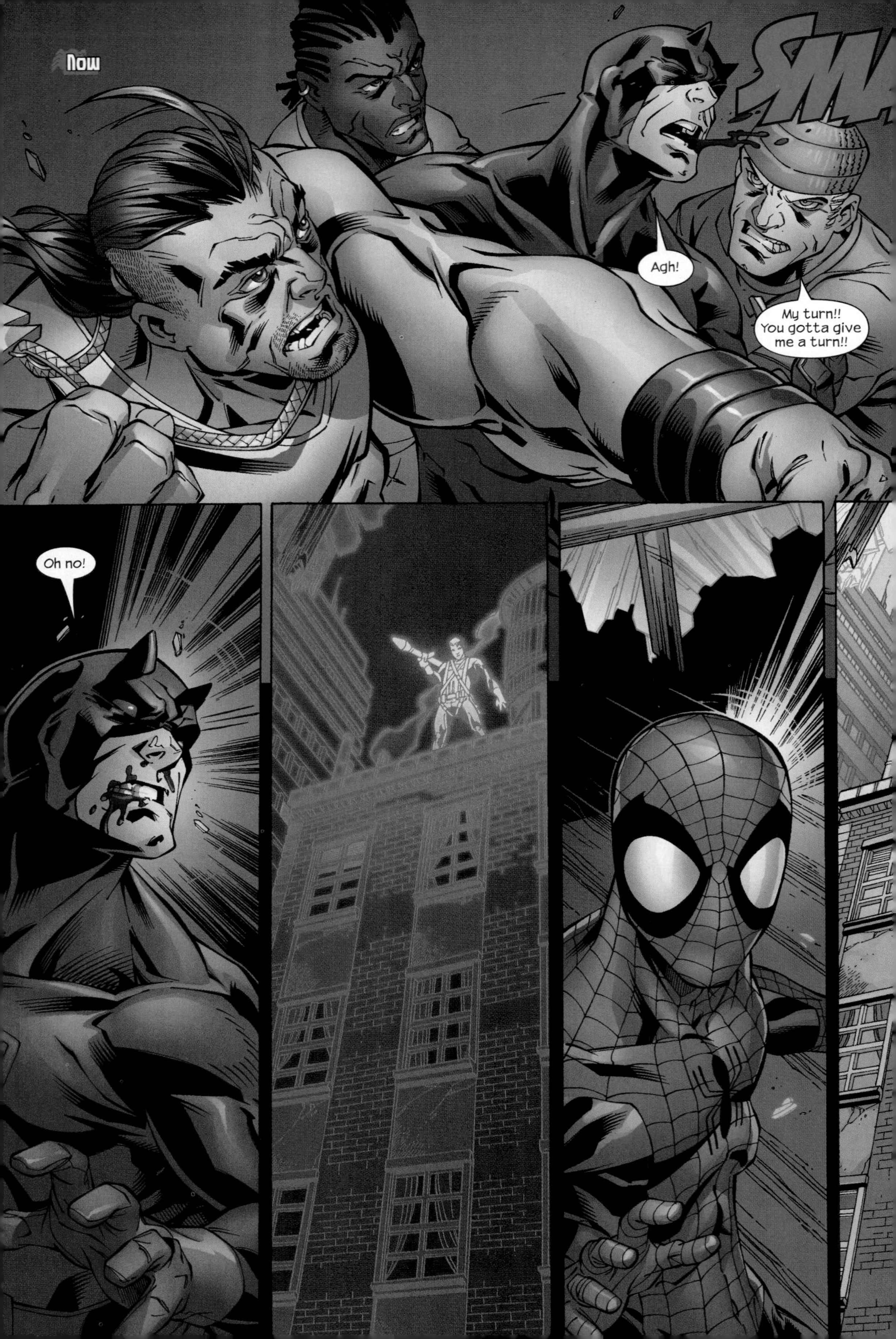
Now
Agh!
My turn!! You gotta give me a turn!!
Oh no!

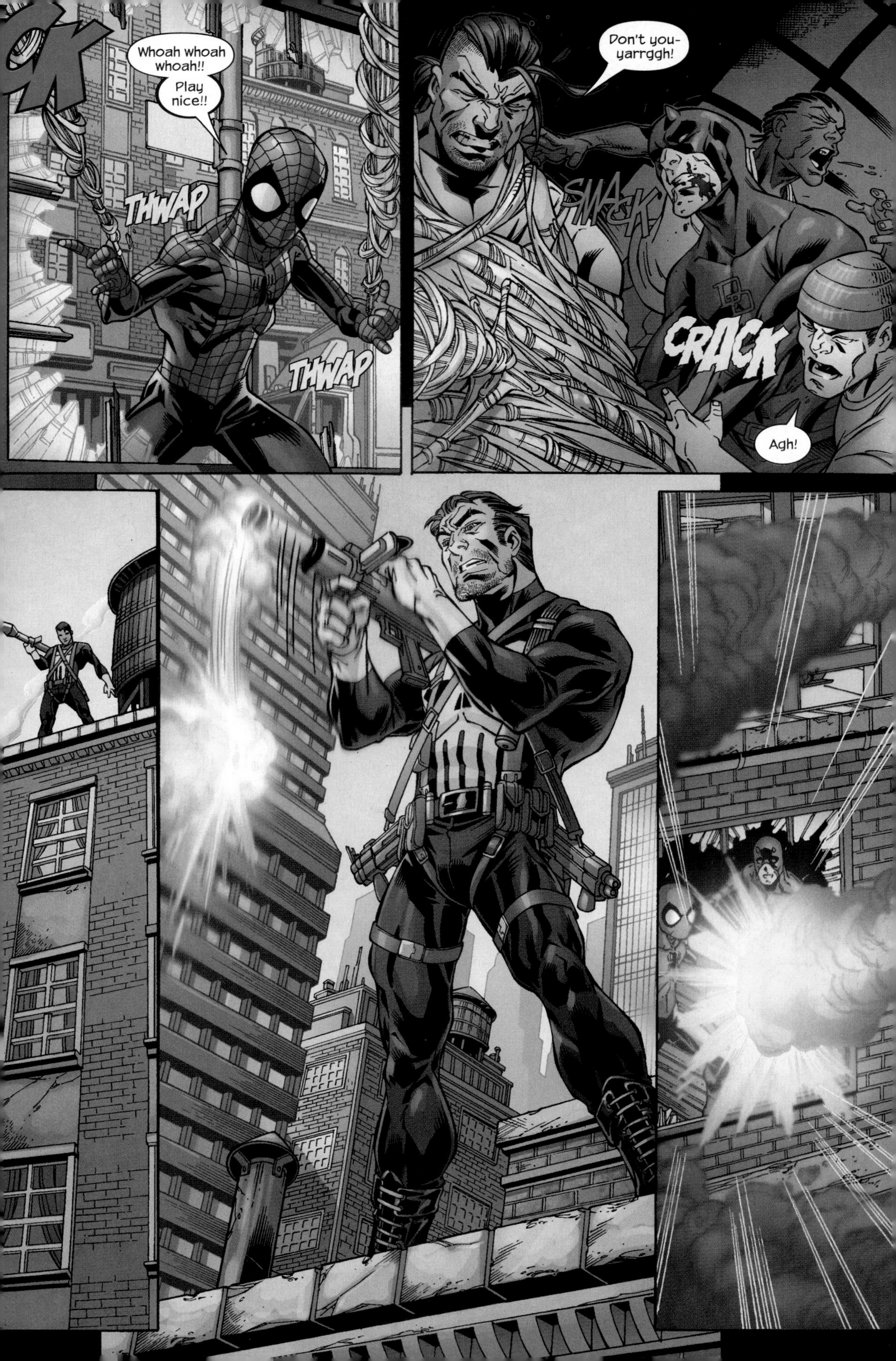

Whoah whoah whoah!!
Play nice!!
THWAP
THWAP
Don't you-yarrggh!
SMACK
CRACK
Agh!

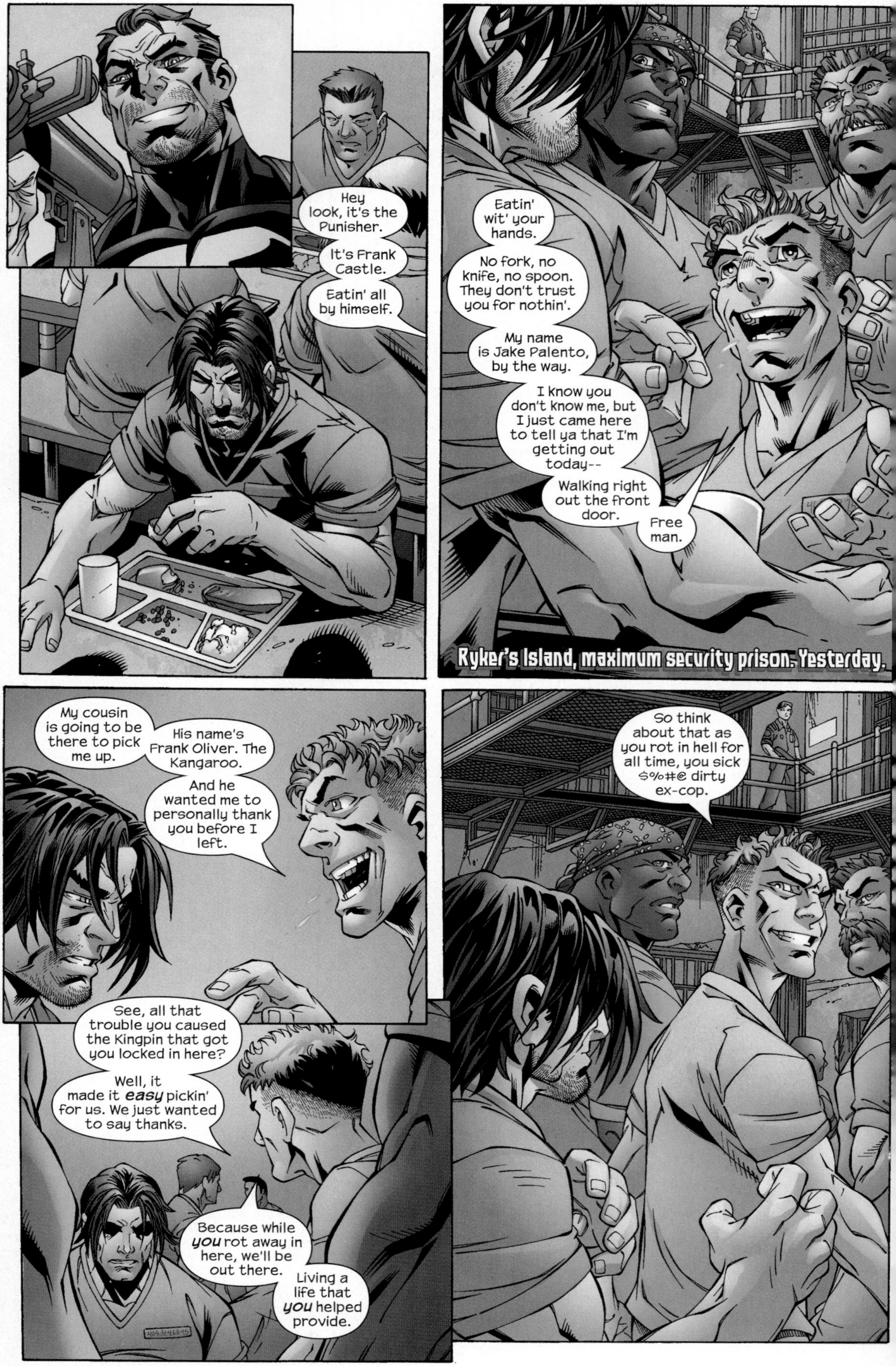

Hey look, it's the Punisher.
It's Frank Castle.
Eatin' all by himself.
Eatin' wit' your hands.
No fork, no knife, no spoon. They don't trust you for nothin'.
My name is Jake Palento, by the way.
I know you don't know me, but I just came here to tell ya that I'm getting out today--
Walking right out the front door.
Free man.
Ryker's Island, maximum security prison. Yesterday.
My cousin is going to be there to pick me up.
His name's Frank Oliver. The Kangaroo.
And he wanted me to personally thank you before I left.
See, all that trouble you caused the Kingpin that got you locked in here?
Well, it made it *easy* pickin' for us. We just wanted to say thanks.
Because while *you* rot away in here, we'll be out there.
Living a life that *you* helped provide.
So think about that as you rot in hell for all time, you sick $%#@ dirty ex-cop.

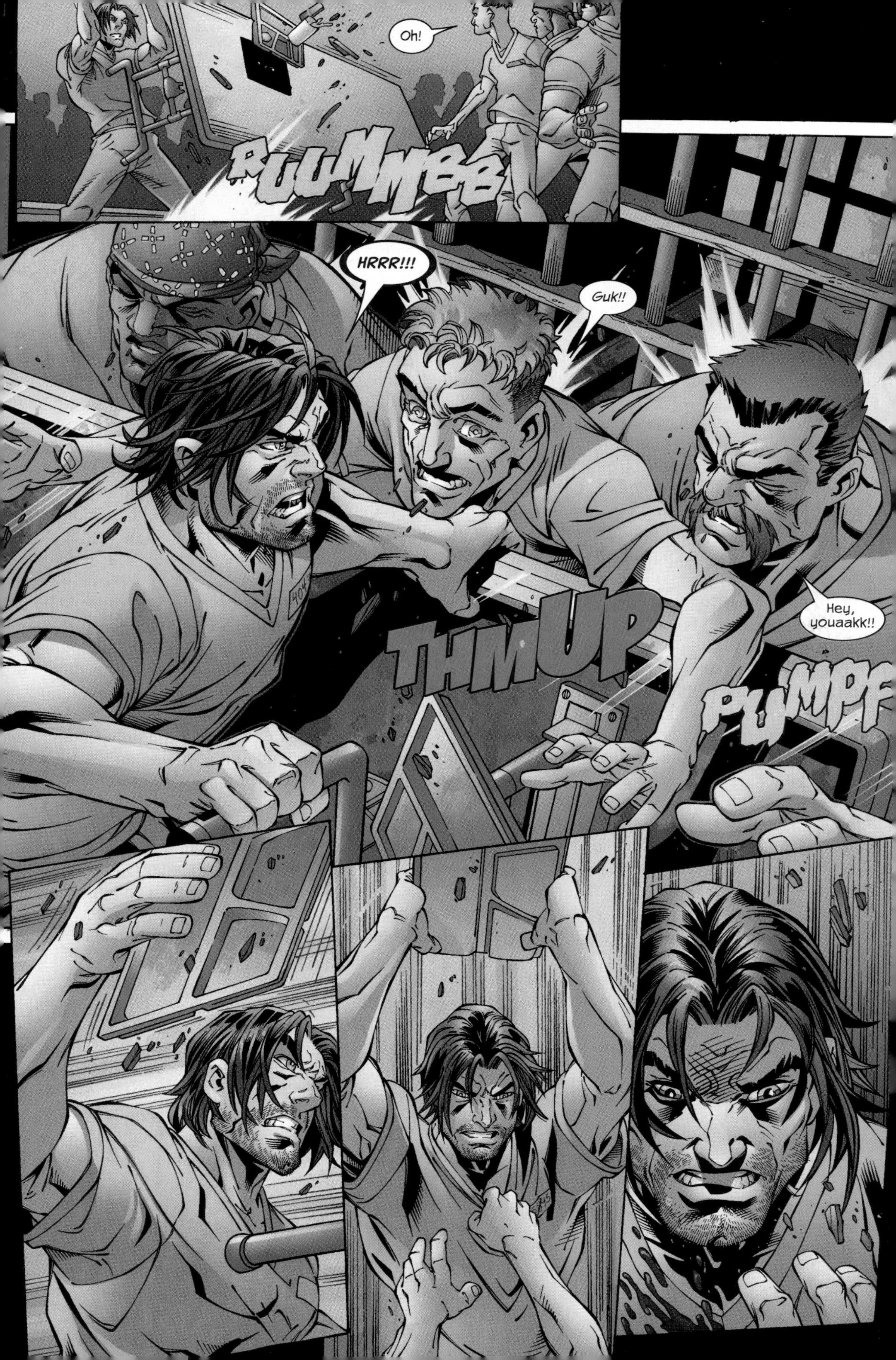
Oh!
RUUMMBB
HRRR!!!
Guk!!
Hey, youaakk!!
THMUP
PUMPF

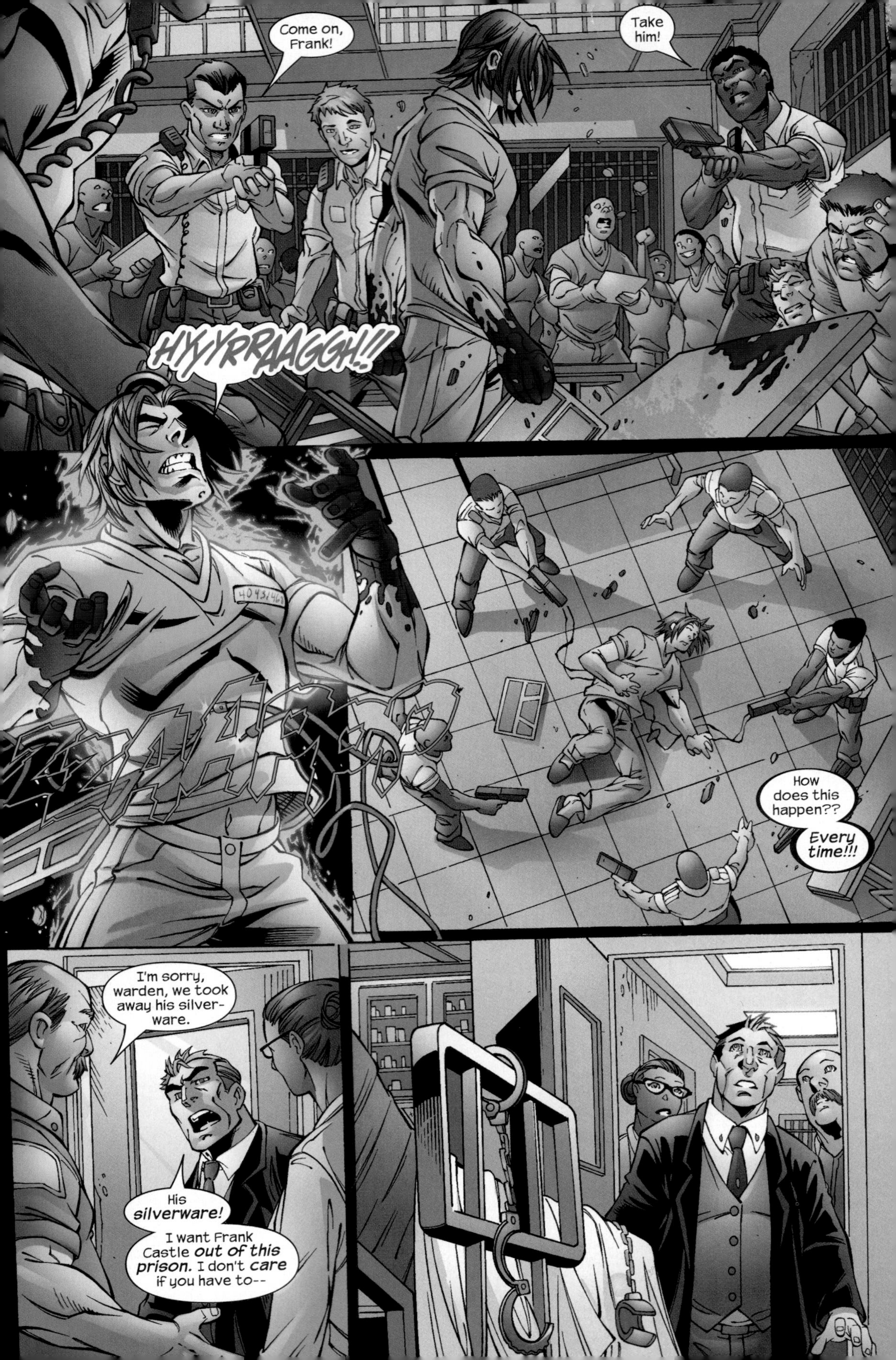
Come on, Frank!
Take him!
HYYRRAAGGH!!
How does this happen??
Every time!!!
I'm sorry, warden, we took away his silver-ware.
His silverware!
I want Frank Castle out of this prison. I don't care if you have to--

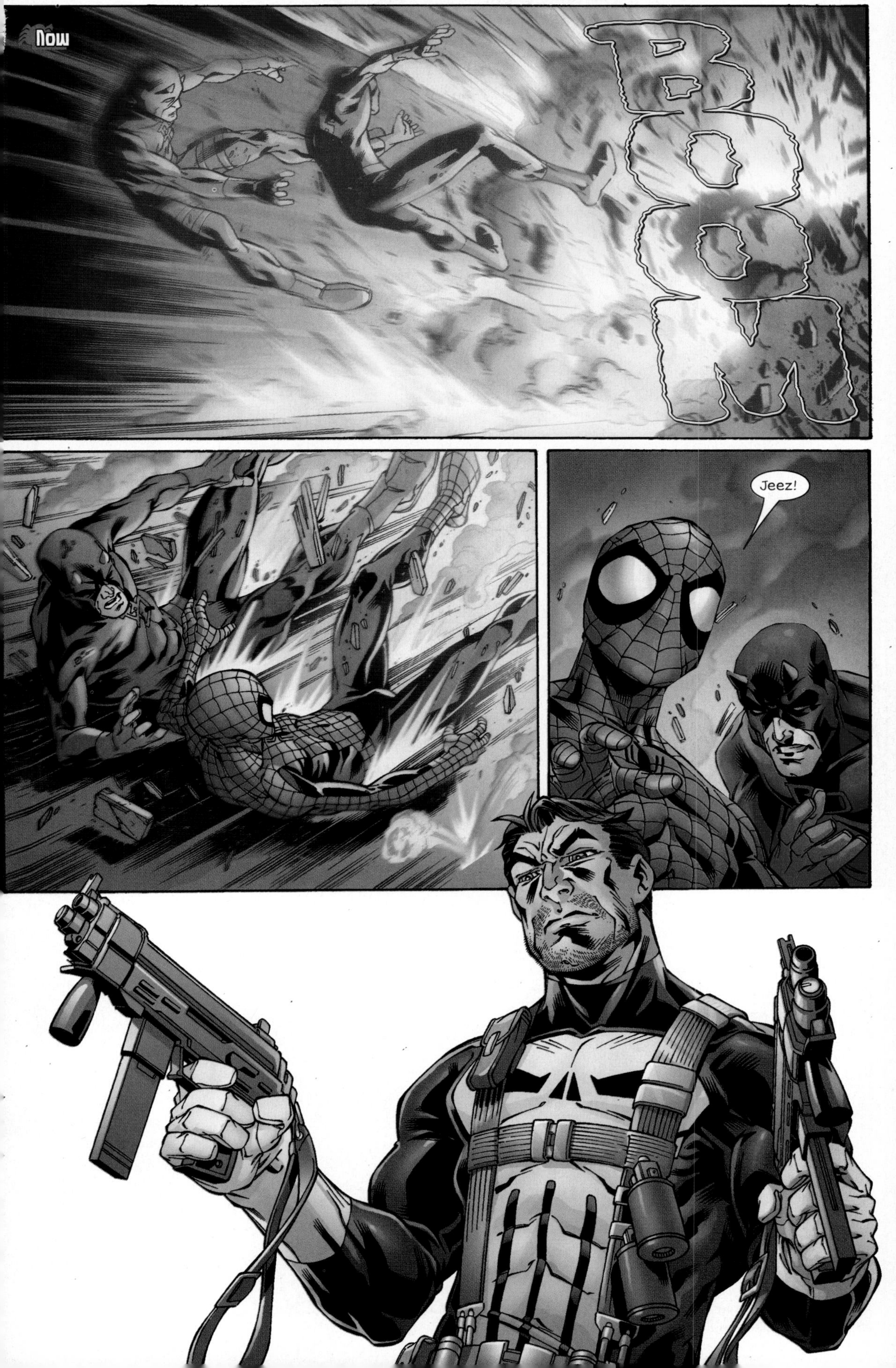
Now
BOOOM
Jeez!

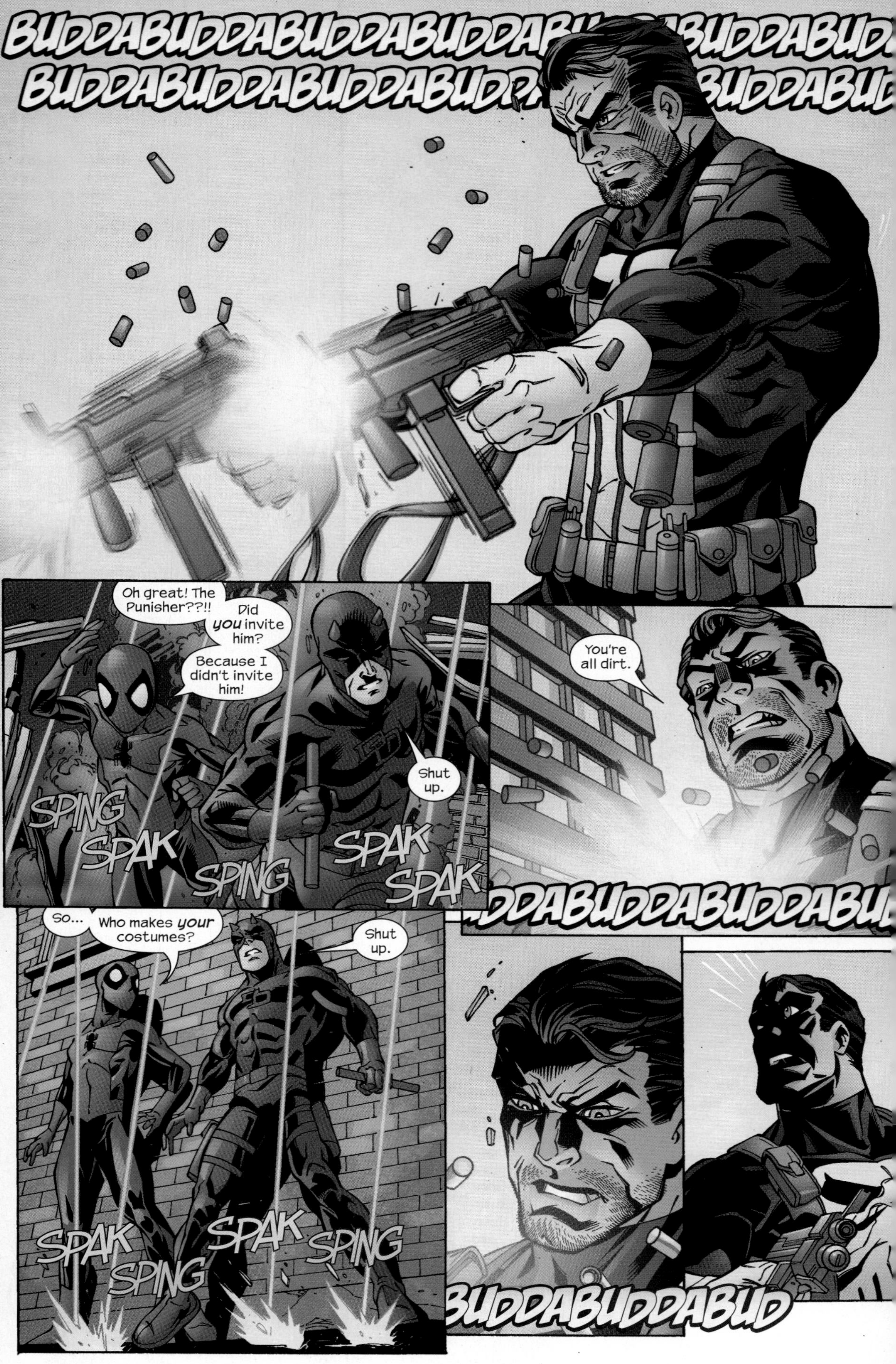
BUDDABUDDABUDDABUDDABU
BUDDABUDDABUDDABUD
Oh great! The Punisher??!!
Did *you* invite him?
Because I didn't invite him!
Shut up.
SPING
SPAK
SPING
SPAK
SPAK
You're all dirt.
DDABUDDABUDDABU
So...
Who makes *your* costumes?
Shut up.
SPAK
SPING
SPAK
SPING
BUDDABUDDABUD

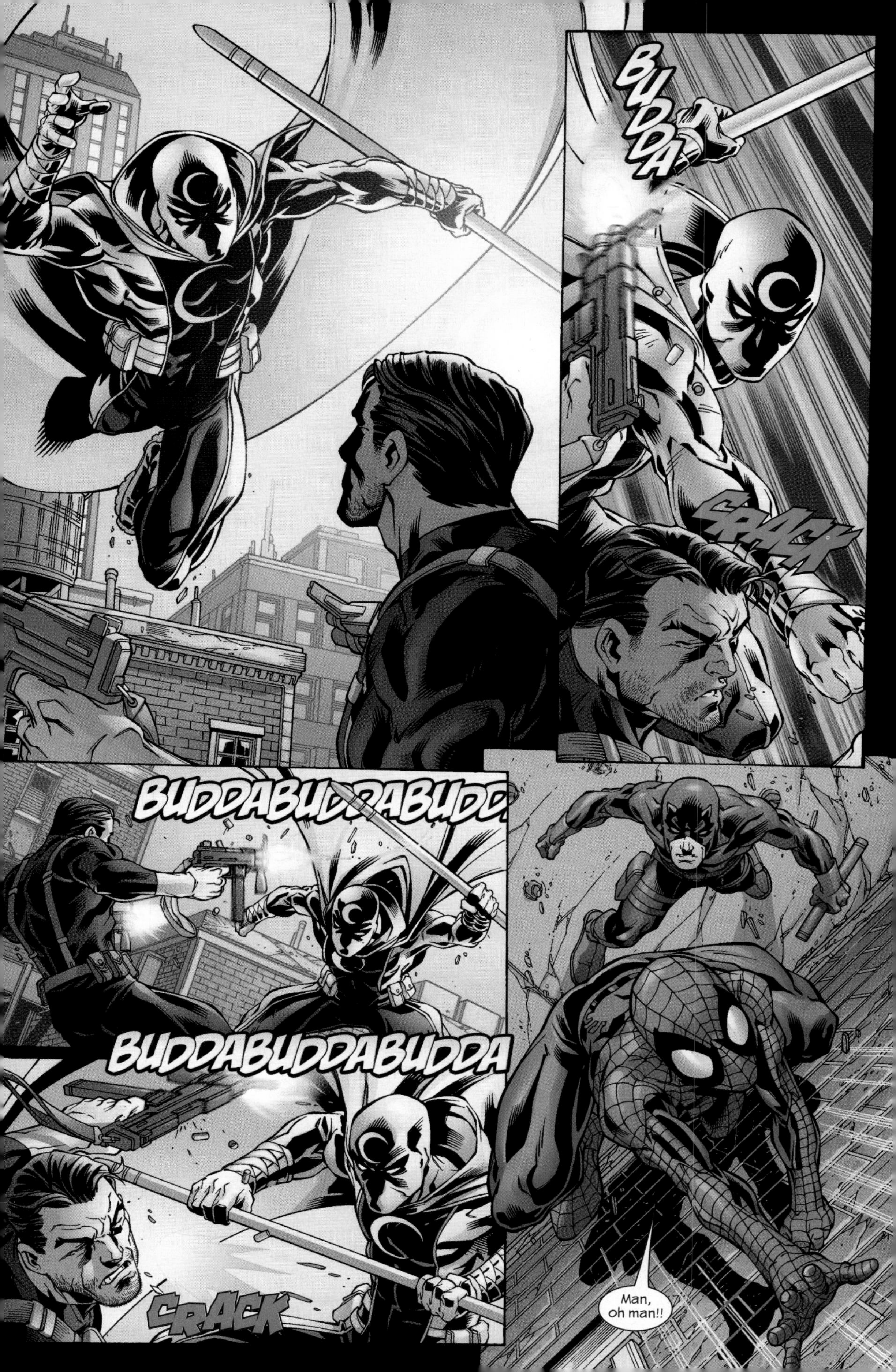
BUDDA
CRACK
BUDDABUDDABUDD
BUDDABUDDABUDDA
CRACK
Man, oh man!!

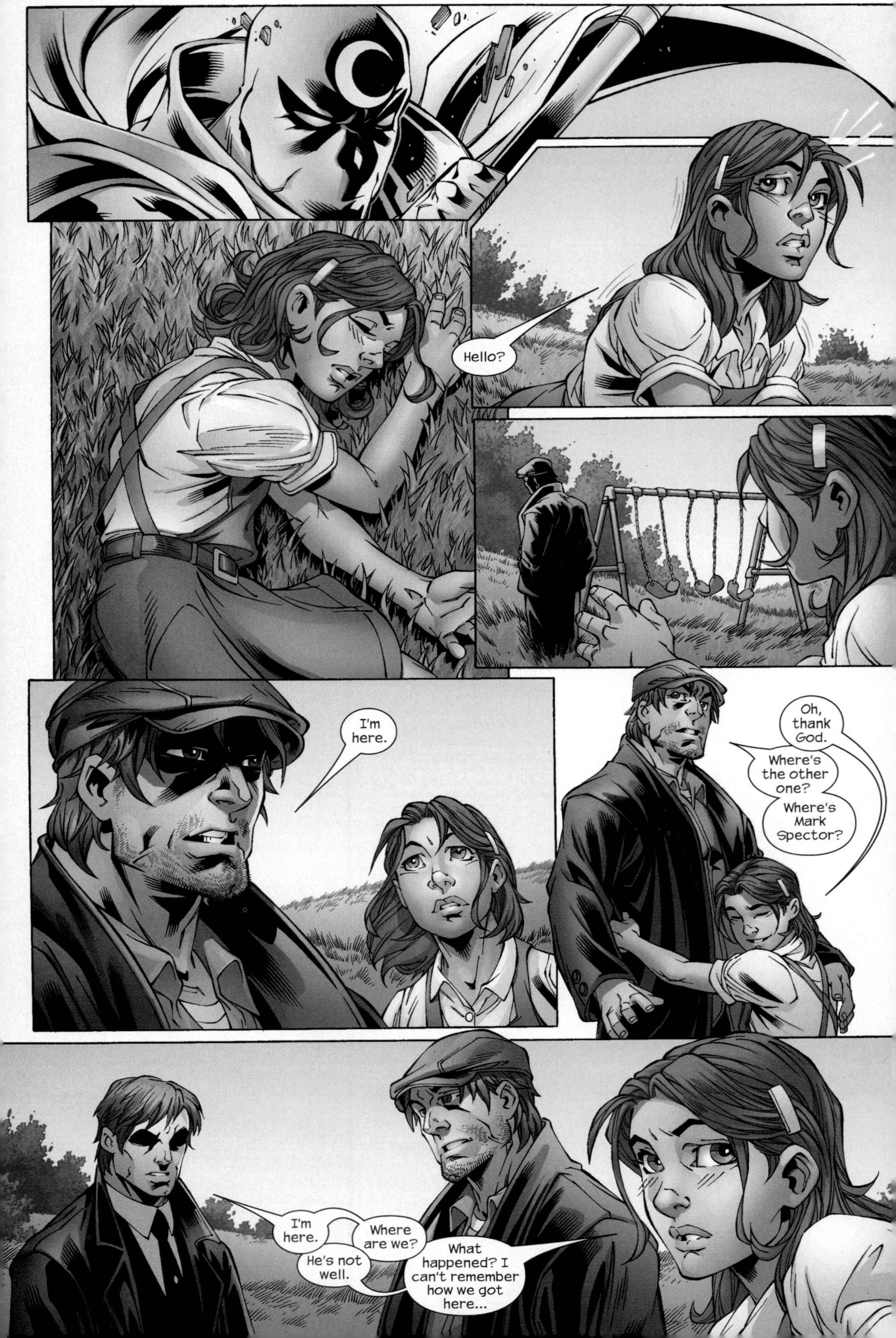
Hello?
I'm here.
Oh, thank God.
Where's the other one?
Where's Mark Spector?
I'm here.
Where are we?
He's not well.
What happened? I can't remember how we got here...

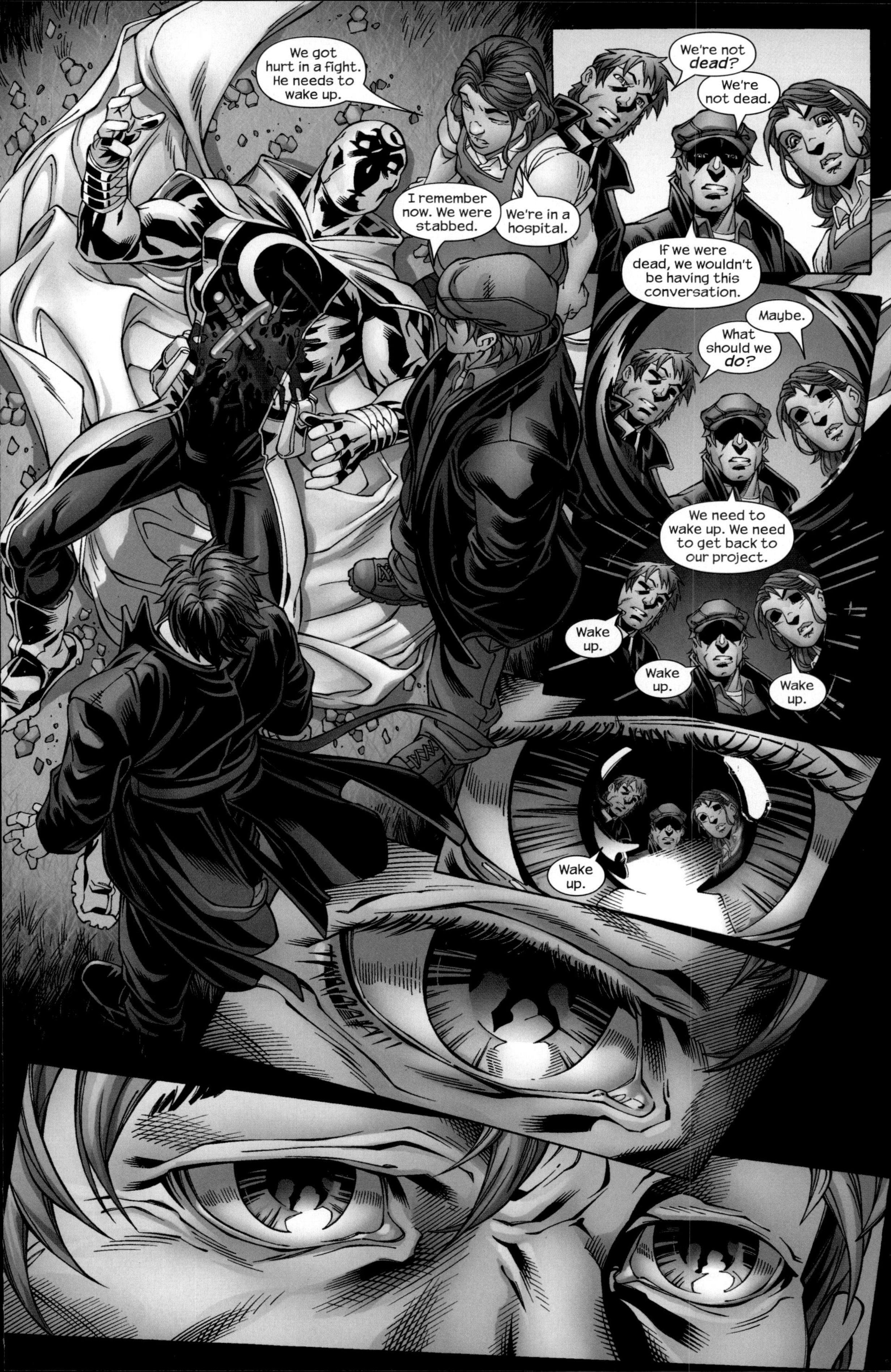
We got hurt in a fight. He needs to wake up.
I remember now. We were stabbed.
We're in a hospital.
We're not *dead?*
We're not dead.
If we were dead, we wouldn't be having this conversation.
Maybe.
What should we *do?*
We need to wake up. We need to get back to our project.
Wake up.
Wake up.
Wake up.
Wake up.

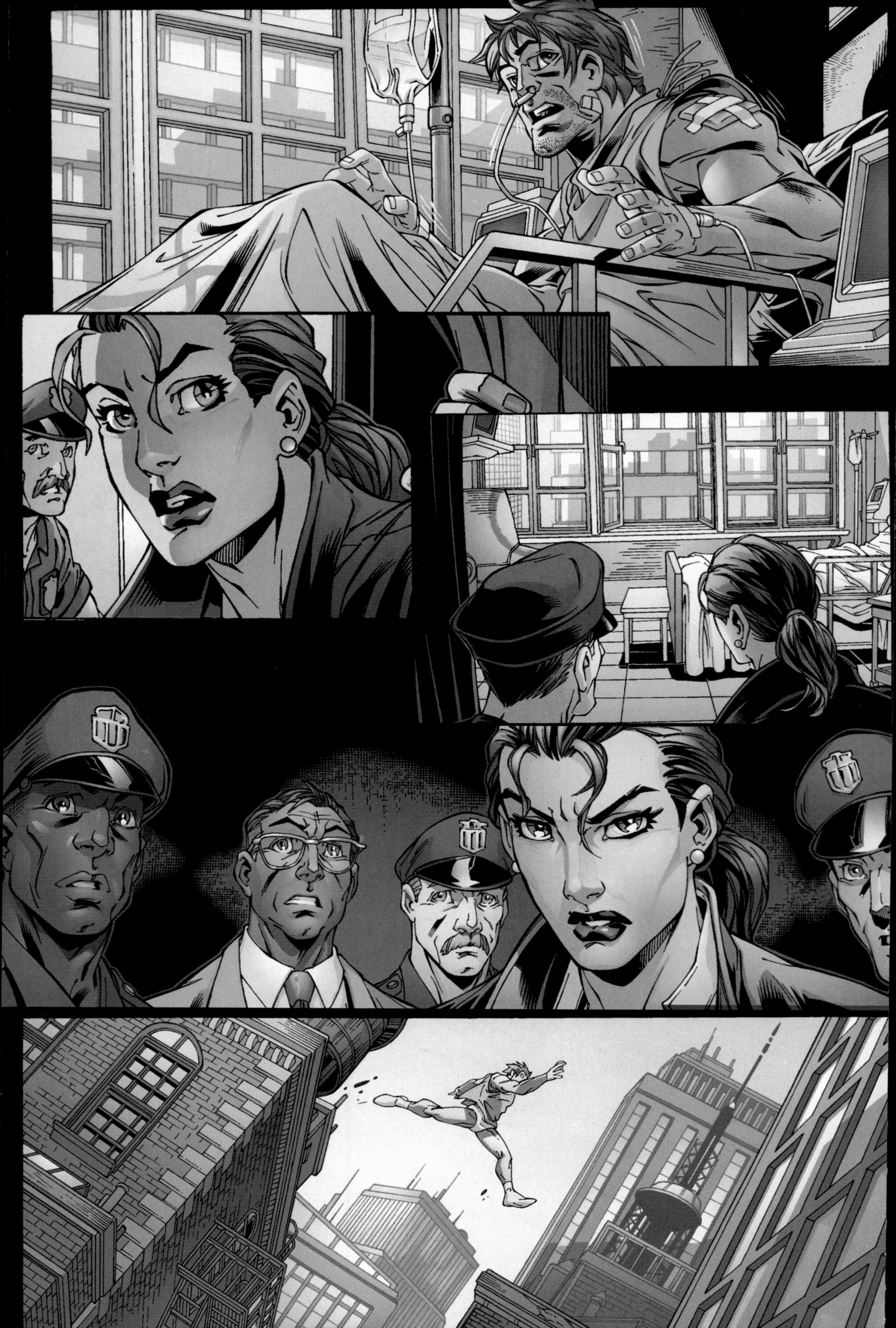

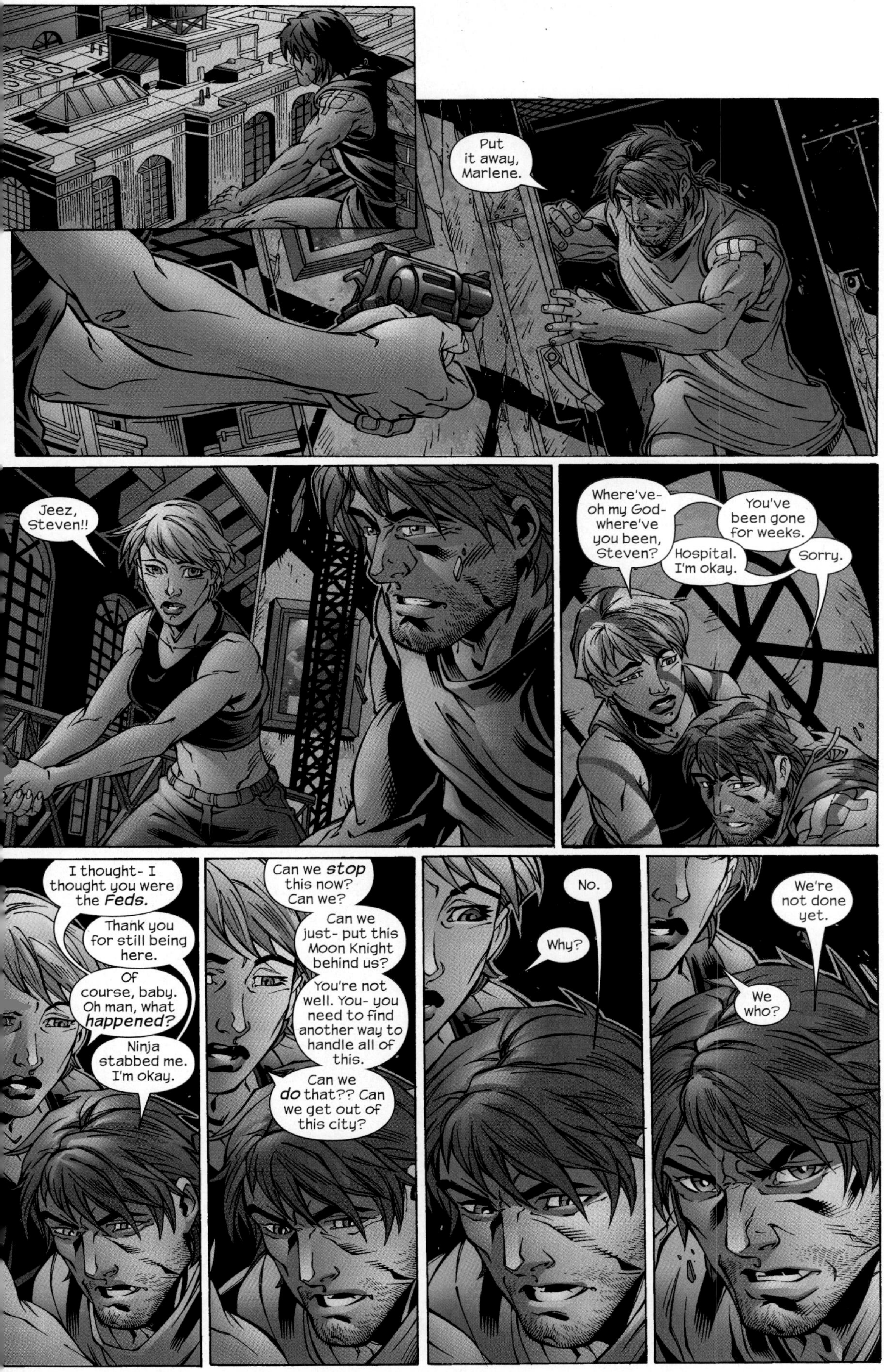
Put it away, Marlene.
Jeez, Steven!!
Where've- oh my God- where've you been, Steven?
You've been gone for weeks.
Hospital. I'm okay.
Sorry.
I thought- I thought you were the Feds.
Thank you for still being here.
Of course, baby. Oh man, what happened?
Ninja stabbed me. I'm okay.
Can we stop this now? Can we?
Can we just- put this Moon Knight behind us?
You're not well. You- you need to find another way to handle all of this.
Can we do that?? Can we get out of this city?
No.
Why?
We're not done yet.
We who?

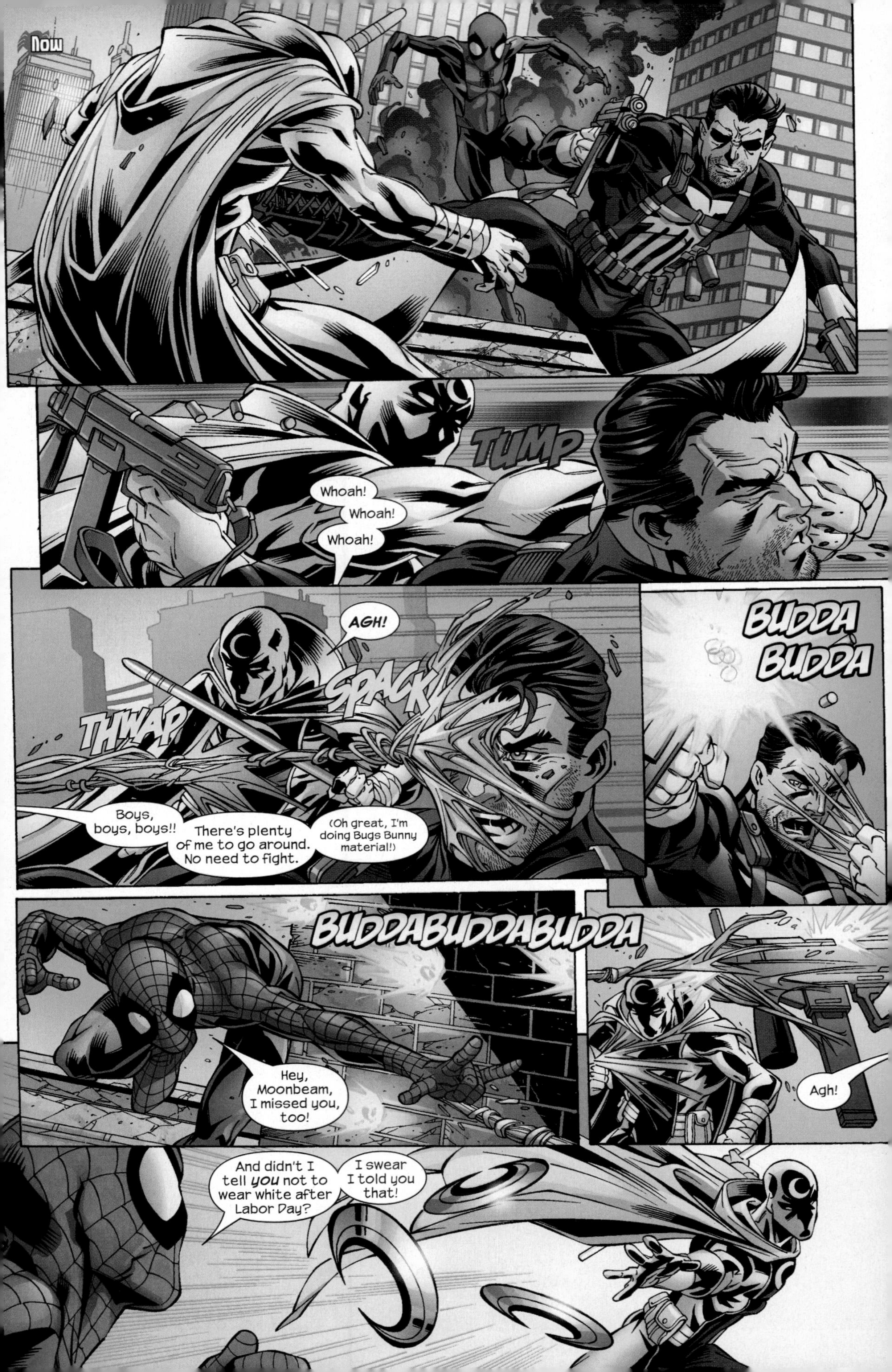
Now
TUMP
Whoah!
Whoah!
Whoah!
AGH!
SPACK
THWAP
Boys, boys, boys!!
There's plenty of me to go around. No need to fight.
(Oh great, I'm doing Bugs Bunny material!)
BUDDA BUDDA
BUDDABUDDABUDDA
Hey, Moonbeam, I missed you, too!
Agh!
And didn't I tell *you* not to wear white after Labor Day?
I swear I told you that!

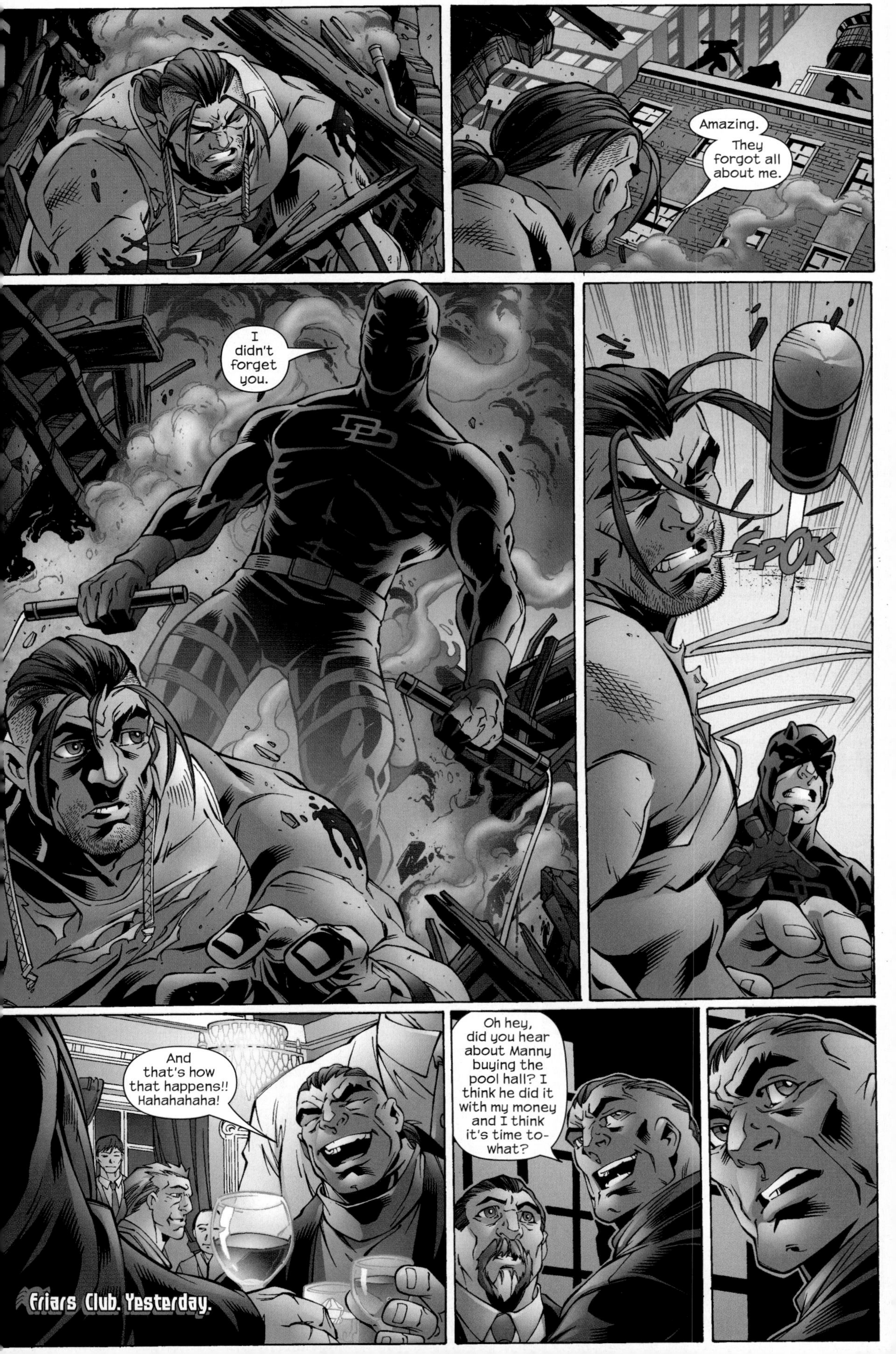

Amazing. They forgot all about me.
I didn't forget you.
SPOK
And that's how that happens!! Hahahahaha!
Friars Club. Yesterday.
Oh hey, did you hear about Manny buying the pool hall? I think he did it with my money and I think it's time to- what?

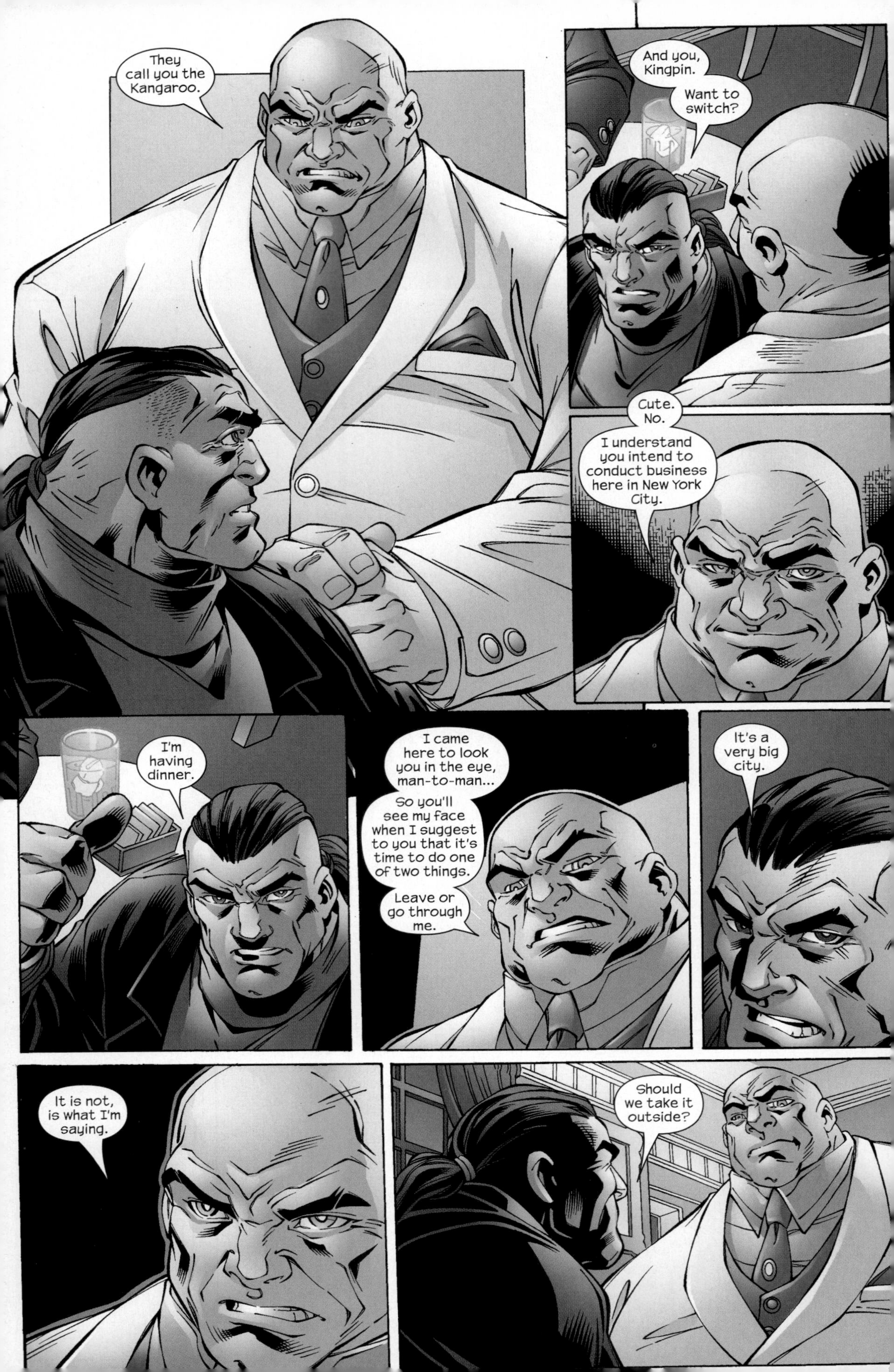
They call you the Kangaroo.
And you, Kingpin.
Want to switch?
Cute. No.
I understand you intend to conduct business here in New York City.
I'm having dinner.
I came here to look you in the eye, man-to-man...
So you'll see my face when I suggest to you that it's time to do one of two things.
Leave or go through me.
It's a very big city.
It is not, is what I'm saying.
Should we take it outside?

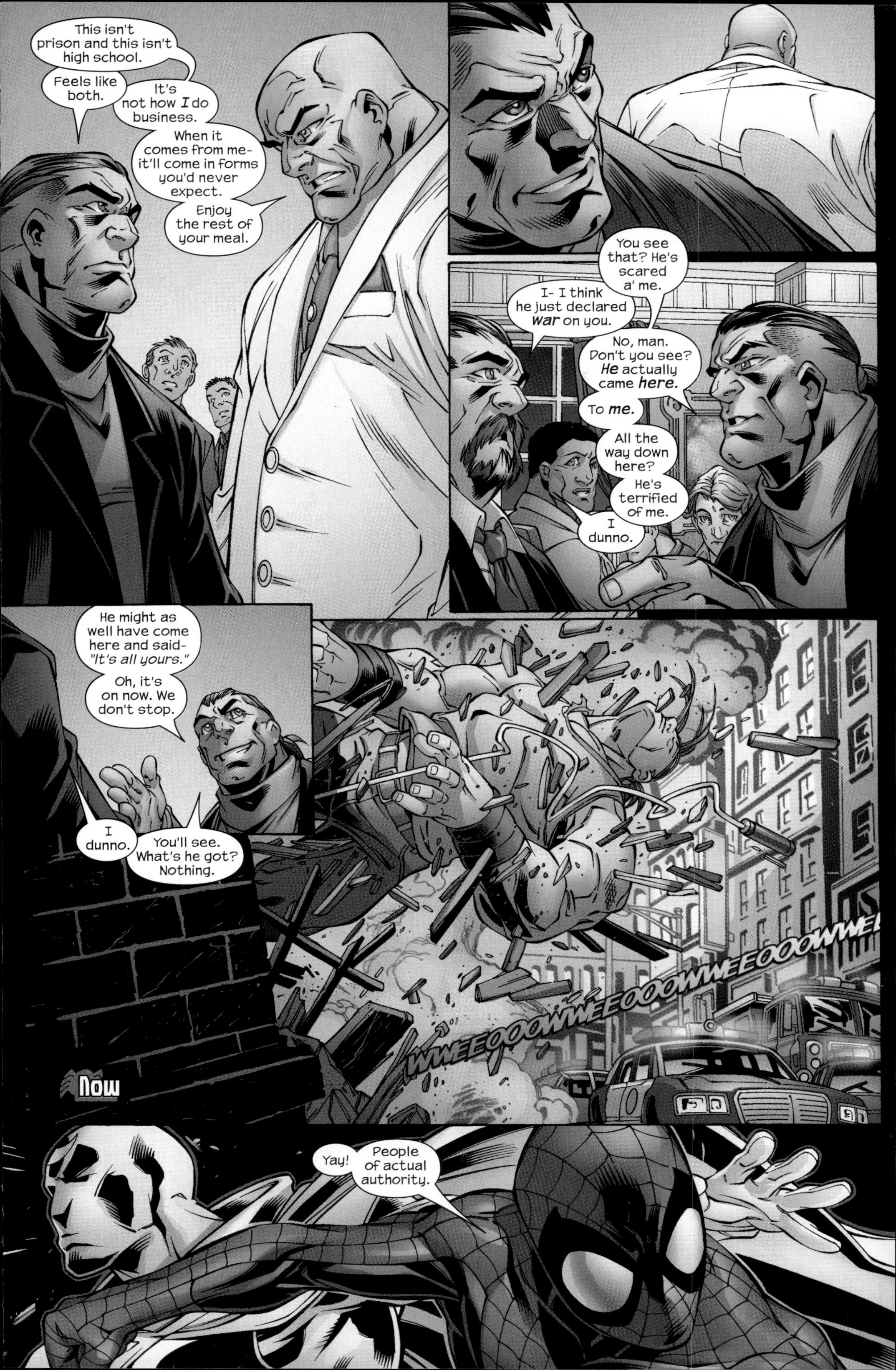
This isn't prison and this isn't high school.
Feels like both.
It's not how *I* do business.
When it comes from me- it'll come in forms you'd never expect.
Enjoy the rest of your meal.
You see that? He's scared a' me.
I- I think he just declared *war* on you.
No, man. Don't you see? *He* actually came *here*.
To *me.*
All the way down here?
He's terrified of me.
I dunno.
He might as well have come here and said- *"It's all yours."*
Oh, it's on now. We don't stop.
I dunno.
You'll see. What's he got? Nothing.
WWEEOOOWWEEOOOWWEEOOOWWE
Now
Yay!
People of actual authority.

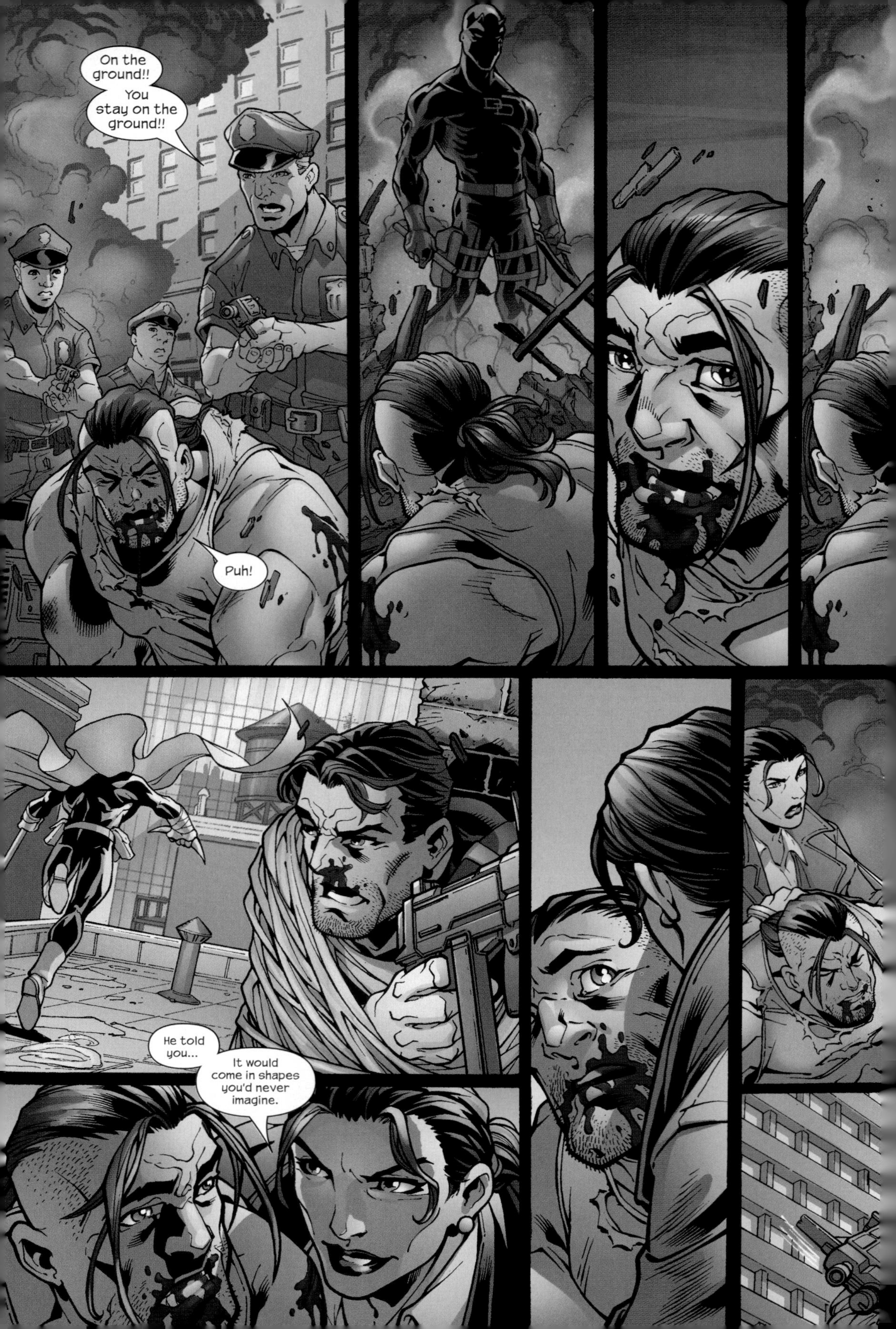

On the ground!!
You stay on the ground!!
Puh!
He told you...
It would come in shapes you'd never imagine.

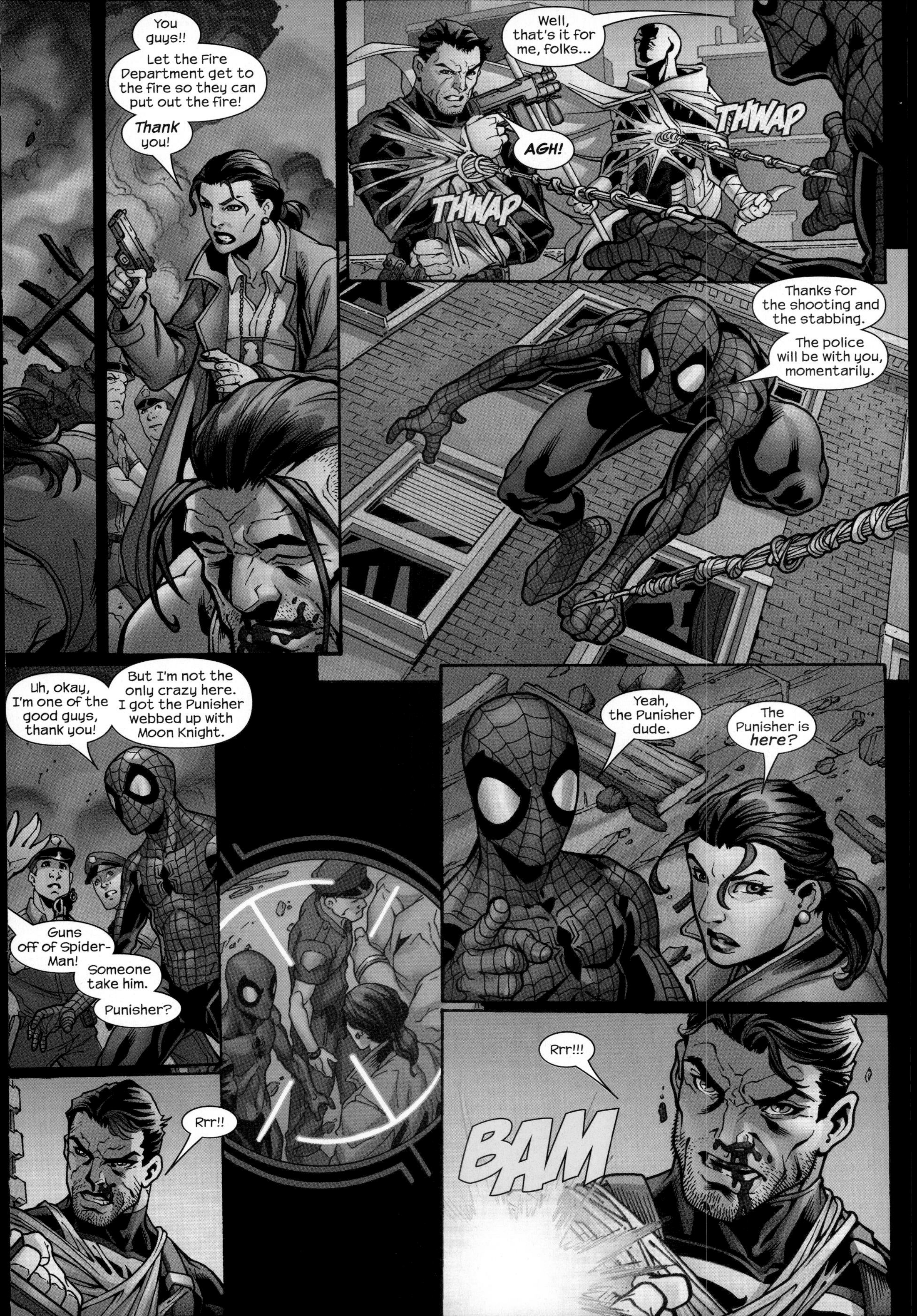

You guys!!
Let the Fire Department get to the fire so they can put out the fire!
Thank you!
Well, that's it for me, folks...
AGH!
THWAP
THWAP
Thanks for the shooting and the stabbing.
The police will be with you, momentarily.
Uh, okay, I'm one of the good guys, thank you!
But I'm not the only crazy here. I got the Punisher webbed up with Moon Knight.
Guns off of Spider-Man!
Someone take him.
Punisher?
Yeah, the Punisher dude.
The Punisher is here?
Rrr!!
Rrr!!!
BAM

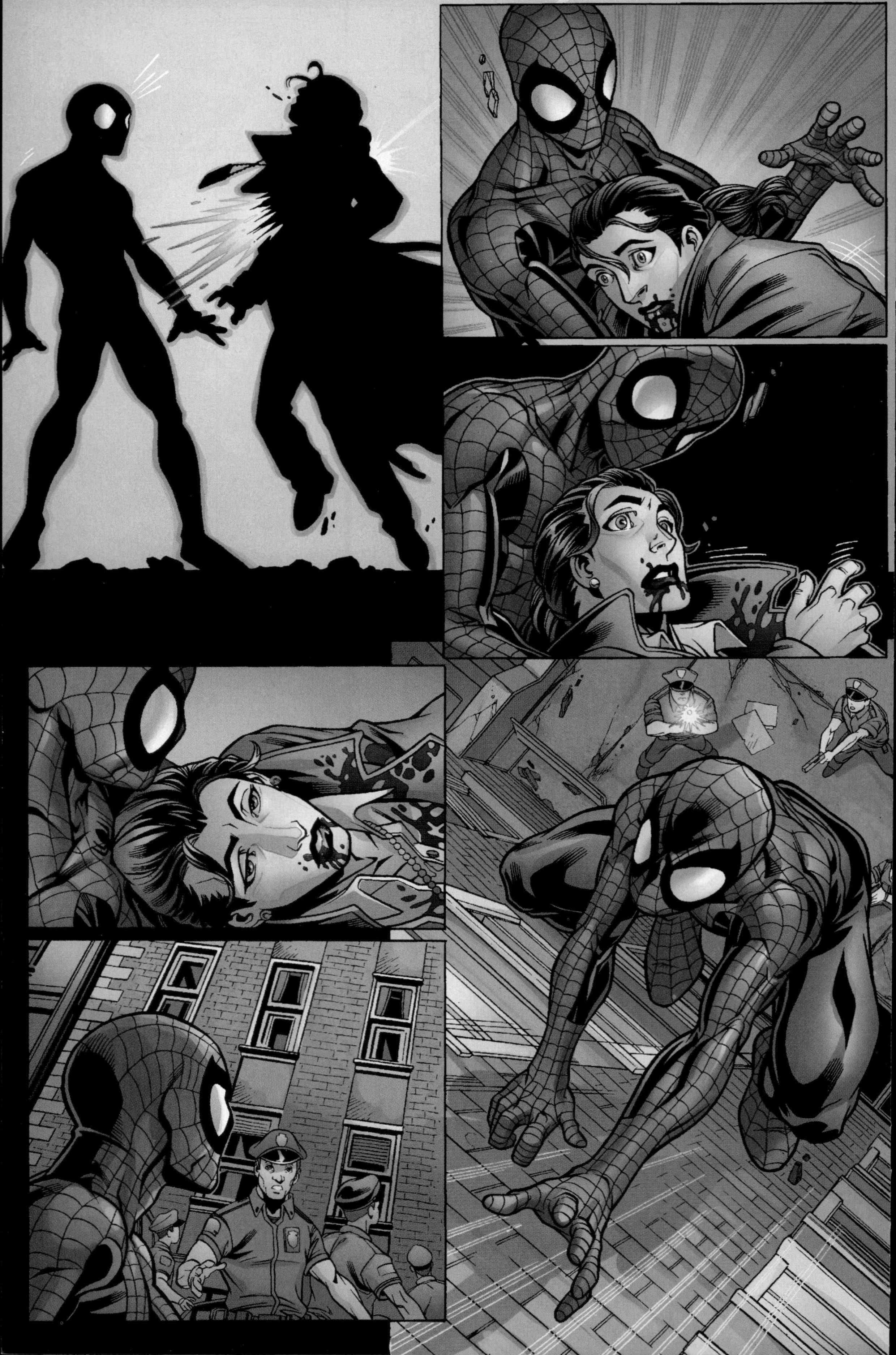

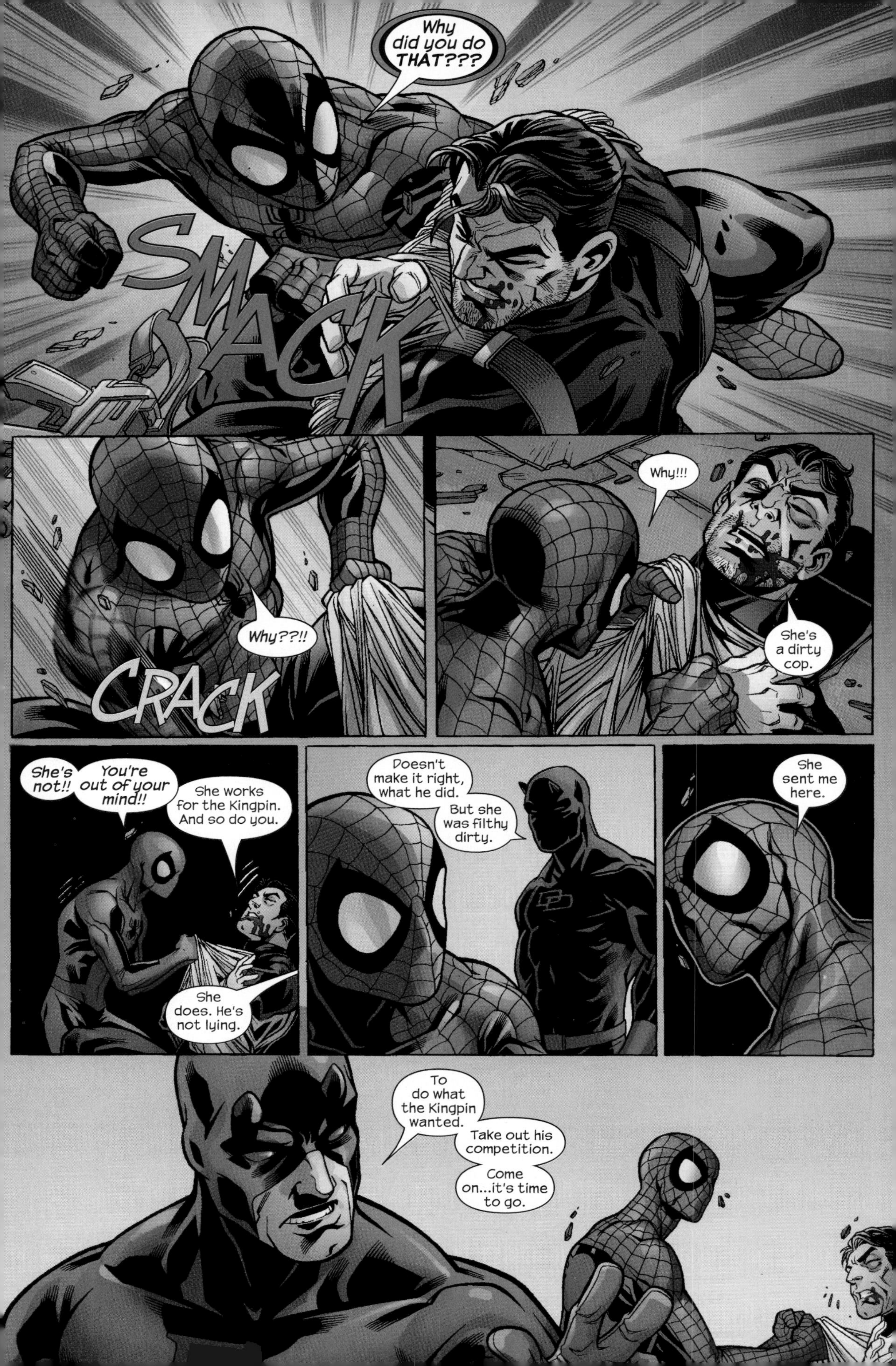
Why did you do THAT???
SMACK
Why??!!
CRACK
Why!!!
She's a dirty cop.
She's not!!
You're out of your mind!!
She works for the Kingpin. And so do you.
She does. He's not lying.
Doesn't make it right, what he did.
But she was filthy dirty.
She sent me here.
To do what the Kingpin wanted.
Take out his competition.
Come on...it's time to go.

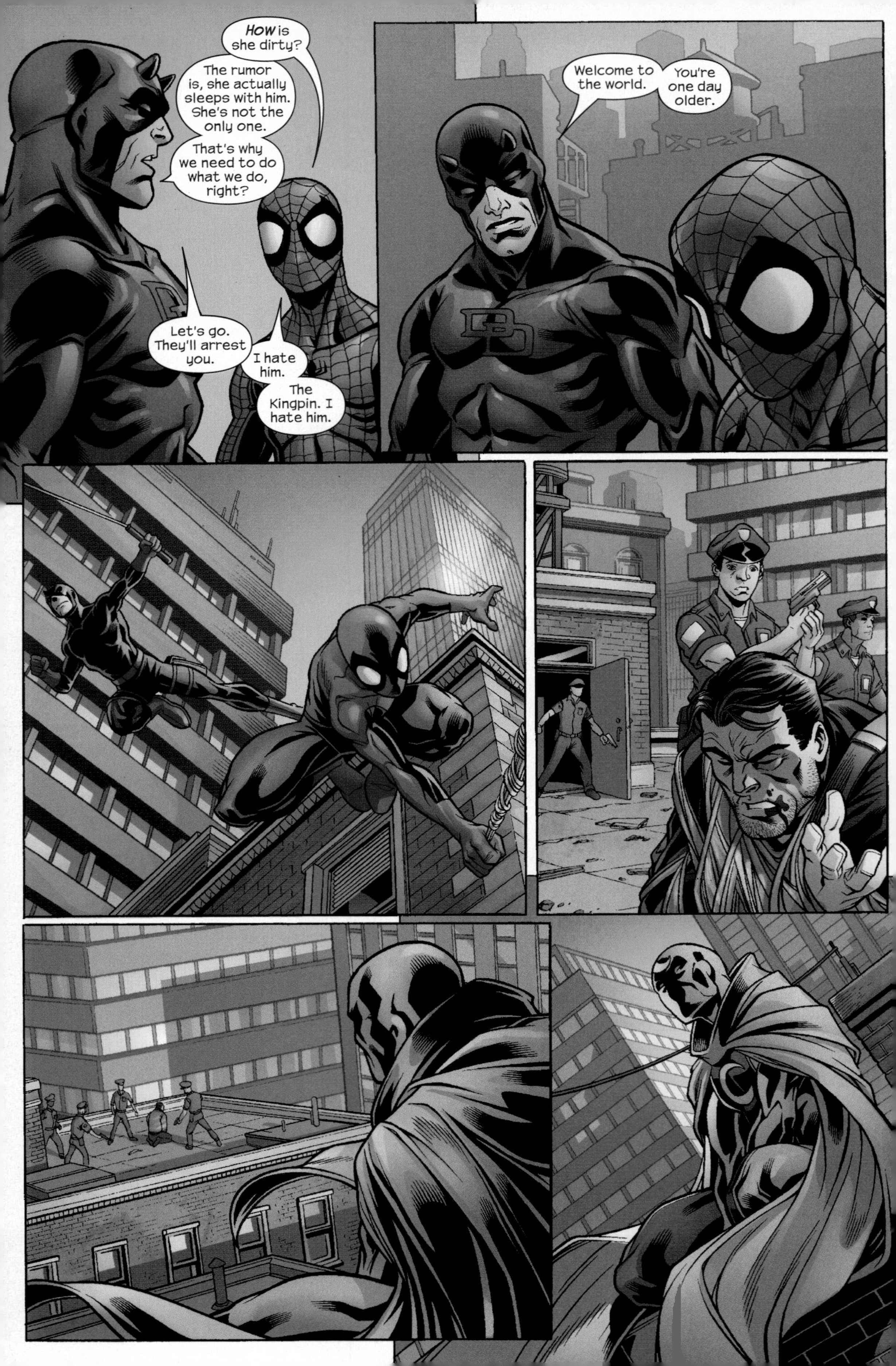
HOW is she dirty?
The rumor is, she actually sleeps with him. She's not the only one.
That's why we need to do what we do, right?
Let's go. They'll arrest you.
I hate him.
The Kingpin. I hate him.
Welcome to the world.
You're one day older.

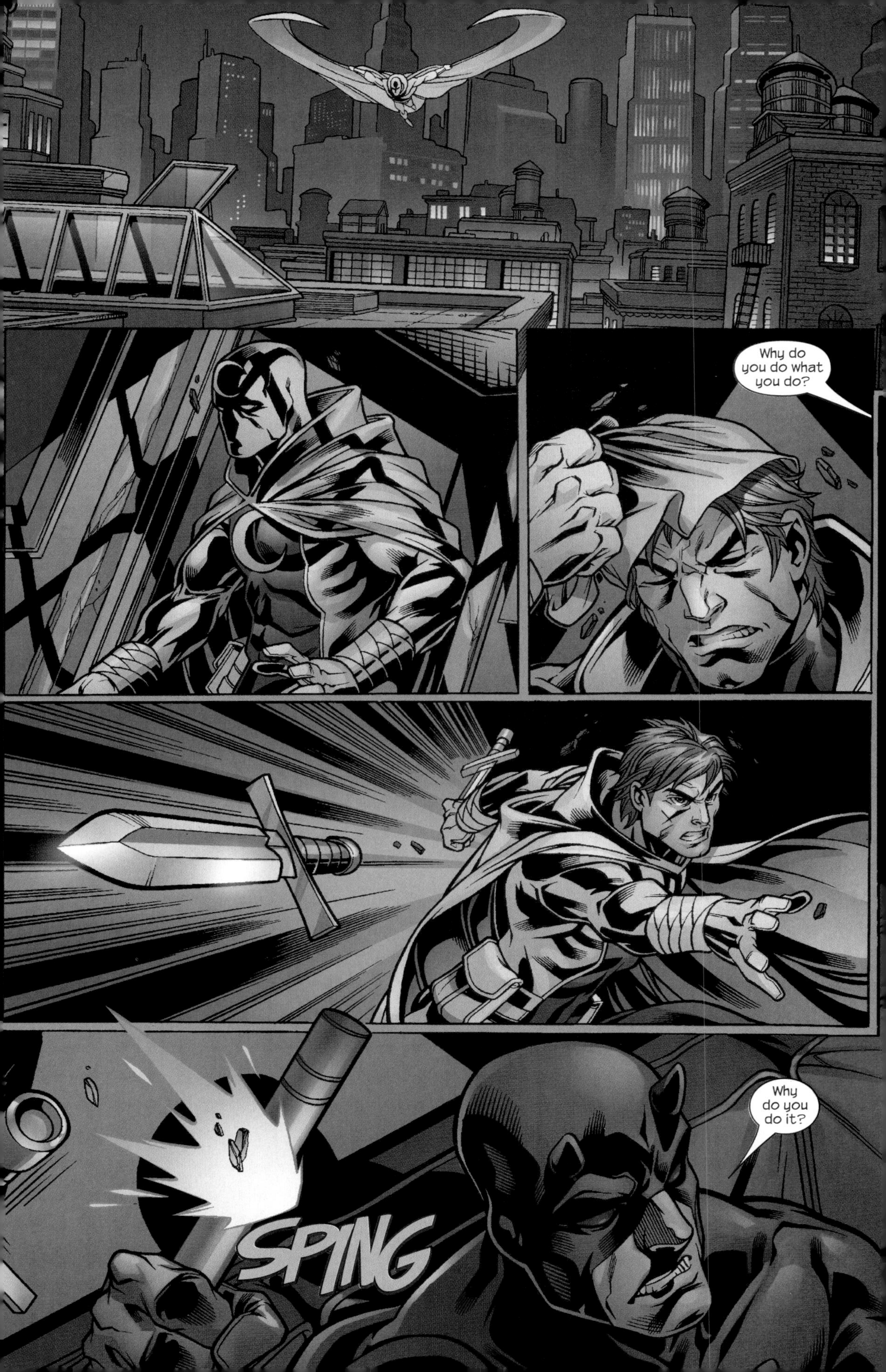
Why do you do what you do?
Why do you do it?
SPING

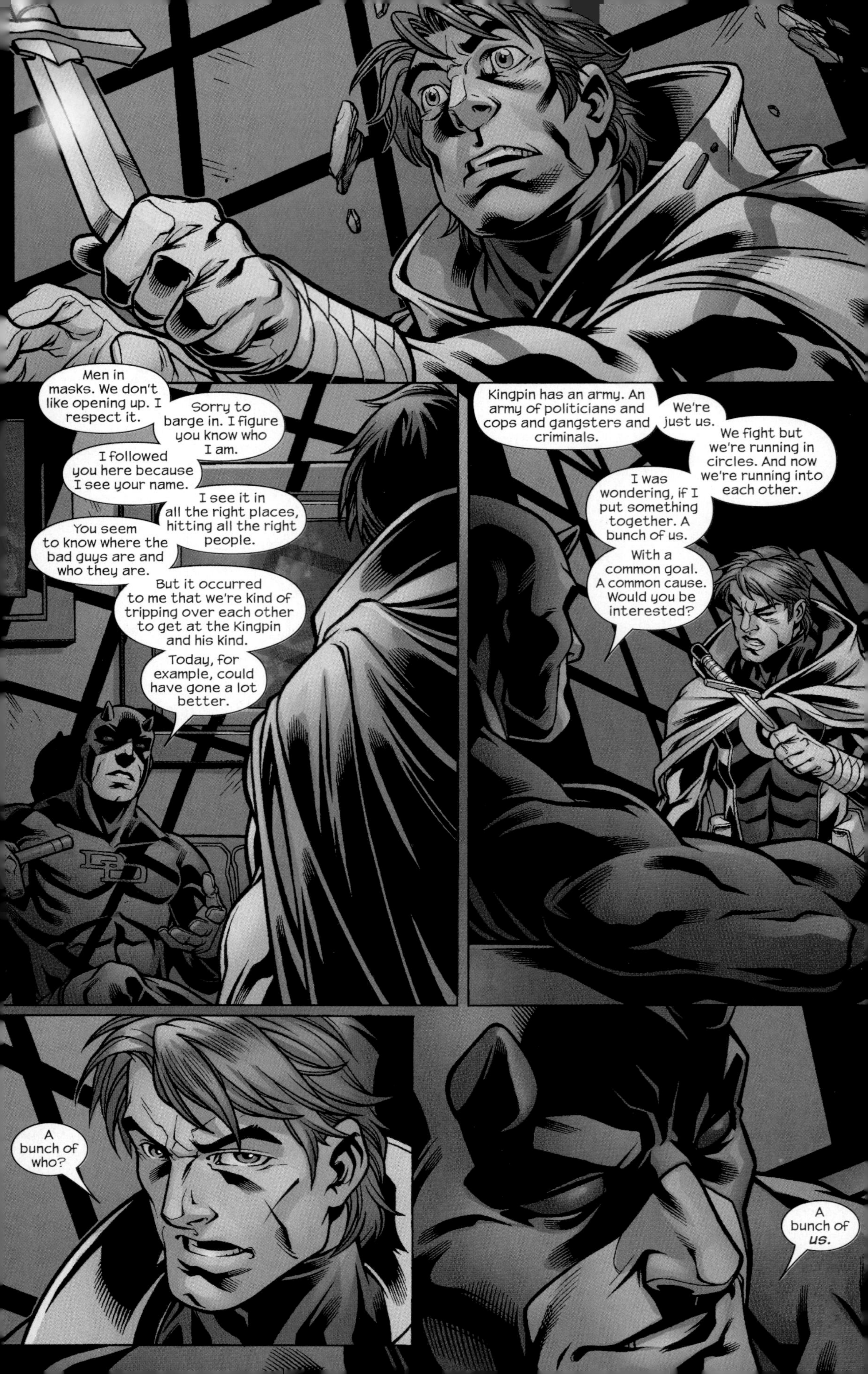

Men in masks. We don't like opening up. I respect it.
Sorry to barge in. I figure you know who I am.
I followed you here because I see your name.
I see it in all the right places, hitting all the right people.
You seem to know where the bad guys are and who they are.
But it occurred to me that we're kind of tripping over each other to get at the Kingpin and his kind.
Today, for example, could have gone a lot better.
Kingpin has an army. An army of politicians and cops and gangsters and criminals.
We're just us.
We fight but we're running in circles. And now we're running into each other.
I was wondering, if I put something together. A bunch of us.
With a common goal. A common cause. Would you be interested?
A bunch of who?
A bunch of *us.*

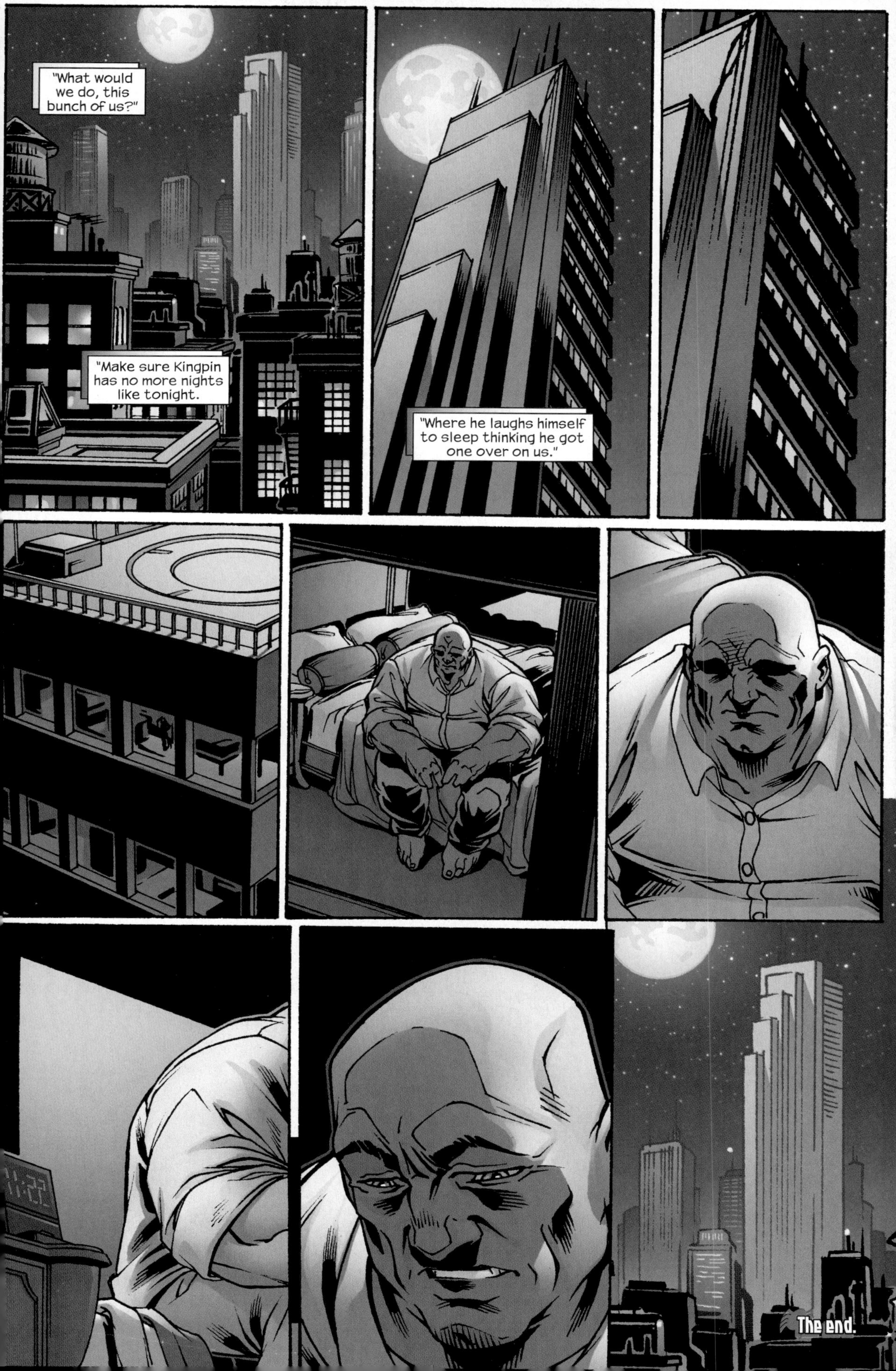
"What would we do, this bunch of us?"
"Make sure Kingpin has no more nights like tonight.
"Where he laughs himself to sleep thinking he got one over on us."
The end.

Cover Pencils by Stuart Immonen

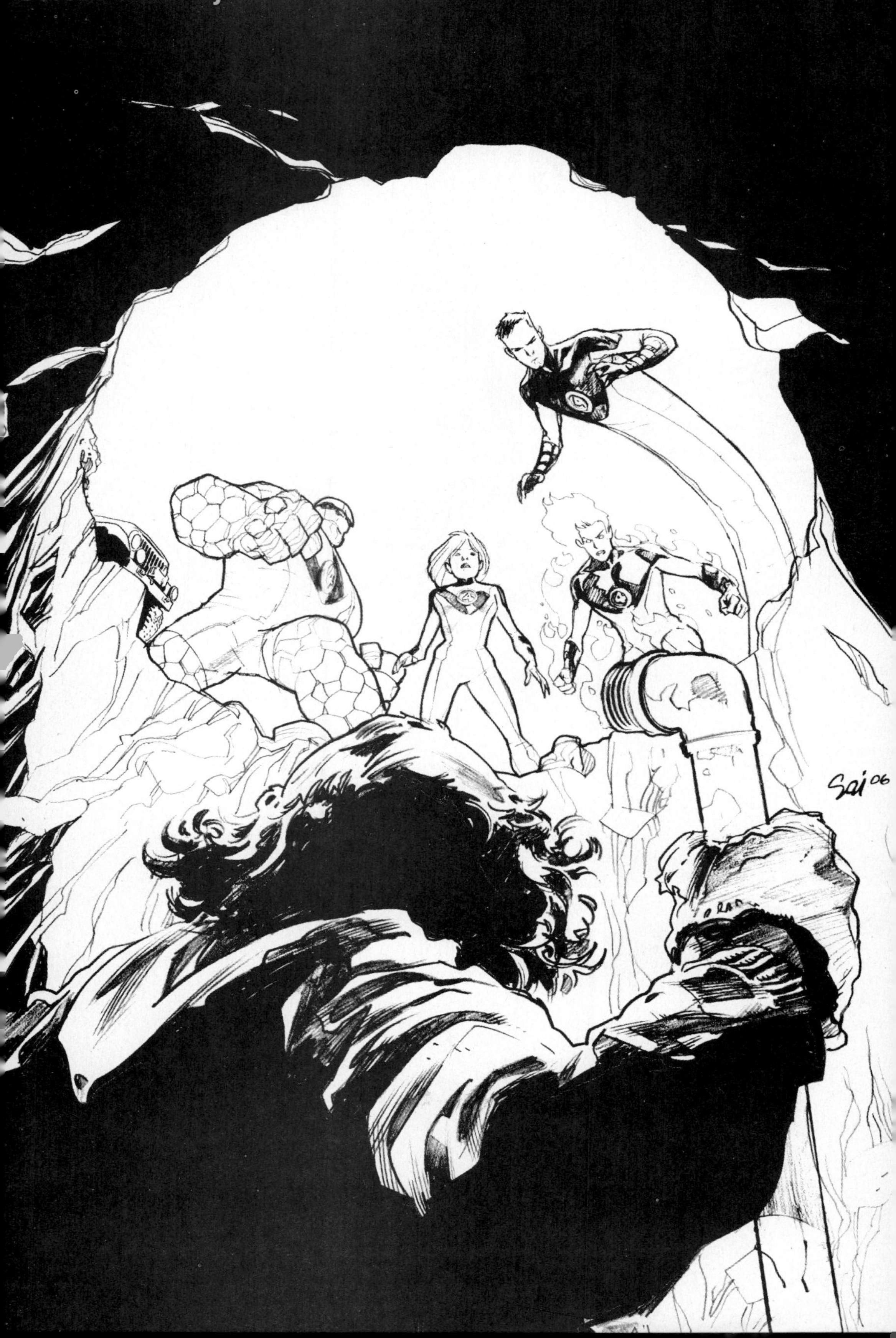